PRAISE FOR *PEOPLE-CENTRIC ORGANIZATIONAL CHANGE*

The book focuses on how to achieve engagement and active participation of stakeholders with organizational change. It introduces a cyclical business transformation framework and its associated principles, which I find particularly appealing as they offer practical guidance on how to establish a change management approach that prioritizes people over processes. Readers will also find the many case studies as a great source of insight that provide valuable lessons learned directly from the field. In essence, this book is an essential read for anyone seeking to navigate the complexities of effecting successful, people-first change in our post-pandemic, fast-paced and hybrid world.

Peter Scheytt, Transformation Manager Cognizant Netcentric, Munich, Germany

People-centric Organizational Change emerges as a beacon of accessible guidance for leaders navigating the post-pandemic and economic crisis era. Bringing us up to date with the impact of generative AI and geopolitical turmoil, the book not only acknowledges the external pressures we face but seamlessly integrates them into its framework, offering a comprehensive guide to managing change amidst adversity. With thought-provoking case-studies, chapter questions and prompts for turning strategy into action, this is not merely a book; it is a manifesto for a new era of leadership—one that recognizes the value of a people-centric approach in achieving lasting transformation.

Jaimie Brown, Senior Director Change Management, Medical Affairs EMEA M&D Communications & Change Management, Astellas, UK

With a clear structure spanning from theory to practice, *People-centric Organizational Change* guides readers through the complex challenges of involving people in transformation processes and preparing them for uncertainties. The selected case studies are like windows into reality, illustrating how theoretical approaches can be brought to life practically. For executives,

change managers, and all those working at the intersection of human dynamics and corporate development, as well as for those who not only lead changes but also shape them with meaning and sensitivity, it deserves a permanent place on the bookshelf.
Daniel Auwermann, TRAFO founder, Berlin, Germany

Professor Julie Hodges presents the inescapable truth that people are at the core of business transformation. As a piece of work it is captivating and inspiring, and just about perfect in the way it is done.
Kathy Gilbert, Executive Management Consultant, Australia

In an environment where we strive to have our leaders ready for future skills, especially in the technology world, this book provides us with an answer – a people-centric approach. This book makes me a believer that equipping teams to cope, limiting pressure, and using dialogue is at the heart of not only successfully leading transformations but also sustaining and improving operations. Any current or aspiring leader will benefit from reading this book. This book will equip any leader with the ability to navigate the ambiguity and uncertainty that team members may feel during transformations.
Inga Grigaliunaite, Global Talent Development and Leadership Programs Lead at Dell Technologies, Ireland

In a landscape where outdated approaches struggle to address the complexity of change management amidst dynamic and chaotic situations, this book emerges as guidance. It recognizes that transformation is not a single linear event but a confluence of simultaneous initiatives, necessitating a focus on agility and adaptability. Dive into this compelling read to discover the essence of people-centric change management and equip yourself with the tools to navigate the intricate web of contemporary business transformation successfully.
Henry Harianto, Group Chief Information Officer, Meratus group., Indonesia

This is a thought-provoking and well-rounded book on organisational change with people at the core! It brings to life some of the key challenges that we face on a daily basis, and as Head of Change, the principles provided reinforce many of the best practices that I follow but take these to another level by giving insightful case studies and examples.
Nic Purvis, Head of Change Management, Sage, UK

People-centric Organizational Change

Engaging employees with business transformation

Julie Hodges

First published in Great Britain and the United States in 2024 by Kogan Page Limited

2nd Floor, 45 Gee Street
London
EC1V 3RS
United Kingdom

8 W 38th Street, Suite 902
New York, NY 10018
USA

4737/23 Ansari Road
Daryaganj
New Delhi 110002
India

www.koganpage.com

Kogan Page books are printed on paper from sustainable forests.

ISBNs

Hardback 978 1 3986 1257 0
Paperback 978 1 3986 1255 6
Ebook 978 1 3986 1256 3

British Library Cataloguing-in-Publication Data
A CIP record for this book is available from the British Library.

Library of Congress Control Number
2023951150

Typeset by Integra Software Services, Pondicherry
Print production managed by Jellyfish
Printed and bound by CPI Group (UK) Ltd, Croydon CR0 4YY

Over the years I have had the honour to teach a wealth of experienced and talented students from across the globe and have had the opportunity to discuss with them the subject that I am most passionate about – people-centric change. Not only have I shared my knowledge and experience with them, but I have also had the privilege of learning from them. I am looking forward to continuing these discussions and debates about change in organisations. This book is dedicated to all the students who I have had the privilege to teach and those I still have the opportunity to meet and teach in the future.

CONTENTS

ABOUT THE AUTHOR

Professor Julie Hodges is an international leading expert on change in organizations, particularly the role and impact of people during transformations. Before entering the academic world Julie worked as a business consultant for over 20 years in several profit and non-profit organizations, including PwC. At PwC Julie was responsible for organizational change and management development in a number of companies include Barclays, Shell, BBC, Lloyds and Reuters. Julie has also worked with Vertex where she set up and led a commercial consultancy team. Her first role was with the British Council where she was the Development Consultancy for East Asia.

Julie has published in a number of international journals on change in organisations. She is the author of several books including *Consultancy, Organizational Development and Change*, *Managing and Leading People through Change* (both Kogan Page), *Sustaining Change in Organizations* (Sage), *Employee Engagement for Organizational Change* (Routledge) and *Organization Development: How organizations change and develop effectively* (Palgrave Macmillan). Her latest book is *Reshaping the HR: the role of HR in organizational change*.

Julie is a Principal Fellow of the Higher Education Academy, Academic Fellow of the ICMCI (International Council of Management Consulting Institutes) and a Senior Fellow of the Foundation for Management Education (FME). She is also a member of the editorial board of the journal *Management Consulting*.

BUSINESS INSIGHTS CONTRIBUTORS

Laura de Ruiter is an Associate Director in the Behavioral Science Consortium at Astellas, a team within the Patient Centricity Division. After a career in academic research, she now applies social science insights in the industry to improve patient outcomes and organizational efficiency.

Douglas Flory is a coach/mentor, consultant, instructor and leader. He has 20+ years of experience leading organizational transformations, change readiness, user experience, communications, training, continuous improvement, project management, data analysis and strategies. He blends human-centred methods, data-informed results, tested experiences, and art+science to create tailored business criteria for success. Douglas serves on the global Board of Directors for the Association of Change Management Professionals (ACMP). He resides in the Rocky Mountains region of the United States with his wife and children.

David Howell is the founder of Able and Rush (People Solutions) Ltd. After leaving school in 1986, David initially became a quantity surveyor within the construction industry but became disenchanted and in 1989 decided to join Staffordshire Police. This led to 31 remarkable and totally unique years. Eighteen of those years were spent serving on police air support, managing and training staff. David's first book, *Speak Up, Listen Down* (2022), highlights that unique career, from walking the back streets of Stoke-on-Trent to protecting President Obama over the skies of London. The book also outlines the serious issue of bullying within policing and how it has been sadly allowed to manifest itself throughout its ranks, whilst offering unique solutions as to how organizations can alleviate the problem to what can be so often a systemic issue. A key part of David's role within air support was facilitating crew resource management – the human factor element of pilot and tactical flight officer training. This training post took David across the whole of the UK and also Jamaica, training the Jamaica Defence Force and the Jamaica Constabulary Force. It was this human factor that fascinated David, and after retiring from policing he took on the role as a Business Change Manager for a digital transformation project within policing. That insight has been further enhanced with the use of innovative psychometric tools that holistically outline an individual's innate talents and how they deal with and adapt to the complexity of the world around them. This work is still ongoing, and a digital application is soon to be released which aids individual self-management of workplace experiences and wellbeing.

David's work continues to make workplaces a safer place to be – where organizations ultimately thrive because of their people and not at the expense of their people.

Zuhair Imran is a digital marketing consultant. Zuhair is an accomplished digital marketing and communications professional with a proven track record of leading successful digital transformation programmes. He has extensive experience in driving change management and process improvement plans for a variety of organizations, including the Bill & Melinda Gates Foundation, Sanofi France and Pakistan, J Walter Thompson (JWT) Pakistan and UK and British Petroleum UK, among others.

In addition to his professional experience, Zuhair is also a respected teacher and coach, having worked with undergraduate, postgraduate and MBA students in multiple countries, including Europe, the UK and Pakistan. He brings a wealth of knowledge and practical experience to his teaching, helping students develop the skills and knowledge they need to succeed in the fast-paced and ever-changing environment. Zuhair's educational credentials include an MBA from Durham University Business School, UK, and a certificate in Social Entrepreneurship from INSEAD, France.

Zoleka Mashiyi is an independent consultant based in South Africa. She is a founder and Managing Director of a consulting and coaching business, Ehlobo Consulting. She is an experienced Prosci® accredited Change Management Practitioner, with over 15 years of experience in the field of enterprise change management, working in the financial industry in the public and private sectors. Zoleka is an International Certified Coach with the Certified Coaches Alliance, specializing in life, leadership and emotional intelligence.

She is a public speaker, a professional with a strong consulting, human resources and organizational development background, skilled in managing projects, building resilient organizations, leading transformational change, leadership and individual/group coaching, employee engagement and designing leadership and organizational development programmes.

David Maybin is a change management and transformation leader who is future-focused and has a proven track record of enabling organizations to thrive, succeed and grow. While adopting new processes and approaches and building highly skilled teams, he has led transformation and change programmes across public and commercial sectors with a focus on people, customer experience and uplifting capabilities. David has also led practice and industry group development and strategic advisory roles in influencing positive change across organizations and in supporting leadership in driving change while embracing the ever-increasing impacts of change.

Carlos Pullen-Ferreira, Vice President, Business Transformation at Sage, has worked in transformation and change for over 20 years. He started his career as a consultant with Accenture, where he was placed on several agile transformations in the banking industry. From these solid foundations, he has led large transformation departments in the lottery, airline, banking and technology industries. His passion for organizational agility and change is founded on a desire for continuous improvement and a belief that anything is possible with hard work and dedication.

Laurence Scates the former Executive Director and Head of the Transformation Office at Astellas. He has an extensive background in project and programme delivery and has long championed the need for understanding the way that change is experienced by organizations and people.

Kathrin Schrepfer is a change management professional, trainer, and business coach. She holds a degree in human resources and organizational development and has more than 20 years of experience in strategic, tactical and operational change management in industry. Over the years, she has trained and coached more than 450 change agents and managers for their tasks. Today, she runs her own training centre to certify change enablers and managers in change management practices and continues to be involved in several client projects.

Steve Tunnicliffe was the Senior Vice President, Global Sales, for ST Engineering iDirect, leading a team of 150 people and accountable for $280 million in revenue. Steve was with iDirect for 16 years and in his tenure with the company undertook a number of senior leadership roles within the sales organization, from running the EMEA region to building the company's global accounts team. Steve completed his Masters of Business Administration (MBA) from Durham University Business School, UK, in 2003 and has been an active alumni mentor on the MBA programme for the past eight years. Steve first graduated from Durham University in 1994 with a degree in Arabic with Middle Eastern and Islamic Studies and on graduation spent the first six years of his career working for a leading Middle Eastern broadcaster based in London before entering the satellite industry in 2000. Prior to working for iDirect, Steve worked for BT Global Services, Plenexis and Loral Space & Communications.

ACKNOWLEDGEMENTS

As with all my others, this book has been a labour of love but would not have been possible without the contribution of many others who were engaged in its creation.

My thanks go to everyone who took the time to contribute their stories, cases studies and experiences for this book (you will find their names and bios at the start of the book). I am also very grateful to everyone at Kogan Page who gave me the opportunity to write this book and contributed to its production – without you this would still be an idea waiting to be shared. Finally, my thanks go to Mick for providing his support, patience and love which got me through the lows and also the highs of writing this book.

01

The rationale for people-centric change

The post-pandemic world

Ayrton Senna once reputedly said that you cannot overtake 15 cars in sunny weather, but you can when it is raining. Well, we have had no shortage of heavy downpours in recent years, including global pandemics, economic retrenchment, creeping inflation, geopolitical conflicts and supply chain constraints, which companies have had to cope with. Globally, the Covid-19 pandemic has created profound changes to how businesses operate and the way in which individuals interact and work. While social movements such as Black Lives Matter, Extinction Rebellion and Stop Oil are causing social and political upheavals around the world, the growth of generative artificial intelligence (AI) is disrupting the way we work and new digital entrants are drastically altering industries, with many capturing more value and significantly higher equity valuations than incumbents. In addition, ecosystem-based strategies are gaining ground; while companies committed to environmental, social and governance (ESG) priorities are increasingly standing out; for others attracting and retaining talent is a key priority as organizations cope with an ongoing shortage of the right capabilities to create value; and for many there is a need to refine hybrid and remote ways of working. In such a dynamic, complex and chaotic environment, organizations are faced with the need to adapt and be agile in order to grow, and in some cases even survive.

At the end of the 1990s the term 'VUCA' (volatile, uncertain, complex and ambiguous) became commonplace. Now we need to add to VUCA: exponential speed; global hyper interconnections; social media; a tsunami of data; intelligent machines; and geopolitical conflict (to name but a few).

Consequently, in many industries change is ongoing and accelerating within an evolving and more fluid business landscape. Many organizations are meeting these challenges by accelerating the pace of change; while others are struggling to pivot in the post-pandemic era. This is not helped by the need to reassess management systems which are based on old rules and emphasize a hierarchy that focuses on uniformity, bureaucracy and control and which is no longer effective or fit for purpose. To cope with this evolving environment necessitates adaption and agility in order to survive and thrive.

The different shifts and disruptions that are occurring are inevitable, interconnected and irreversible, and are dramatically reshaping the business landscape. In order to adapt to them, companies are having to make fundamental changes to work, the workforce and the workplace. Research suggests that organizations are estimated to have carried out five business transformations in the past three years and nearly 75 per cent expect to increase the types of major change initiatives they will undertake in the next three years.[1] McKinsey's Global Leadership Survey, which included 900 senior executives from nine industries, revealed that participants were focused on the need for speed in organizational changes, with the majority saying that they expect transformational change in almost every area of their business.[2] The survey further highlights that fundamental and lasting shifts are predicted in everything from how and where people work to the role of management, and from core processes and technology to talent, skills and organizational culture. Yet, despite what appears to be an exponential increase in organizational change, Paul Polman and Andrew Winston stress in their book *Net Positive* that the pace of change may never again be as slow as it is now.[3] Although the need for speed is acute, this speed needs to be sustainable. However, this is proving to be a challenge because, even though change is accelerating, the people who have to cope with it have hit a barrier, with employees' willingness to support change having fallen from 74 per cent in 2016 to 38 per cent in 2022.[4] This gap between the required effort needed to change and employee willingness to change is termed the 'transformation deficit' and unless it is addressed it will hamper organizational ambitions and decrease employee engagement with change.[5] This deficit is partly due to employees still recovering from the turmoil of navigating and surviving the pandemic. Despite being challenged during the early months of the pandemic, organizations and their employees made remarkable changes that were fuelled by adrenaline and a sense of urgency, which showed how adaptable everyone was and how they could find ways to make things work. The acceleration and amount of change predicated by the Covid-19 pandemic has, however, been, in many cases, difficult to maintain and individuals have become weary of the speed that was witnessed in the early months of the pandemic. Speed is not, however, just about going faster; it is also about being more efficient and effective, and, importantly, having the energy and enthusiasm to move at a quicker pace.

Simultaneous transformations

The inexorably accelerating pace of change means that, whereas in the past organizations could expect one major change to rejuvenate and sustain them for some time, this is no longer the case because whereas previously there was a tendency to complete one transformation at a time, organizations are now having to embark on several, often simultaneously. Consequently, they are faced with innumerable challenges, no matter how successful their previous transformations have been. Such challenges include: How do we prepare for what is coming next while we are busy implementing the current transformation? How do we keep up with the external forces for change? How can we convince exhausted workers to join the next transformation? For many organizations addressing such questions means that there is no time to rest, no time to admire their efforts and no time to think.

Shifts from top-down linear change

Transformations are notoriously challenging, especially because they are no longer a one-off single activity but are multiple simultaneous events. Despite this shift, there is still an over-reliance on linear n-step process frameworks, for managing change, that tend to be based on one-size-fits-all, top-down strategies. The idea that a major change can be designed and managed as a discrete episode of activity is no longer fit for purpose and indeed rarely has such an approach achieved the speed or new behaviours that are required. Such frameworks don't tend to reflect the complexity and multiplicity of most transformation initiatives but instead try to simplify what is a dynamic process that is becoming more so as change continues to happen in non-linear ways. Since organizations are filled with chaos and complexity, periods of order and disorder, linearity and non-linearity, business transformations rarely fall into a neat checklist of x number of steps. In spite of this, many transformations still tend to be driven from the top down in a linear way. This typically means that the executive team exclusively makes strategic decisions, creates implementation plans and then rolls out organization-wide communication to gain employee commitment to the imposed change. Such efforts are often reduced to convincing people that what is proposed is a good idea, although it is often more like a public relations campaign than an engagement effort, with an attempt to reassure people that what they want and need is for the proposed transformation to happen, and that the plan as presented is already as good as it can get. This common strategy might enable change where organizations are vertical, in that leaders hold all the key information and employees are structured in hierarchical reporting lines, so that the top-down change reflects the organization's structure and workflow, but it is no longer appropriate in workplaces where there are more flexible modes of working and where employees' expectations have moved on and staff have more access to information about their jobs, business environment and each other, as well as there being more matrixed reporting lines and interdependencies. Top-down, process-only transformation strategies are disconnected from the workforce, and ultimately a 'my way or the highway' diktat is out of date in an age of disruption and fails to engage people with the change or sustain its benefits. Consider for a moment the transformation instituted by Ginni Rometty, the former Chief Executive and Chair of IBM.[6] Rometty and some of her colleagues say she was pivotal in transforming the company by: reinventing half its portfolio of businesses; building its cloud computing division; and establishing its leadership in artificial intelligence and quantum computing. In contrast, critics argue that she was too slow at taking decisive action to move the old global tech company forward, unlike its competitors such as Amazon Web Services, Microsoft and Google parent Alphabet. There is evidence to support such concerns, for at one time IBM suffered 22 consecutive quarters of falling revenue, and during Rometty's eight years as CEO the company's share price fell 25 per cent, when the broader US stock market rose more than 150 per cent. Subsequently, the company was forced to divest assets that were bringing in $9 billion in annual revenue, including semiconductor manufacturing and some lower-profit services and software businesses. They also acquired 68 companies, including open-source software pioneer Red Hat, and spent a total of $133 billion on deals, research and development, and capital expenditure.[7] To do this, a significant top-down transformation was implemented which took considerable time. Such a traditional management-driven strategy for business transformations with little employee involvement has been successful for many companies, but due to the internal and external drivers for change which are impacting the workplace, workers and work it is becoming redundant. Any organization that believes change can be launched from the top down without considering the impact, reaction and involvement of people is deeply deluded. For organizations do not create, implement or sustain change purely through the application of a top-down process – instead, people do. Processes may well be needed but not on their own – instead, people and processes together provide the main levers for business transformations.

Often, change driven from the top down fails to engage properly with the frontline operational staff who are essential for the delivery of high-quality products and high levels of customer service. Successful organizational change does not happen because of one leader and the executive team driving the change on their own and taking all the credit for it, but instead it requires the involvement of key internal and external stakeholders who are able to contribute effectively to co-creating business transformations. Internal stakeholders, such as frontline staff, can play a significant role in advocating for the transformations that they want to see, as well as contributing to ideas and their implementation; while managers can support the interests of those both above and below them, as accurately and positively as possible. External stakeholders, such as customers, also have a key part to play in contributing to ideas, opportunities and what needs to change and how. Business transformations can, therefore, be achieved more effectively when stakeholders, that is, those who are affected by it and/or can influence it, are given a chance to engage with change, rather than having it imposed on them from above.

When organizations are faced with the prospect and speed of a transformation, involving the key relevant stakeholders in the process can help to achieve success. Gartner, in their survey of more than 6,500 employees and over 100 chief human resources officers (CHRO) around the globe, found that the organizations that are most effective at transformations rely on their workforce, not executives, to lead change.[8] This suggests that, whenever feasible to do so (and I appreciate that there are times when it is not always feasible, such as in a crisis situation), people should be engaged in and accountable for organizational changes, and should not have to wait for the executive team to tell them what to do but should have the autonomy to help each other to navigate the disruption and uncertainty impacting on their work and workplace. This requires leaders and managers to be able to appreciate the need for distributed responsibility – that is, responsibility being shared amongst relevant stakeholders – although simply understanding the need for distributed responsibility for change is not sufficient. Leaders and managers also need to be willing to engage people with business transformations as early as possible, and to ensure locally anchored ownership of the change. To do this effectively requires clarity on who the impacted stakeholders are and who can influence the change, including those external to the organization such as vendors, partners and social groups. This means securing shared commitment and engagement from a diverse community of multiple stakeholders, which is vital for enabling organizations to adapt and rejuvenate.

Changing mindsets

Change is only embedded when individuals and teams in the organization begin to work in new ways, adopt new mindsets, display new behaviours, use new tools and apply new processes and procedures. Yet the role of individuals has often been ignored in the change management literature; those studies that have examined individual roles have often favoured a leader-centric perspective that focuses on the strategic and/or personal nature of transformational leadership. This has often been at the cost of focusing attention on those at different levels of the organization and inside the change process whose decision-making and subsequent actions can have a determining impact on the overall effectiveness of a business transformation. In an increasingly dynamic context where workplaces are breaking down and work is becoming more diverse, it is vital and more important than ever to engage people with change rather than imposing it on them. To do this effectively requires a shift in mindset, as was seen during the Covid-19 pandemic.

The pandemic forced organizations around the globe to implement radically new ways of managing and implementing change, because they had to respond to a sudden, unforeseen crisis whose rapidly emerging nature made it difficult to predict and plan for events. This brought to the fore the pitfalls of strategies that envision moving in a linear way from point A to point B on a static path, and that assume that there are years, rather than months or weeks, in which to rethink outdated views and transform existing ways of working. Having a process and a plan to deal with the unexpected is important, but not the only thing that is needed. Even more vital is to make a fundamental mindset shift: from a focus on purely process to one on process and people, and from surviving to the pursuit of thriving. A thriving mindset recognizes that disruption is continuous and embraces it as a catalyst to move the organization forward. Such a shift from survive to thrive depends on an organization becoming and remaining distinctly people-centric at its core. This is not just a different way of thinking and acting but a different way of being, one that approaches every change from a distinctly people angle first, rather than just a process one. To do this, an organization needs to ground itself in principles such as engagement, collaboration, communications, diversity, inclusion, equality and wellbeing. These people-centric change principles enable an organization to be agile and to adapt to the perpetual disruption of the heavy downpour of changes.

People-centric change

Reframing change management

Organizations are having to implement business transformations in hybrid and remote work environments which classic change management approaches were never designed to do. This is driving a need to reframe how change is conceived, agreed and implemented, and how people are engaged with transformations, because traditional top-down linear models of change that have had a pervasive influence in practice are no longer as relevant as they used to be. Yet, much of the literature on organizational change focuses on designing the perfect implementation checklist,[9] or improving the implementation of an existing transformation process.[10] Such frameworks adopt a linear, structural-functionalist view where the role of change agents is to align, fit or adapt organizations through interventions to their organizational vision. The overall objective is often to find the best way to manage change that will enable individuals to adopt the required behaviours to enact the desired organizational state. Research suggests that this model of change is limited because it treats change as a single, momentary disturbance that must be stabilized and controlled, and is, at its core, top-down in nature and focused on leaders maintaining control.[11] The view that conventional change management models have is that the development of ideas for change is the reserved prerogative of senior management (and often consultants); while employees' involvement is largely confined to unquestioning implementation. This top-down approach frequently results in an impoverished and unsustainable change process that is no longer fit for purpose in the changing workplace.

To address the limitations of a linear approach to change there have been calls from academics to reframe change management as a micro-situated, everyday, distributed practice, similar to Gronn's notion of distributed leadership, which demands a shift from the dominant perspective that treats it as a strategic tool deployed by key players in the organizational hierarchy.[12] In other words, a move from a traditional top-down process to a more emergent concept involving employees across the organization. This is the basis of people-centric change (outlined in this book), which proposes that people are at the heart of a transformation and that stakeholders including employees, who often have valuable insights into how the work they do could be improved, are given the space and autonomy to contribute and engage with organizational change as early as possible. The rationale for this is that, as organizations fundamentally re-imagine their operating models, rethink their product and service portfolios, reinvent their supply chains and rebuild to correct inequality and racism, the type of approach to the business transformations required is quick, agile and, in many cases, virtual. The opportunity lies not in doing change the same way as it has always been done and a little bit better and a little bit faster, but instead doing it differently. When organizations are facing the demand for transformational change there is a need to enable and engage people who are best positioned to drive change from its inception. This means creating a way of doing transformations that fully resonates with the organization's purpose and values, that acknowledges the capabilities and motivations of employees and that ultimately increases productivity and impacts positively on wellbeing.

Re-aligning transformations as inclusive

In the post-pandemic world there is a need to rethink not only how change is managed but also how teams and others are engaged equally and inclusively with it and inspired to contribute to it. This is about recognizing that any individual in the organization can influence change and its outcomes, and means everyone has the permission and autonomy to think beyond their job description, is able to look for ways to contribute to the broader organization's goals, and can help to transform the workplace and the work that they do. This means being able to reshape how business transformations are done by finding ways to engage people with them. This is what happened during the crisis of the pandemic when organizations had to rethink what had to change and how this could be done remotely, which resulted in the reshaping of organizational change according to a different set of assumptions. Reshaping approaches to organizational change does, however, mean more than just redesigning tasks and activities; it also involves reconfiguring how change is done by leveraging the capabilities that different people can bring to the entire journey of a transformation, from its inception to its sustainability. A people-centric approach to change is, therefore, inclusive and recognizes the need for equality and diversity in how change is enacted.

Putting people at the heart of change

People play a vital part in organizational change, but often it does not seem like it. Organizations put effort, energy, time and money into the activities of change, such as: writing new procedures and processes, designing development and training courses; building systems; looking for ways to digitize and rationalize work; launching new products and services; creating brands; and opening new facilities. But the people who will implement and work with such new initiatives are often an afterthought, despite the fact that change is only achieved and sustained when it is accepted and adopted by people, which means that they should be involved in the process and even drive it. For instance, consider the example of a global insurance company that was hit with regulatory findings that required it to overhaul its work processes. The company needed to make an inventory of all its customer terms, conditions and supporting processes, assess whether any of those violated the regulations and then create new controls to avoid future violations. This was an enormous undertaking that involved several consultants and thousands of dollars, but the company did not have a plan for sustaining the work after the consultants left, and subsequently it continued to have regulatory issues. Consider for a moment what might have been different if the leaders had, from the beginning, engaged some of their employees in the transformation and if they had made sure that those people had the resources to continue the work after the consultants left; perhaps then the company's ongoing regulatory challenges might have been avoided.[13] A people-centric approach is, therefore, a way to ensure that business transformations achieve their purpose by encouraging people to drive positive and sustainable change rather than having it imposed upon them.

A people-centric approach to change will provide significant benefits. For instance, positioning people at the forefront of a transformation and giving them space to contribute will help to give voice to the voiceless, provide opportunities for diversity of thought and ideas, and create an inclusive approach to decision-making. To put individuals, such as frontline staff, at the heart of decisions about changes related to their work and workplace entails: creating a shared sense of purpose and meaning of change; enabling people to engage as early as is feasible with a transformation; and trusting them to engage with change in a way that allows them to fulfil their potential, by providing them with a degree of autonomy over what needs to change, why it needs to change, and how it will change and when.

For effective planned transformations, people need to be centre stage in evolving the change. Traditional change management as we knew it is now obsolete, and the very notion that change can be managed in a top-down way feels absurd given the reality and pace of business, especially since the context in which organizations operate is fundamentally shifting. Engaging people in a business transformation has, therefore, never been more important, and to do this successfully organizations need a culture as well as the capabilities and capacity which supports people-centric change. In order to justify and help advance a people-centric approach to change, this book outlines some of the key arguments for doing so and proposes a practical framework with several key principles for implementing such an approach. The book also brings together insights from individuals and organizations from across the globe that have experience of business transformations and have experienced the benefits of people-centric change.

The aim of this book

As the global pandemic ebbs, its impact on the world of work is becoming more evident. Working in an office five days a week from 9 am to 5 pm – 'what a way to make a living' as Dolly Parton once said – looks like it might be over for many people. Hybrid and flexible work arrangements are becoming the norm and although there are good reasons why organizations are keen on a mix of in-person and remote working, there are also reasons why this shift is raising concerns, especially when one considers how organizational changes are enacted. The changes in the workplace, such as the move to hybrid working, are turning how organizational change is done upside-down, and in turn demanding different or new approaches to the traditional linear models of change management, which are long overdue for an overhaul. Indeed, the shift to more flexible working is highlighting how essential it is to democratize how business transformations are conducted and to build a change-capable organization with the capacity for major changes.

This book considers how change can be delivered *with* rather than *to* the people who are part of a transformation process. In it I attempt to question existing ways of doing business transformations, and to encourage you to think and act a little differently. The perspectives within the book are based on my research, teaching and consultancy work on organizational change over several decades and also conversations I have had with people from many different sectors and countries. As a Professor at Durham University Business School, I have over the years also had the opportunity to hear the views of thousands of students whom I have taught and this has helped me to fine-tune my own thinking and ideas about organizational change (and continues to do so). These ideas have been translated into action through my research and writing, culminating in this book on the concept of people-centric change, which focuses on the importance of engaging people with business transformations. To help illustrate how people-centric change works in practice I have brought together insights from business people across the globe in a series of 'business insights' at the end of each chapter. I hope that you will consider the questions I have included at the end of each of these, and how the lessons which they highlight might be applied to organizations you are either working in or ones that you are familiar with. I have also drawn from a range of frameworks that will help you to bring some structure to how you engage people with change, but importantly, also, how you contribute to and actively participate in business transformations.

I have studied organizational change since I completed my Ph.D. nearly 30 years ago, and have worked with many organizations that have been engaged in business transformations. Over the years I have been brought in at various junctures, such as: the inception of an idea for change; when root causes have to be identified and ways to address them considered; after things have started to go wrong; and even at the rescue stage when it is evident that the proposed change is sinking. Throughout my career I have witnessed ideas and learning about how planned organizational change is evolving, from a top-down project management approach to one that is iterative and focuses on employee participation. It is heartening to see and hear the need for more people-focused approaches to planned transformations but the challenge is not just talking the talk but actually enacting a people-centric approach to change in practice.

In recent conversations with senior leaders and managers across the globe and also with frontline staff, I have heard similar concerns being raised about business transformations in the changing workplace. Some of the most important concerns raised can be grouped under the challenges of: how to engage stakeholders in change; engaging opposing voices; creating effective communications; positioning change as an opportunity rather than a threat; the evolving nature of the role of managers in transformations; the impact of change on wellbeing; and fostering collaboration and inclusivity. This book has emerged from those conversations and focuses specifically on these challenges and how to address them. In the process, due consideration is given to how adopting a people-centric approach to business transformations is essential, as employees, leaders, managers and organizations navigate the reshaped world of work. The focus of the book is, therefore, on creating change in a people-centric way because the successful achievement of major change necessitates not only involving people in conversations about change and idea generation but also in realizing and sustaining the benefits of business transformations. How this is done in changing work environments poses significant issues some of which this book will examine, as well as considering some practical solutions. Furthermore, this book is a call to action to cultivate and implement a more people-centric approach to business transformations, to consider different perspectives and, importantly, to make the leap from the rhetoric of ideas to the action of creation and implementation. I have therefore written this book in a practical way, to support you and your organization to make that leap with business transformations, because the success of organizational change in a world of increasing volatility, complexity and chaos is highly dependent on the advocacy of people.

Although leadership envisions and drives change, success is largely contingent on the engagement of stakeholders (internal and external to the organization). Research shows that only by engaging stakeholders does change have a chance to be successful.[14] The underlying assumption of this book is, therefore, that the engagement and active participation of stakeholders with organizational change is a must-do, not a nice-to-have activity, because there are benefits for the organization when people are able to share a diversity of perspectives and ideas to help drive improvements and innovation and engagement with making change happen.

This book stresses that stakeholder participation is a key success factor, no matter what the driving forces are and how the change process is initiated and managed, because only by gaining the commitment of all those concerned, through their full involvement in planned transformational change, will change be successful – a claim that has been supported empirically.[15] For instance, research suggests that participation is important for building and maintaining trust not only in the change process but also between management and employees.[16] Participation also reduces opposition to change through improved information sharing, decision-making and organizational commitment.[17] This book does, however, go further than these assumptions and posits that individuals and teams should not merely participate but also be responsible for developing solutions, which means involving key stakeholders and stakeholder groups, as early as possible, in identifying what needs to change. Business transformations should, therefore, whenever it is feasible to do so, be constructed or negotiated *with* rather than *for* stakeholders, thereby reflecting the plurality of stakeholder interests. To explore how this can be done, this book breaks fresh ground and sets out frameworks, perspectives, practical approaches and recommendations for successfully engaging people in business transformations. It does this in several ways, including: providing real-world experiences from individuals across the globe and from different sectors; considering prevalent types of change scenarios such as mergers and acquisitions, restructures and downsizing and digital transformations; identifying the key capabilities required to engage people with organizational change now and in the future; and providing culturally transferable tools, frameworks and practical approaches which can be adapted, depending on the context of the organization.

I hope that, whether you are a frontline or leading worker and/or managing a team of people, or a multinational company employing thousands of people across the globe, or a student studying organizational change, this book will help you to:

- appreciate the importance of the people dynamics of change
- engage others and become engaged yourself with change within different working contexts
- achieve the benefits accrued from sustaining change with other key stakeholders and
- apply the practical skills mentioned throughout the book to ensure you and others are a proactive part of a business transformation

Structure of the book

To help to expand your knowledge and understanding of people-centric change and how to apply it in practice, this book is structured into the following chapters, with each focusing on a key theme that is relevant to people-centric change.

Chapter 1: The rationale for people-centric change

The complexity and fluidity of organizational change means that how it is managed now and in the future needs to be very different from the prescriptive linear approaches that have been popular for several decades. This chapter discusses the need for a shift from top-down change to a more people-centric approach. The rationale for reframing how change is enacted is considered within the context of changing work environments. The chapter concludes by outlining the key themes covered in the book.

Chapter 2: Why engaging people in business change is crucial

This chapter examines the context in which organizations are operating and some of the forces that are driving the need for transformation and affecting the way that it is done. Consideration is given to some of the reasons why organizations cannot afford to ignore engaging people with change and goes on to discuss how successful transformations require attention to the people dynamics of change, stressing that it is individuals and teams who ultimately implement and sustain change by adapting how they work and behave. The chapter concludes with the case of ST Engineering iDirect written by Steve Tunnicliffe, the company's ex-Senior Vice President, Global Sales. This thought-provoking business insight highlights the fact that effective employee engagement with a business transformation comprises numerous factors including: transparency and frequent communications from leaders; a clear mission that everyone, irrespective of role or position, can support and feel that they can make a contribution to; and also an effective work culture that mobilizes and empowers the workforce.

Chapter 3: Engaging stakeholders

People-centric change is about engaging people proactively in transformations. This chapter on how to engage stakeholders explores several of the key principles and practices that underpin the way that engagement with a business transformation can be generated and sustained. Particular attention is paid to some of the important factors that influence stakeholders' engagement with change, such as autonomy, relationships and the opportunities to co-create change. The chapter also reflects on a number of important challenges, such as: how to engage people in change in a limited period of time when a change is the result of urgent pressures requiring a rapid response; and how employees' visibility and involvement with a transformation can be ensured in a hybrid work environment. Emphasis is given as to how engagement with a business transformation does not just happen but involves people having the opportunity to be proactive in mobilizing change.

This vital point is illustrated in the business insight written by Carlos Pullen-Ferreira, Vice President, Business Transformation at Sage. Carlos stresses how employees are by no means passive actors in organizations but can be proactive in making change happen.

Chapter 4: Engaging opposing voices

People can represent the greatest challenge to organizational change by the different ways in which they react, especially if they oppose it. This chapter reflects on how to address opposing voices by seeing them through a positive lens rather than a negative one, and by appreciating why they may be resisting change. Instead of dismissing what 'opposers' have to say, people-centric change proposes welcoming their views by respecting and empathizing with them. How and why people oppose change is explored in this chapter, with particular deliberation on how to address opposition by: making change meaningful; giving people a voice (even if it is one of opposition); and taking time to understand the perspective of others. In particular, emphasis is given to the importance of listening to dissenting voices, especially in pressurized situations such as when there is a need to drive the transformation through to a specific deadline. The chapter concludes with a business insight written by independent consultant Zoleka Mashiyi, who outlines the challenges of implementing a transformation within a public sector department in South Africa where there was opposition and apathy to changing the culture of the department to one that was more service orientated.

Chapter 5: Communication of change

Communications play a pivotal role in people-centric change before, during and after a transformation is implemented. Yet, despite this, communication is often done badly, as a mono-directional transfer of instructions and explanations. This chapter contemplates what can be done to make the communication of change more effective by discussing some of the practical challenges of communication and by suggesting how these can be addressed. In particular, the chapter focuses on the need for conversations and the ways that dialogue can help to ensure meaningful change. To help stimulate conversations, consideration is given to some of the ways of creating space for dialogue and impromptu conversations. Furthermore, attention is given to the communication of change in hybrid and remote working environments and some of the challenges such as encouraging people to speak up online and join conversations. The importance of having flexible multi-level communication plans is illustrated in the business insight written by Laura de Ruiter, Associate Director in the Behavioural Science Consortium and Laurence Scates, the former Executive Director and Head of the Transformation from Astellas Pharma Inc. Laura and Laurence espouse the need for consistent and targeted communications of change. The chapter concludes with some practical suggestions for the effective communication of change.

Chapter 6: Change as an opportunity, not a threat

Change is often viewed as a threat or risk. People-centric change proposes reframing business transformations so that they are seen not merely as threats but also opportunities. To achieve this shift in mindset, the challenge is how to convince people who are surrounded by threatening disruptions that they should not look at them as just risks, but as opportunities, especially when they are tired and exhausted from ongoing changes. In an attempt to help people reassess their perspectives of change, this chapter begins by discussing the reasons why a business transformation should be looked at as an opportunity, and the ways of repositioning a transformational change so that it is seen in a positive light. The chapter goes on to explore how to facilitate and align people to see change as an opportunity through several approaches, such as encouraging innovation, experimentation and a learning environment. The importance of learning during a business transformation and how to position a transformation as an opportunity rather than a threat is described in the business insight of a pharmaceutical company in Pakistan. The case is written by Zuhair Imran, a digital consultant, who provides an open and honest account of the challenges he faced in shifting the view about a digital transformation from a negative to a positive one.

Chapter 7: Re-imaging the role of managers in change

The role of managers is critical in people-centric change. The traditional approach to the management of change has conventionally been hierarchical, which may have made sense when jobs were fixed, workplaces were physical, information flowed downwards and change management was seen as an isolated project, actioned only when adaptions or improvements were needed. Nevertheless, that is no longer the case, especially since the world of work is being rapidly enabled by technology that is driving a prioritization on agility, adaptability, speed, innovation, responsibility and connectivity. Consequently, managers are facing increasing ambiguity in their role as they try to manage change in a world of advancing technology as well as hybrid and remote environments where there is less control and visibility of the processes of change and fewer opportunities for impromptu conversations. At the same time, managers are also trying to recreate the cohesiveness, collaboration and camaraderie of the office through the freedom and flexibility of remote working. These demands are driving the need to reframe the role of managers, which is explored in this chapter. It begins by considering the evolving role of managers and goes on to discuss the need for them to pivot to people-centric change. Particular attention is given to the need for managers to shift their role from micromanaging a transformation, particularly in remote and hybrid work environments, to one of micro-understanding. To prevent the risk of micromanagement and to help to reframe their role, the chapter explores the need for a shift in mindset as well as the key capabilities required for people-centric change. The changing role of managers is highlighted in the business insight written by Kathrin Schrepfer, a change management professional, trainer and business coach, about the merger between two medium-sized international cyber security companies based in France, Germany and the UK. Kathrin discusses what happened when different styles of management surfaced post-merger and the importance of ensuring the buy-in and ability of managers to effectively manage the merger. The chapter concludes with some practical recommendations for managing transformations in hybrid environments.

Chapter 8: Wellbeing during change

Frequently, the people element of change is only considered once a transformation has started, and often not until the process is about to finish, which is too late and unlikely to create the necessary changes in the working practices, skills, knowledge and behaviour required to deliver the benefits of the change. Such an approach may also adversely affect the health and wellbeing of individuals, which in turn can have a detrimental impact on the effectiveness and performance of teams, and eventually the organization. In contrast, people-centric change stresses the need to build wellbeing into transformations because employees with higher levels of wellbeing are more likely to enjoy their work and to have higher levels of engagement and adaptability during transformations. To support the need for transformations to build wellbeing into their plans, this chapter examines the importance of ensuring the positive impact of change on people. It begins by examining the concept of wellbeing, followed by the impact that a transformation can have on individual, team and organizational wellbeing. The chapter includes a business insight written by David Howell, the founder of Able and Rush (People Solutions) Ltd, of a transformation within a police service in the Midlands, UK. The case emphasizes the need for wellbeing and mental health as an intrinsic part of a business transformation rather than an extrinsic one. As David explains, this can help to increase the likelihood of successful outcomes as well as ensuring a healthy transformation journey both mentally and physically for everyone involved and impacted. The chapter concludes by discussing potential practices for ensuring positive health and wellbeing as part of organizational transformations.

Chapter 9: Equality, diversity, inclusion and change

Although much organizational effort appears to be based on the belief that employees are not responsible adults and they need to be 'managed' into transformations, this is a very narrow-sighted view. On the contrary, people-centric change stresses the need for organizational transformations to be characterized by equality, diversity and inclusion (EDI). This chapter emphasizes the importance of the EDI inside a business transformation and considers practices for giving voice to the often voiceless. In this era of hybrid working attention is also given to how a sense of inclusion, unity and alignment can be created when some employees are working remotely. The importance of integrating EDI into an organizational culture is outlined in the business insight written by Douglas Flory, a change management and transformation expert, which describes how a global IT company succeeded in doing this. Douglas stresses the need for education, data, sponsorship, stakeholder engagement and communication for driving EDI into a culture.

Chapter 10: Fostering collaboration

A key element of people-centric change is collaboration. As workplaces break down and work becomes more diverse, it is more important than ever to foster collaboration with transformational change, whenever feasible to do so, rather than imposing it on people. This chapter explores how to establish a collaborative environment for change, including when people no longer sit in the same space or office, are dispersed across many offices or are working from home. Some of the practical ways that collaboration and ownership of change can be created in these different situations and amongst individuals and teams working in flexible ways are explored. The chapter emphasizes the importance of teaming for collaboration, including the emergence of superteams, which are combinations of people and technology, using their complementary capabilities to pursue business transformations at a speed and scale not otherwise possible. The importance of collaboration in people-centric change is illustrated in the case of Lamu Island, Kenya which highlights that change that is inclusive and collaborative can strengthen partnerships across communities, the organization, industries and national borders. The importance of collaboration is further stressed in the business insight written by David Maybin, a Senior Change Lead based in the Victorian Department of Health, Australia, in which he describes the implementation of a new customer relationship management (CRM) system within a large Australian government department. The chapter concludes with some practical implications for effective collaboration.

Chapter 11: How to build a people-centric change strategy

This concluding chapter pulls together the main themes discussed throughout the book and proposes a framework for people-centric change, along with principles to support it, based on my research and consultancy work. The chapter outlines how the elements of the framework, which moves away from a traditional linear approach to a cyclical model, are linked together, with eight key principles comprising: build engagement; foster collaboration; encourage dialogue; promote reflection and enquiry; stimulate innovation; enhance wellbeing; develop managers; and build transformational capabilities. The chapter concludes by considering how the framework can be applied in practice.

Summary

Before the Covid-19 pandemic, organizations assumed that they knew best how to implement a business transformation, but the pandemic brought to light that change can be more effective when employees are allowed to take more initiative, in other words when the change is more people-centric. This reframing of change is not based on what employees were recruited to do, or what they are certified to do, or even what organizations or leaders want them to do, but it is about giving people more autonomy to choose how they can help to tackle critical business problems and/or opportunities. For change to be successful, people need to be included in the process from the start, given opportunities to engage with it, be committed to it, and be willing to embed it. Too often, the people dimension is only considered after a transformation has started, and in many cases not until the end of the process, which is often too little, too late. This can lead to a failure to create the desired changes in working practices, skills, knowledge and behaviour that are needed to deliver the business benefits. To create a successful transformation, people must feel that they are instrumental in influencing the direction of change, which means that employees and other key stakeholders need to be not just participants but also protagonists in business transformations, thus necessitating a shift from the conventional strategies. Traditional change management, often top-down and characterized by linear processes, lengthy timelines and faltering implementations, is no longer adequate and, in an era of disruption and digitization, is outdated. Instead of top-down linear strategies, there is a need to consider adopting a people-centric approach that is less prescriptive, more collaborative and involves stakeholders throughout the process, instead of simply telling them what will happen and what they must do.

It is important to pursue a people-centric approach to planned business transformations not as an end in itself but as a means of improving change in organizations and working lives. A people-centric approach to change is not a one-time event or even a process, but goes far beyond the strategies for consultation and participation that most organizations embrace. Putting people at the heart of a business transformation, enables agility and adaptability which are vital for organizations that are having to frequently rejuvenate due to the changing environments in which they operate.

Notes

1 Gartner. Gartner organizational change management case studies, Gartner, nd. www.gartner.com/en/human-resources/insights/organizational-change-management (archived at https://perma.cc/DV92-4QU8)

2 E Mygatt, A Padhi, C Relyea and B Weddle. Organizing for speed in advanced industries, McKinsey, 20 August 2020. www.mckinsey.com/industries/industrials-and-electronics/our-insights/organizing-for-speed-in-advanced-industries (archived at https://perma.cc/GNF6-F26S)

3 P Polman and A Winston (2021) *Net Positive: How courageous companies thrive by giving more than they take*, Harvard Business Review Press, Boston, 247

4 J Turner. This new strategy could be your ticket to change management success, Gartner, 28 November 2022. www.gartner.com/en/articles/this-new-strategy-could-be-your-ticket-to-change-management-success (archived at https://perma.cc/X9RB-FG34)

5 C O Morain and P Aykens. Employees are losing patience with change initiatives, *Harvard Business Review*, 9 May 2023. hbr.org/2023/05/employees-are-losing-patience-with-change-initiatives (archived at https://perma.cc/VM6C-2YSS)

6 G Rometty. Ginni Rometty: Leadership, legacy and a new mission, *Financial Times*, 8 March 2023. www.ft.com/content/beae436b-ce83-43ab-9254-70f9f3b6b1b3 (archived at https://perma.cc/9M6A-CXDC)

7 G Rometty. Ginni Rometty: Leadership, legacy and a new mission, *Financial Times*, 8 March 2023. www.ft.com/content/beae436b-ce83-43ab-9254-70f9f3b6b1b3 (archived at https://perma.cc/63BC-N8HY)

8 Gartner. Changing change management: Effectively preserve order during major changes, from M&As to culture changes, nd. www.gartner.com/en/human-resources/trends/changing-change-management (archived at https://perma.cc/AG6B-RR8H)

9 J P Kotter (2012) *Leading Change*, Harvard Business School Press, Cambridge, MA

10 S Fernandez and H G Rainey. Managing successful organizational change in the public sector, *Public Administration Review*, 2006, 66 (2), 168–76

11 D A Blackman, F Buick, M E O'Donnell and N Ilahee. Changing the conversation to create organizational change, *Journal of Change Management*, 2022, 22 (3), 252–72. www.researchgate.net/publication/358697039_Changing_the_Conversation_to_Create_Organizational_Change (archived at https://perma.cc/V776-T8QC)

12 P Gronn. Distributed leadership as a unit of analysis, *The Leadership Quarterly*, 2002, 13 (4), 423–51. www.sciencedirect.com/science/article/abs/pii/S1048984302001200 (archived at https://perma.cc/Z867-LRJJ)

13 A Giacoman and C Hapelt. Making transformation stick, Strategy + Business, 19 July 2021. www.strategy-business.com/blog/Making-transformation-stick (archived at https://perma.cc/9KXY-TLQY)

14 J Hodges (2019) *Employee Engagement for Organizational Change: The theory and practice of stakeholder engagement*, Routledge, London

15 S Fuchs and R Prouska. Creating positive employee change evaluation: The role of different levels of organizational support and change participation, *Journal of Change Management*, 2014, 14 (3), 361–83. www.tandfonline.com/doi/abs/10.1080/14697017.2014.885460?journalCode=rjcm20 (archived at https://perma.cc/62W7-3MDC)

16 C A Yue, L R Men and M A Ferguson. Bridging transformational leadership, transparent communication, and employee openness to change: The mediating role of trust, *Public Relations Review*, Setember 2019, 45 (3), 101779. www.sciencedirect.com/science/article/abs/pii/S0363811119300360 (archived at https://perma.cc/38AL-DULX)

17 R Lines. The structure and function of attitudes toward organizational change, *Human Resource Development Review*, 2005, 4 (1), 8–32. journals.sagepub.com/doi/10.1177/1534484304273818 (archived at https://perma.cc/P7L4-775X)

02

Why engaging people in business change is crucial

Introduction

In his book *Hit Refresh*, Microsoft CEO Satya Nadella writes that great leaders recognize the true signal within a lot of noise and act accordingly.[1] The torrent of trends, ideas and data that is sweeping through organizations makes knowing what to change, when and how quickly, more difficult than ever, especially as the need for change is speeding up as existential challenges grow – for example, global inequality continues to soar; the world's biophysical health keeps deteriorating; and climate change is on the increase. It is not, however, a totally negative picture, since there are some positive trends that are also speeding up – for instance, technology such as generative AI is getting smarter and more efficient and providing us with more tools and different ways of working; and the costs of building a clean economy are continuing to decrease. Addressing these trends (and others) requires many organizations to transform, which can no longer be done by the senior leadership team alone but instead requires engaging others to ensure success. As Paul Polman and Andrew Winston point out in their book *Net Positive*, leaders have to demonstrate that they are open to working with others, and rather than just commanding from behind a desk they have to engage people to work with them to solve challenges.[2] In other words, the bias that a leader may have for a top-down command-and-control strategy for change needs to become a bias for transformative, collaborative action. This means treating everyone equally, and encouraging engagement and innovation amongst staff, particularly those on the frontline, to rethink how products and services are delivered, rather than just pressurizing them to do better and implement what has already been decided by the senior team.

Engaging stakeholders in organizational change is critical, because most business transformations do not deliver their expected benefits. This is evident in a study of hundreds of companies executing major changes which found that few achieved or exceeded expectations but instead 50 per cent settled for dilution of value and mediocre results, and 38 per cent fell well short of expected results.[3] With such poor results it is, therefore, of little surprise when employees retort 'Here we go again' when they are told about another impending change that has been developed without their involvement and which will likely deliver results that are only short-term. To avoid this happening, employees, including those on the frontline, should not be treated simply as mere conduits for top-down decisions, nor as mediums for ensuring compliance to the implementation of a transformation, but instead their engagement and involvement should be sought from the beginning. Nevertheless, it is important to recognize that there may be times when it is not always possible to engage others in organizational change – for instance, when a situation arises suddenly (such as a pandemic), when there is a crisis (for example a cybersecurity breach or attack) or when new laws and/or regulations must be adhered to. But, whenever feasible to do so, stakeholders must be involved from the inception of a business transformation.

Aim of chapter

To set the scene for people-centric change, this chapter considers the context in which organizations are operating by exploring some of the forces that are driving the need for business transformations and affecting the way that change is done. It begins by discussing some of the global forces driving change, then goes on to explore why transformations are necessary. The chapter concludes with the case of ST Engineering iDirect, written by Steve Tunnicliffe, previously the company's Senior Vice President of Global Sales. The case highlights that effective employee engagement with a business transformation comprises numerous factors, including the need for: transparency and frequent communications from leaders; a clear mission that everyone, irrespective of role or position, can support change and make a contribution; and an effective work culture that mobilizes and empowers the workforce.

Global forces for change

The pandemic has both revealed and accelerated a number of trends that are playing a substantial role in shaping the future of organizations and that are impacting on the workplace, the nature of work and the role of workers. Some of these forces for change can be controlled, while others must be navigated, but few of them can be ignored. Globalization, for instance, is changing, but it is not disappearing, as there are new dynamics around countries such as Russia and China, as well as shifts in the global economic power, with rapidly developing nations, for example some African states, which, with large working-age populations, are embracing a business ethos, attracting investment and improving their education systems. A further trend is resource scarcity and climate change, with the demand for energy and water forecast to increase by as much as 50 per cent and 40 per cent respectively by 2030.[4] Moreover, the changing size, distribution and aging profile of the world's population is putting pressure on business, social institutions and economies. Longer lifespans are affecting business models, talent ambitions and pension costs, and driving the need for older workers to learn new skills and work longer. Added to this is a shortage of people and capabilities in the workforce in a number of rapidly ageing economies, for instance in the UK, USA and European Union (EU), where job vacancies have increased and outstrip the availability of people. In the UK this is most noticeable in the public sector, especially health, education and transport, although the shortage is also affecting private companies, too. In Europe, a study by the German Chambers of Commerce and Industry (DIHK) in January 2023 reported that more than half of the 22,000 companies surveyed had experienced difficulties in recruiting staff, especially in technology, and that, based on its digital ambitions, the EU needs 20 million technology specialists.[5] This demand for expertise is being driven by technological advancements.

Technological breakthroughs

The rapid advances in technological innovations such as automation, robotics and generative AI are dramatically changing the nature of work and impacting on how work is done, as well as increasing cybersecurity issues. As Al Gore said, 'We are at the early stages of a technology led sustainability revolution which has the scale of the Industrial Revolution and the pace of the digital revolution'.[6] Technology has the power to improve lives, raise productivity, living standards and average lifespan but it also brings the threat of disruption, which is seen in a number of ways, including:

- ***Automating work:*** Spending on technology is going up because it is displacing things which organizations used to do manually. For example, Walmart, an American multinational retail corporation, has used automation to halve the number of steps needed to ship products from some of its e-commerce distribution centres, and healthcare provider Humana has leveraged technology to reduce administrative tasks.
- ***Metaverse:*** The metaverse is driving a shift from global business models, standards and homogeneity to highly targeted interactions to, and among, heterogeneous communities composed of individuals with common interests, irrespective of their location. This shift is creating new business opportunities, but also requires investments in workforce capabilities and development to ensure effective engagement with these micro-communities. There is also, however, a need to manage the complexities and risks of the metaverse, including security, privacy and accessibility.

Technology innovations are thus bringing advancements but also threats, along with companies facing impediments such as a lack of expertise and resistance for fear of job losses. To address these threats, the need for people and technology to collaborate and work together has to be recognized and developed so that technology is viewed as a supplement to human input, not a replacement. The development and collaboration of superteams (see Chapter 10) can help to reposition workers in roles where they work alongside technology and are not replaced by it. Inevitably, in an increasingly digital world we need to understand technology, and particularly AI, because it is becoming an increasing part of the way that we work, whatever we do, whether it is in a supermarket, a farm or a university. We also need have to be cognizant about technology's limitations, as well as how we can be manipulated by the technology we use to connect and entertain ourselves. Whether we embrace it or not, advances in technology are reshaping both the challenges and possibilities of work and how change is being enacted in organizations.

Rise of stakeholder capitalism

In a post-pandemic world, CEOs and boards are focusing more on their organization's impact on the long-term welfare of multiple stakeholders, not just their stockholders. This has led to the resurgence and growing importance of stakeholder capitalism, which focuses on the needs and interests not just of shareholders but of all constituents, such as customers, employees, suppliers, partners, communities and the natural environment. The rise of stakeholder capitalism has been spurred on by the climate crisis and increasing social challenges, such as rising inequality. Increasingly, there is a sense among business leaders that the prevailing ideology of putting shareholders above everyone else needs to change. As Microsoft's CEO Satya Nadella puts it, the job is all about customers, partners, employees, investors and governments, and is about all of them, all of the time.[7] Within the context of a business transformation, this translates as the need to effectively engage and interact with internal and external stakeholders.

People-centric change is highly dependent on the advocacy of all key stakeholder groups, which is the link between strategic decision-making and effective implementation, between individual motivation and product innovation, and between delighted customers and growing revenues. Research suggests that a company's relationship with external stakeholders can influence as much as 30 per cent of corporate earnings.[8] So, although leadership may envision and drive change, success is largely contingent on the engagement of stakeholders. This means that the involvement of stakeholders with a business transformation is a must-do, not nice-to-have, activity since there are benefits for the organization when people externally engage and those internally interact across functional and business unit boundaries to bring a range of perspectives and help to drive change and innovation. Studies show that highly engaged employees tend to support organizational change initiatives and are more resilient in the face of change.[9] Organizational change should, therefore, whenever feasible, be constructed or negotiated *with* rather than *to* stakeholders, thereby reflecting the plurality of stakeholder interests.

Impact of the forces for change

Nature of work

As organizational strategies evolve in the face of disruption caused by the global forces for change, companies are being challenged to rethink outdated views, especially since employees expect more from their employers in terms of more meaningful work and more flexibility in when and where they work. As work has become less mechanistic, jobs have become increasingly more fluid and dynamic, giving individuals and teams the potential autonomy to shape what they do and how they do it. This is evident in the increased application of job crafting, which involves taking proactive steps and actions to redesign what people do at work, essentially changing tasks, relationships and perceptions of their jobs. The use of such approaches is accelerating, particularly as ways of working move away from rigid reporting lines to networks of teams, from prescribed routines and job descriptions to expanded job canvases, and from narrow skills to broad capabilities. The implication for workers is that they need to be viewed not as interchangeable cogs in an organization's wheels, but rather as individuals with unique and disparate experiences, thoughts, attitudes, needs and values – all of which makes the need to engage them in business transformations more important and complex than ever before.

Shift to hybrid and remote working

The impact of global trends, as well as the aftermath of the Covid-19 pandemic, has meant that the nature and role of work is being redefined around the world. The concept of remote working as an element of more flexible working has been adopted by a significant number of organizations in line with employee expectations. Surveys indicate that 75 per cent of hybrid or remote knowledge workers agree that their expectations for working flexibly have increased and that if an organization were to go back to a fully on-site working, it would risk losing up to 39 per cent of its workforce.[10]

For employees, hybrid working provides greater flexibility between working and personal time, which contributes to improved work–life balance, as well as a reduction in the time and cost spent commuting. There are, however, challenges with implementing business transformations across remote work environments. For instance, remote working creates a distance between employees and their workplace by restricting or removing the opportunity for them to engage in informal exchanges with managers and colleagues. Furthermore, it reduces the opportunity to share tacit knowledge and information and also risks reducing opportunities to engage in the collaborative sharing of ideas and hence the promotion of creativity and innovation. A further challenge is invisibility, in that managers may not be aware of the capability and potential of an individual to contribute to and engage with a business transformation because they do not see that individual at work if they are working remotely. It can also be harder to build and maintain trust without proximity. Moreover, there is the risk of individuals losing touch with what is happening with a transformation if they are away from the office for long periods of time.[11] The impact of so many more people working remotely is that inflexible, all-consuming workplace change management models may no longer be fit for purpose. Organizations will, therefore, need to look for different ways to implement business transformations, because managing change remotely and in hybrid environments is very much an active process and requires maintaining close and personal contact with individuals and teams.

Changing employee experience

With the workforce undergoing upheaval, the employee experience has never been more important. Different generations, each with different values, needs and expectations, such as working conditions or work–life balance, are working alongside one another, raising new challenges for finding ways of engaging them with a business transformation. For instance, the way that employees want to work is changing, with more people working outside the traditional office space and the 9 to 5 schedule, which affects how and when they engage with change. As a result, stakeholder engagement is growing in complexity, especially since globalization and technology are shifting organized work onto a different level, in terms of connectivity and the mobility of people. There is, thus, a need to be more flexible in how business transformations are organized and implemented.

Threat to wellbeing

The global trends and their impact on stakeholder engagement have the potential to affect work-related wellbeing. For example, while technology can provide benefits, leading to the automation of routine activities, providing opportunities to work from home, and giving greater access to information, it can also present challenges to employee wellbeing, such as creating work overload, blurring the boundaries between the work–home interface, and eventually increasing stress levels. Furthermore, home working can be difficult for some people because of the isolation it may bring, which in turn can impact on their wellbeing. To address such issues, wellbeing needs to be moved up the agenda of organizational change and focused on the individual in work, not just the individual at work. This necessitates shifting from designing wellbeing programmes that are separate from a business transformation, to designing wellbeing into the transformation processes (see Chapter 8 for further discussion on this). By doing so, organizations can help workers not only feel their best but also perform at their best by strengthening the tie between wellbeing and the outcomes and effectiveness of business transformations.

In sum, the post-pandemic world is creating and accelerating business and societal shifts that are altering the trajectory of organizations since they impact on the future of work, the workforce and the workplace, and drive the need for faster and sustainable decision-making. These trends present huge opportunities as well as threats to organizations and to the people who work within them. When so many complex forces are at play, process-based linear models of organizational change are too simplistic. Instead there is a need for a clear and meaningful approach for business transformations involving the engagement of stakeholders.

Business transformations

Change as a dynamic process

Organizational change is a dynamic process that unfolds intentionally or emerges, and is characterized by content and the context of the organization.[12] The *content* is *what* actually changes in the organization (such as the structure, process, systems and behaviour) and can be small (incremental) or radical (transformational) alterations to the whole or parts of an organization in order to improve its effectiveness, efficiency and wellbeing. The *process* comprises *how* the change occurs, that is the pace, timing and sequence, as well as: how the need for change emerges; the way decisions are made and communicated; how people are engaged with change; and how they respond to it. It is a process that is sometimes planned and managed with the intention of securing anticipated objectives and benefits and is, at other times, unplanned and emergent. The *context* is the *environment* (internal and external) in which an organization operates and the situation in which the change is being implemented. Institutional theory tells us that the environment in which an organization operates can strongly influence the development of an organization, so to survive organizations must conform to the trends prevailing in the environment. In other words, they must adapt either in a planned or emergent way to the complex and chaotic environment in which they operate.

Transformational change

Bruce Feiler, in his book *Life is in the Transitions*, refers to 'lifequakes' – a forceful burst of change that leads to a period of upheaval, transition and renewal.[13] Lifequakes involve a fundamental shift in meaning, purpose or direction and are massive, messy and often miserable. This is similar to business transformations that involve radical changes not only in how an organization operates but also in how people perceive, think and behave at work that go far beyond merely fine-tuning the status quo. Transformations are either derivatives or combinations of various prototypical quests such as:[14]

- ***Global presence:*** Extending market reach and becoming more international in terms of leadership, innovation, talent flows, capabilities and best practices.
- ***Customer focus:*** Understanding customers' needs and providing enhanced insights, experiences, or outcomes (integrated solutions) rather than just products or services.
- ***Nimbleness:*** Simplifying how work gets done so that it becomes agile.
- ***Innovation:*** Incorporating ideas and approaches from fresh sources, both internal and external, to expand the organization's options for exploiting new opportunities.
- ***Sustainability:*** Becoming greener and more socially responsible in positioning and implementation.

Each of these quests has its own focus, enablers and derailers, and each requires the organization to do something more or different with its operating model, customers, partners, internal processes and resources. These quests were evident in a transformation implemented by Medialaan NV, a leading free-to-air video broadcaster in Belgium. When the company spotted the shift in video viewing by young people to platforms such as Netflix or YouTube it bought Mobile Vikings, a mobile virtual operator with attractive data plans. Consequently, Medialaan not only diversified its revenue base to include data plans but was also able to re-engage with a lost segment of its market – teenagers – thus transforming itself into a leading online social video platform and one of the few traditional broadcast companies to grow its TV audience amongst the youth.[15] Thus, transformational change involves a shift in the purpose or direction of a company.

Why begin a transformation?

Behind every transformational change there are motivating forces, that is the internal factors and external trends that create the impetus for change, such as the need to: capture value creation opportunities; realize gains in growth or efficiencies; tackle disruptive new market entrants; adapt to the impact of technology on consumer behaviour; or address macroeconomic pressures such as supply chain issues. To address such demands organizations will often implement various changes, such as: carrying out a merger or acquisition; portfolio moves; restructuring; and/or identifying new market opportunities. A planned business transformation is, therefore, often driven by forces for change that have the potential to significantly impact on an organization and its ways of working.

Who is involved in a transformation?

To be effective, a transformation needs more than one person at the top of the company deciding what has to be changed and when and how this should be done. Nevertheless, the role of the CEO and senior executive team is important in several ways, including: defining a vision of the future and the impact of this on the organization's mission and strategy; communicating the significance of a transformation; sponsoring the transformation journey; and modelling any desired behavioural changes. There are a multitude of senior people who also need to be involved. For example, in some organizations there may be a chief transformation officer (CTO) who will act as the high-level orchestrator of the transformation process and have the mandate and authority to make decisions about personnel, investments and operations. Particularly in large companies, planned transformations are often supported by a programme office or a transformation office (TO) led by the CTO. The aim of the TO tends to be to define goals, model new ways of working and ensure that the overall programme and specific workstreams stay on track. The TO may also provide a repository of information and support where those engaged in the transformation can get help when faced with difficulties and also guidance with the development of new skills. Moreover, the TO can monitor results through weekly, action-oriented meetings where attendees might include the CTO, a sponsor from each of the workstreams and other key initiative owners, plus representation from functions such as finance and HR. The TO may also assist in ensuring that benefits from the organizational changes are sustained and that individuals and teams do not revert to old ways of working as transformation initiatives are completed. Although the CTO and TO may be in charge of several transformations, the responsibility for making day-to-day decisions and implementing those initiatives lies with line managers, transformation managers and frontline staff. So, while the contribution of the executive team and other senior leaders is crucial, a lot more people across the organization are needed to make a transformation work through their involvement, engagement and ownership and to ensure that it does not fail.

What can go wrong?

Transformations may fail to deliver their full potential due to a lack of opportunities for engagement and a lack of ownership by staff at the frontline. There may also be confusion around roles and responsibilities, with staff constantly having to escalate requests to take action or a decision. When only a fraction of the workforce gets involved with a transformation, the rest may feel disengaged and may not want to contribute their ideas or participate in the process. Consequently, the desired benefits and results might never be achieved. Moreover, highly centralized transformations often fail to capture (or even ask for) the ideas for improvement initiatives from frontline employees or even to consider employee knowledge that is vital to the effectiveness of the transformation. For example, as part of a centralized cost-cutting approach a major supermarket chain decided to reduce the number of hours worked by staff in all its shops. This led to long queues at the checkouts and significant frustration and annoyance amongst customers. To prevent this from happening, an alternative approach would have been to put the stakeholders at the heart of the transformation and to get their views on what could be done differently so that the change was co-created in a collaborative way (see Chapter 10 on fostering collaboration) rather than imposing the wrong change which eventually failed.

Engaging people in business transformations

Rationale for involving people in transformations

A transformation is twice as likely to achieve its goal, and to sustain its benefits, when engagement in the effort is effective and starts early with key stakeholders. Unfortunately, too many boardroom conversations and plans for change underestimate the people element and either miss it out altogether, or delegate it to human resources (HR) or the organizational development (OD) team to sort out. Even when attempts are made to engage stakeholders, they fail to be effective and tend to fall into two traps. The first is to frame engagement as a communications issue, which usually means top-down, one-way communication with no real dialogue or engagement.

An external consultancy might be recruited to run a communications campaign with straplines and slogans, which usually feels rather abstract and rarely creates the right conditions for engagement. The second trap is when an attempt is made to start engaging stakeholders only once everything is clear and aligned at the top of the organization by the executive team. The rationale for this is that people can't be involved when the executive team are not yet clear on the answer. While this desire for conclusive clarity is understandable, the reality is that engagement is important from as early as possible, as is evident in the example of a transformation in a global manufacturing company that has 12,000 people around the world. Due to the impact of technological advancements, the company needed to be transformed and restructured in a completely different way, which meant that it had to close nearly a quarter of its factories and refurbish the remaining ones. This meant that an estimated one-third of roles had to made redundant and the remaining staff had to be upskilled. After spending some time reflecting on the approach that they should take, the executive team decided to abandon their usual top-down strategy and instead put engagement at the centre of the transformation right from the start. Consequently, even in the initial months when the executive team were still designing the transformation roadmap, they included some key frontline employees in their team meetings and spent time with them articulating and defining the narrative of why they needed to change and what that would mean for everyone. The team also mapped out the different stakeholder groups who might be affected most, and how critical they were to engage, and began engaging with these groups early on, in both one-on-one and small team meetings, in-person and online, sharing what they could, and when the answer was not yet fully clear they shared at least the process and rough timelines. They also mapped out an engagement plan that aligned with the timeline of the transformation. The feedback from the employees, even those whose roles were impacted, was positive because they felt listened to, involved and respected. On the whole, employees supported the change and helped to implement it. This example illustrates that even when a transformation has a negative impact on job roles it is vital to engage key frontline employees as early as possible in the process to ensure their commitment and participation with it.

Change is all about people

Academics and practitioners are continually producing literature on organizational change. While some academic studies provide new and useful theoretical insights, others stress academic rigour but lack practical relevance. Many of the practitioner books on organizational change are dedicated to describing what change looks like, what instigates it and how it can and should be managed. The perspective in these books tends to be that of management, with little attention being given to what change looks and feels like for employees in the organization, or how they can be effectively engaged in business transformations. This is a gap which needs to be bridged, since change is all about people, especially as all change affects someone and needs individuals and teams to implement and sustain it effectively.

Preparing, planning, implementing and sustaining change in organizations are all done by people and in turn impact on individuals and teams who are doing the work. The vast majority of business transformations, however, tend to be managed from a technical and process perspective without recognizing or understanding how the people element influences the success or failure of the transformation, because it is often easier to focus attention on, and to become preoccupied with, the technical and process sides of change, dealing with quantifiable and predictable issues such as developing strategies and action plans, calculating profitability and rationalizing resources rather than the unpredictable, complex and chaotic human dimension. There is, therefore, a tendency to neglect and, in some cases, to ignore the important people element not only in the literature but also in practice when implementing change. Any organization that believes change can take hold without considering how people need to be involved in it is in deep delusion, for frontline individuals and other key stakeholder groups are vital to any business transformation.

Drive for agency

Engaging stakeholders in business transformations means shifting the power and agency of change from employer to employee. The desire for this shift is evident in the changing expectations of employees due to changes in the nature of work, partly due to technological advancements and also due to employees wanting more from their employer, including more meaningful work and more time and place flexibility. The difficulties with achieving this alteration are that organizational change has traditionally been something that has been undertaken by leaders, managers and consultants portrayed as having agency, as change agents and change leaders, with employees positioned as recipients of change and depicted as relatively agentless. Agency, as the psychologist Bessel van der Kolk defined it, is the feeling of being in charge and control: knowing where you stand, knowing that you have a say in what happens to you and that you have some ability to shape your circumstances. In practice, this means that employees and other stakeholders do not want to just let change happen to them but instead they want to affect, shape, curtail, expand and temper what happens in their working lives. In other words, employees no longer want to be merely passive actors in business transformations but instead want to be proactive in mobilizing their own part in the process. The most important way that organizations can help employees to do this is by empowering them to act with agency and choice over what they do. Employees who feel that they have autonomy and control are more likely to actively create their own engagement experiences with business transformations. This approach is in juxtaposition to the traditional assumption that organizations know best about how change should be imposed on people. But, as the pandemic has taught us, change can be done quicker and in a more agile way when employees are allowed to take more initiative. Giving people a voice in transformations helps organizations to act more dynamically and quicker. In contrast, top-down strategies based on identifying business needs and then finding or developing the solutions to address them, and then imposing them on frontline staff, will always be slower and less inclusive than approaches that allow employees and other key stakeholders to make decisions based on their experience and knowledge.

People-centric change is about giving employees more agency and autonomy to choose how they can best tackle critical workplace challenges as well as opportunities. Organizations that follow this path will benefit from the increased engagement and inclusivity of stakeholders in transformations that are critical to adapting to disruption and being agile.

Growth of agility

Adaptation is vital if an organization is to keep up with, and get the most out of, the accelerating forces for change, as well as soften the blows of their impact. In order to be adaptable, organizations also need to be agile, that is to swiftly turn decisions into actions, to manage change effectively, to focus on customers and to optimize the value of knowledge and innovation. To achieve this necessitates asking: can we enable more effective decision-making about business transformations by pushing decisions to the edges of the organization and creating psychological safety (see Chapter 4) that empowers people, and creates agency? To do this effectively and drive better and faster decisions across teams, managers and leaders must avoid intervening and micromanaging, which they will tend to do because they think that when decisions are delegated down to the appropriate level the frontline employees who are empowered to decide are too siloed and have individual accountabilities that are too tactical. To avoid this, there is a need for agility and adaptability at all levels. The benefit of this can be illustrated by the example of the Card Factory – a greetings card business. When its UK shops were in lockdown, the company's Christmas displays continued to be on show until the spring when staff came back from furlough and had to destock and restock the entire business within two weeks in the face of serious logistical challenges. Despite the teams having the Shipfinder app on their mobile phones for tracking ships that were supplying their stock, employees had to be extremely agile since they did not know when the ships were going to dock or when the stock would arrive. To address this, they were empowered by senior management to make decisions in real time, so that if they needed to change the display in a store because one product had not arrived but another had they were able to do so, without the decision having to be ratified by the board. Since the staff were given clarity on what they were able to make decisions about, they were able to make changes quickly. This shows the need for agility and adaptability, but also the importance of enabling people to make decisions about changes that impact their work.

People's knowledge, experience and ideas

The process of a planned transformation will be much smoother if people are engaged early with it and are asked for input on issues that will affect their work. Frontline employees, especially, tend to be rich repositories of knowledge about where potential issues may occur, what technical and logistical challenges need to be addressed and how customers might react to changes. In addition, the early engagement of frontline workers can help to ensure successful implementation, whereas their disengagement can make implementation difficult.

Managers who resist engaging stakeholders early in a transformation often do so because they believe that the process will be more efficient and quicker the fewer people that are involved in the planning. This is, of course, short-sighted, since involving as many people as is feasible to do so will actually help enable stakeholders to have agency and to take ownership of the change. This is evident in the production system of Toyota – a Japanese multinational automotive manufacturer – known as Lean manufacturing, which pushes decision-making to the lowest level. Since the workers on the assembly line are the ones who see problems first and are closest to any malfunctions that are inevitable in any manufacturing process, they have the authority to stop the manufacturing process using the Andon cord. In the event of a potential problem, a team member on the production line can pull the cord to flag up the issue, stop the process and receive immediate assistance. Even though potentially stopping the entire production line seems like a costly measure in terms of time and productivity, it actually enables the root cause of the problem to be identified, thereby allowing the issue to be eliminated and the manufacturing process to be improved.[16] Just as in Toyota, every person is an expert at something and has the right to make decisions about what needs to be improved and also how their job and workplace needs to change. This is highlighted in the following case by Steve Tunnicliffe, the ex-Senior Vice President of Engineering iDirect, in which he describes his experience of engaging stakeholders with a business transformation and why this is important.

CASE STUDY

Business Insight: ST Engineering iDirect

ST Engineering iDirect (iDirect) is a Singaporean owned technology company in the satellite industry headquartered in Herndon, Virginia in the United States. The company employs approximately 1,000 people across two main locations at Herndon and St Nikalaas in Belgium, and is a leading player in the satellite industry in the provision of ground segment networking technology. The company was founded in 1994 as ComSoft Systems, and in 2000 with private equity investment by Amp Capital Partners changed its name to iDirect Technologies. In 2001 a new management team made up of principally ex-McKinsey Consulting partners, led by John Kealey and Kevin Calderwood, was put in place. The company was turned around and sold on to Singapore Technologies (ST) in 2005 as a subsidiary of Vision Technologies Systems. In 2007 iDirect had approximately 130 employees with a turnover of US$ 100 million. From 2007 to 2017 the company's growth was exponential and it was winning market share in key markets such as defence, maritime and aeronautical connectivity, and enterprise networking. In 2011 Inmarsat selected iDirect as its ground segment partner for its next generation high speed ground network infrastructure globally. Winning this deal was transformational, and the company quickly grew to develop next generation technology used by every leading satellite company. In 2019 iDirect's parent company – ST Engineering – acquired one of iDirect's main competitors – Newtec, a Belgium headquarter company with a legacy of doing business in broadcast and enterprise networks. The acquisition was completed just five months before the start of the first Covid-19 lockdown. ST Engineering merged the legacy entities into a unified company, which represented a combined workforce of 1,000 people and in 2022 a combined revenue of $320 million.

The two legacy companies' respective corporate cultures were very different: iDirect was hierarchical with a centralized functional structure and a more direct CEO-led management culture. Conversely, Newtec had a flatter hierarchy with transversal decision-making, which was a more informal group-based approach than iDirect. When the companies came together, the CEO of iDirect continued as CEO of the combined entity and the former CEO of Newtec was appointed President and Chief Commercial and Strategy Officer. For all intents and purposes, the legacy management structure remained intact in the two principal locations.

For two years through the course of the pandemic there was little in the way of meaningful integration, and the legacy entities continued to operate as effectively two separate companies. The company did not consolidate platforms, engineering teams or other functions in a meaningful way, and understandably the pandemic did not help. Working in an online environment, primarily over Microsoft Teams, did not help either, with work–life balance blurring adding to fatigue and stress among the employees.

As time unfolded, frustration emerged. Technology direction became contested and strained, as did management decision-making between the legacy business leaders. In the summer of 2021 there was a change at the management level at ST Engineering, iDirect's parent company, when it became clear to iDirect's owners (ST Engineering) that the integration was not going well and that intervention was required. There was a need for the iDirect management team to address some of the challenges faced by the lack of people integration and collaboration. Integration had been naturally challenging and a number of people-orientated engagement plans were put into place through the latter half of 2021 and into 2022. The following initiatives were kicked off:

1. A Regional Ambassadors Council (RAC) was set up to advise on and provide feedback to the executive leadership team. This was initially trialled in Europe with the objective of creating other RACs in other regions. This was a new role created to drive engagement and better informal communications. Initially, candidates were nominated by the executive team.
2. HR-led focus groups were held in multiple locations (the US, Belgium, the UK, Ireland, Germany, the UAE, and Singapore) where there was a high concentration of people. People in every region and department were encouraged to participate on a voluntary basis.
3. A Management Channel was launched on Microsoft Teams to encourage the cascading of information and the devolvement of decision-making. The channel

encourages managers to ask questions on issues such as the 'return to office' policy after the pandemic.

4. An iDirect Culture Code was launched and those values were communicated internally and externally. This was an opportunity for people to share what they thought the values should be through the various forums (focus groups, engagement surveys, etc.) and ideas were distilled and submitted in an online survey for polling. The results were then shared in a 'fireside chat' as well as in electronic communications.
5. Collaboration Days were set up in each key location to encourage cross-team/function collaboration and to assist with the company's return-to-work policy. Tuesdays and/or Thursdays were nominated as the Collaboration Days, with the executive sponsor encouraged to come up with ideas such as a team lunch, or something informal that would encourage people to come together and talk.
6. The company kicked off in December 2021 with an engagement survey facilitated by a third party, Energage.
7. Meeting-less Fridays were initiated to try and create space and time for people to complete work.
8. Core hours were implemented, and meetings discouraged during unsociable times and outside business hours.

Furthermore, in parallel throughout the two-year period of the pandemic, iDirect developed a transformational strategy to move the company from a hardware-centric product company to a customer-centric software company, which was a similar transformation to that of other historically hardware-based companies such as IBM and Cisco. The transformation was approved by the ST Engineering Board in July 2022 given the sizeable investment ask from iDirect to ST Engineering.

Core to the transformation was not only evolving and positioning the business for the future but also addressing some of the integration activities that had not been undertaken. Each aspect of the transformation was allocated a nominated executive sponsor who is responsible for engaging other managers in supporting the transformation. The deliverables of the transformation are key performance indicators which are owned by key stakeholders such as the executive team.

A central aspect to the transformation execution is talent acquisition and retention, particularly with the recruitment of a significant number of engineers, which is extremely challenging, particularly in a highly competitive technology environment.

The summer of 2022 saw the exit of both the CEO and President of iDirect, who were the legacy CEOs prior to the acquisition. ST Engineering appointed the President of the Global Business Area from Singapore as interim CEO and initiated a search for a new CEO.

When considering the lessons learnt, it is fair to say that the timing of the pandemic was not helpful at all and effectively delayed the start of the integration. Integration is not just about systems and processes but fundamentally about people and culture, and consequently if people can't get together, learn from each other and collaborate then it is very challenging to execute. Combined with the pandemic was the move to home-working and the adoption of Microsoft Teams. Again, the effect was to blur the work–life balance and create fatigue, stress and even in some cases burnout among employees. The pandemic really challenged the business from a people perspective. However, whilst the company is now healing and recovering, it could be argued that the integration initially failed, and it failed because the acquisition of Newtec was positioned as a merger rather than an acquisition. This led to strain at a management level with weak decision-making and inefficiency, with each of the former CEOs claiming ownership for the company's go-to-market strategy. Furthermore, roles and responsibilities were not clearly defined, and the management chain was at times ambiguous. What should have occurred was change management with clearly defined roles and responsibilities.

Empowerment of people and managers should have also occurred sooner. At the very beginning of the integration, the former senior managers perpetuated the differences between locations and a culture of 'them and us' was allowed to fester.

The fastest team to integrate was the global sales team, which was perhaps to be expected since their mission was clear, collaboration is at the heart of their philosophy and they were already remotely based prior to the pandemic, in that they were already working using online tools, such as WebEx, and working remotely.

Now that the company has to execute against the transformational strategy and there has been far more collaboration and teamwork than at any time over the past two years, people are quickly seeing the opportunity that flows from having a clear direction and an inclusive organizational culture. All of this said, a fundamental reason for the lack of integration has been that the company has not had a unified cause around which the whole company could get behind. Without a cause people have been internally focused, stuck in their silos and struggled to collaborate to address business problems. Fortunately, with the kick-off of the transformation, it has become increasingly clear to the staff what the company's direction and business objectives are.

iDirect haven't implemented any formal change management model but it could be argued that over the past three years the approach taken is most aligned with the Satir change management model.[17] Initially under the Satir model iDirect have gone through the following phases:

- *late status quo,* where, immediately post acquisition of Newtec, each legacy organization operated 'as is' in silos

- *resistance,* the natural response to integration, which has been endemic for the first two years post acquisition
- *chaos,* where change management has been challenging to implement and there remains confusion and resistance even to some degree today
- *integration,* when productivity begins to level out and iDirect have started to achieve alignment, suggesting general acceptance. iDirect are not there yet but arguably this phase is building and in progress
- *practice and new status quo,* when staff accept the new normal; the company has not reached this point yet

What this case study shows is that employee engagement is critical to business transformation and success. Effective employee engagement requires numerous factors, including: leaders to be transparent and communicate often; a clear mission that everyone, irrespective of role or position, can get behind and feel that they can make a contribution to; and an effective work culture that mobilizes and empowers the workforce, reduces staff attrition, increases productivity and builds better work and customer relationships, and fundamentally improves the company's financial performance. In the case of ST Engineering iDirect, the timing of the acquisition of Newtec and the pandemic certainly did not help and contributed to a delayed integration phase. However, it also highlighted some serious failings in leadership that fortunately the company has been able to identify and resolve effectively. The company now is on the right trajectory for success, learning from its experiences.

Questions

1. What were the key difficulties faced with the transformation and how were they addressed?
2. The case indicates that the integration initially failed. What could have been done differently to ensure that the key stakeholders were engaged fully with the transformation?
3. Consider a transformation you are currently working on or are familiar with. How might the lessons learnt be applied to it?

SUMMARY

In an age of disruption and digitalization organizations need to be ready to respond to the significant forces driving change, such as a global pandemic, economic turbulence, rising political and military tensions, and the rapid advancement of intelligent machines. The speed of such forces has not only increased but new driving forces for change are constantly occurring, such as cybersecurity breaches and attacks, which are jolting organizations into action and forcing them to transform rapidly and, in some cases, become more complex with an increase in flexible modes of working. These forces are impacting on the need to engage stakeholders more than ever with organizational changes and provide the opportunity to set a people-centric agenda for transformations that enables and empowers individuals, teams and organizations to build agility and resilience.

Changes in employee expectations, especially their desire to enhance and develop their sense of agency, is also driving the need for a more people-centric approach to change. This necessitates putting boundaries in place that channel employees' decisions and ideas towards the benefit of the organization and its workers, allowing participation not just for its own sake but because what is chosen helps the organization and its employees grow and thrive. People-centric change thus involves giving employees more agency and autonomy to choose how they can best tackle critical workplace challenges as well as opportunities. Organizations that follow this path will benefit from the increased engagement and inclusivity of stakeholders in transformations that are critical to adapting to disruption and creating sustainable change. People-centric change is, therefore, highly dependent on the advocacy and engagement of all key stakeholder groups, because without stakeholder engagement in the transformation process the likelihood of success will diminish. So keeping employees engaged in a change-saturated environment is vital to ensure that people are inside the transformation process rather than on the outside looking in.

PRACTICAL IMPLICATIONS

The practical implications that can be drawn from this chapter are:

- *Engage frontline workers in decisions about what needs to change and how.* The person who is the receptionist or the janitor will know more about receiving people or cleaning offices than anyone else, and it is incredibly wasteful if an organization does not take advantage of their knowledge and include them in decisions about changes which affect their work. Although such an approach may take longer in the beginning, ensuring inclusivity will avoid mistakes and failures. In addition, not only will more ideas be raised, but people will also be more committed to implementing changes because they have been involved and engaged in developing the plan for change.

- *Give people more agency with change.*
  Give people more agency and autonomy to choose how they can best tackle critical workplace challenges as well as opportunities. Although, remember to put boundaries in place that channel employees' decisions and ideas towards the benefit of the organization and its workers, thereby allowing participation not just for its own sake but because what is chosen helps the organization and its workers to grow and thrive.

Notes

1. S Nadella (2017) *Hit Refresh*, Collins, London
2. P Polman and A Winston (2021) *Net Positive: How courageous companies thrive by giving more than they take*, Harvard Business Review Press, Boston
3. L Methot, J Melton and J Breidenthal. How to unleash the power of the front line, Bain & Company, 5 April 2018. www.bain.com/insights/how-to-unleash-the-power-of-the-frontline-change-management-blog (archived at https://perma.cc/89WG-L5CC)
4. F Harvey. Global fresh water demand will outstrip supply by 40% by 2030, say experts, *Guardian*, 17 March 2023. www.theguardian.com/environment/2023/mar/17/global-fresh-water-demand-outstrip-supply-by-2030 (archived at https://perma.cc/CEE3-UVSB)
5. L Colback. Technology and the skills shortage, *Financial Times*, 18 May 2023. www.ft.com/content/b1b710a1-6d12-43e5-8508-ae4584a7289a (archived at https://perma.cc/Z3NH-EAZE)
6. P Polman and A Winston (2021) *Net Positive: How courageous companies thrive by giving more than they take*, Harvard Business Review Press, Boston, 247
7. S Nadella (2017) *Hit Refresh*, Collins, London
8. J Browne, R Nuttal and T Stadlen (2016) *Connect: How companies succeed by engaging radically with society*, Public Affairs, New York
9. For example, L Holbeche and G Matthews (2012) *Engaged: Unleashing your organization's potential through employee engagement*, Wiley, London
10. E R McRae and P Aykens. 9 future of work trends for 2023, Gartner, 22 December 2022. www.gartner.com/smarterwithgartner/9-future-of-work-trends-post-covid-19 (archived at https://perma.cc/QNZ3-64NQ)
11. K Delany. What challenges will organisations face transitioning for the first time to the new normal of remote working? *Human Resource Development International*, 2022, 25 (5), 642–50. www.tandfonline.com/doi/abs/10.1080/13678868.2021.2017391 (archived at https://perma.cc/L62M-3HL4)

12 J Hodges (2021) *Managing and Leading People Through Organizational Change: The theory and practice of sustaining change through practice*, 2nd edn, Kogan Page, London

13 B Feiler (2020) *Life is in the Transitions,* Penguin Press, New York

14 N Anand and J L Barsoux. What everyone gets wrong about change management, *Harvard Business Review*, November–December 2017, 78–85. hbr.org/2017/11/what-everyone-gets-wrong-about-change-management (archived at https://perma.cc/BQV4-CD9F)

15 J Bughin and N van Zeebroeck. The best response to digital disruption, McKinsey, 9 May 2017. www.mckinsey.com/mgi/overview/in-the-news/the-right-response-to-digital-disruption (archived at https://perma.cc/ZPP7-N9GT)

16 A Biddle. TMUK's 25 objects – 19: Andon Cord, Toyota, 11 December 2017. mag.toyota.co.uk/toyota-manufacturing-25-objects-andon-cord (archived at https://perma.cc/3ZN2-D43G)

17 Satir Transformational Systemic Therapy (STST), also known as the Satir method, was designed to improve relationships and communication within the family structure by addressing a person's actions, emotions and perceptions as they relate to that person's dynamic within the family unit. The Satir Change Model says that as we cope with unexpected or significant change, we predictably move through six stages: late status quo, resistance, chaos, integration, practice and new status quo.

03

Engaging stakeholders

Introduction

In a post-pandemic world, to create people-centric change requires embracing a multi-stakeholder approach and engaging internal and external stakeholder groups in order to create agility, adaptability and resilience. This involves mobilizing the energy of people in order to leverage their skills, knowledge, experience, passion, judgement and creativity. Engaging stakeholders in this way with a business transformation is, however, challenging and demands attention. The literature is awash with generic checklists for improving engagement with organizational change, which are full of good things to do but tend to be pitched at such a level of generality that they do not provide a clear basis of action for fostering engagement. Such checklists tend to have limitations because they view individuals, particularly employees in a passive role, while engagement is seen as something that is driven by the organization rather than something that is also under the control of employees themselves. Furthermore, there is an assumption in the literature that stakeholders are either engaged or not, and that, once engaged, the impact on their performance is linear, in that a bit more engagement equals just that bit more performance. This is an overly simplified explanation, and yet much of the change management literature presents this picture. Hence, there is a lack of clarity about what organizations can do to generate engagement with business transformations.

In an attempt to address this issue, the aim of this chapter is to identify some key principles and practices underpinning the way that engagement can be generated and sustained for people-centric change. Particular consideration is given as to how engagement with a business transformation can be fostered and maintained as a shared responsibility. The chapter begins by discussing some of the factors that influence stakeholder engagement, including the history of change in the company and the organizational culture. The chapter also explores the importance of stakeholder relations and some of the challenges faced in building such relationships, including power and politics. It goes on to discuss how stakeholders can be active agents in the co-creation of a business transformation, with attention being paid to how organizations can avoid being paralyzed by opinion overload. Throughout, the focus is on how stakeholder engagement does not just happen to individuals but involves them having the opportunity to be proactive in mobilizing change. This is illustrated in detail in the business insight about a transformation in an airline company, written by Carlos Pullen-Ferreira, Vice President, Business Transformation at Sage. The case highlights that employees are by no means passive actors in organizations but need to have the autonomy and opportunity to be proactive in making change happen.

Factors that influence stakeholder engagement

Before even examining how to engage stakeholders it is worth considering what might be influencing whether or not individuals and groups are open to engage with business transformations (I discuss the antecedents of stakeholder engagement in more detail in *Employee Engagement for Organizational Change*[1]). Some of the key influences on stakeholder engagement are outlined in other chapters in this book and include, but are not limited to; uncertainty (see Chapter 8); transformation saturation (see Chapter 8); a lack of equality, diversity and inclusion in transformations (see Chapter 9); and the mismanagement and micromanagement of change (see Chapter 7). Other key influencers include the history of transformations and the culture of the organization, which are discussed below.

History of transformations in the organization

Engagement can be influenced by an organization's history of transformations, including the frequency, pace and success of previous transformational changes, which can impact on an individual's and/or team's experience of change in the organization. This can shape attitudes towards future transformations and behavioural responses to them. It is similar to when you are driving a car, and before signalling to change direction you look in your rear-view mirror; likewise, changing the direction of an organization involves people doing a rear-view inspection of the history of transformations, including what have been the successes and what have been the failures, and the reasons for both as well, as lessons learnt. Ignoring the impact of previous changes, particularly if they have failed, can cause negative attitudes towards transformations, which can result in a vicious cycle whereby stakeholders will avoid engaging in change and consequently prejudice the success of future changes due to their perceptions and experience of past changes. Similarly, the personal experiences of individuals and teams can have either positive or negative effects on their willingness to engage with a transformation. Those who have experienced past successes might be more likely to commit to future transformations, whereas those who have experienced failed changes might be more cynical about the motives for yet another change and/or sceptical about their ability to support it and make the necessary changes. Experience of previous changes can thus influence the willingness of stakeholders to engage in future transformations. It is, therefore, worth considering the impact that previous transformations might have on current and future changes and ensuring that there is time for reflection during and at the end of a transformation, and that the lessons learnt are identified and shared. This can help to build learning and reflection into a transformation and the culture of the organization.

Culture

For stakeholder engagement to become real, commitment needs to start from the top, that is, the board or executive team. Encouragement from the top to participate and get involved in the transformation process can help to create an organizational culture that is conducive to engagement and learning. This is illustrated in a study of a transformation project at a leading cardiology department in Denmark, where senior management defined the scope of a change process and championed its implementation but left the analysis, diagnosis and solution development to the departmental staff.[2] To do this, the department cascaded responsibility in a transparent way for the diagnostic and analytical activities, as well as the development of solutions. The application of such an orchestrated approach meant that senior management set a direction by formulating the general themes and scope of possible changes that they would accommodate but the scope was sufficiently broad to provide leeway for stakeholders to develop solutions. Information sharing and transparency were similarly important because they allowed all participants, not just management, to engage with the process. Those employees responsible for the change provided continuous progress updates to the senior team and other stakeholders so that the progress and status was available for everyone to see. Such a strategy, when change is driven from the top down and the bottom up, creates a dynamic that is referred to as 'book-ending' because there is support for the change from both directions. In turn, this can help to create a culture of engagement with change based on trust and transparency, which helps to strengthen both the probability that people will engage with the change and stakeholder relations.

Stakeholder relationships

People-centric change focuses on a stakeholder approach which involves including relevant individuals in the identification, design and implementation of business transformations. Stakeholders include those internal and external to the organization, including employees, shareholders, customers, investors, trade unions, suppliers, partners and distributors, as well as local communities, government and non-governmental organizations. According to stakeholder theory, stakeholder engagement is about developing relationships, inspiring stakeholders and creating communities where people strive to give their best and where the relationships with stakeholders are managed in an action-oriented way.[3] This requires an understanding of who will be impacted by change, when, where, how and why they will be affected, as well as their influence on proposed transformations. There are likely to be multiple stakeholders and several stakeholder groups who will need to be identified, and their levels of interest and influence and what matters to each of them must be understood. Different stakeholders are likely to act in ways that maximize their own influence and interest to secure their preferred outcomes. The most powerful stakeholders are those who are in a position to influence the important aspects of the transformation, such as timing, pace and employee engagement, and have control over the resources it requires. There is, therefore, a need to be able to identify key stakeholders and their influence and impact.

Stakeholder identification and mapping

To identify key stakeholders requires firstly identifying who they are by asking the following questions:

- Who will gain or lose something from the transformation?
- Who has the power to make or break the transformation?
- Who controls critical resources and/or the expertise required to make the transformation successful?

Once the key stakeholders (individuals and groups) are identified, the next step is to assess the level of influence they have and the impact the transformation will have on them. This can be done by considering:

- How much influence each stakeholder/group has to make the transformation happen, or to prevent it from happening and whether it is high, medium or low.
- What level of interest each stakeholder/group has and whether it is high, medium or low.
- What impact the transformation will have on each stakeholder/group and whether this is high, medium or low.

Those individuals and groups identified then need to be plotted onto a stakeholder map (see Figure 3.1)

This exercise of analysing and mapping stakeholders will provide a guide as to where, and with whom, there is a need to devote time, energy and effort. It is worth remembering when doing this that stakeholders who are not committed to the transformation but who can influence it represent a potential risk, so they need to be proactively managed because they can impact (positively and negatively) the progress and success of the transformation. The stakeholders who are optimistic and supportive will need to be engaged as soon as possible, as they will help to ensure that the transformation is supported, owned, implemented and sustained successfully across the organization.

As a business transformation progresses, the stakeholders may change. For instance, some individuals/groups might become less relevant, some may lose interest, new stakeholders may emerge and others might leave the organization or move to another role where they are no longer involved in or impacted by the transformation. The engagement and management of stakeholders is, therefore, an ongoing and dynamic part of people-centric change.

FIGURE 3.1 Stakeholder map

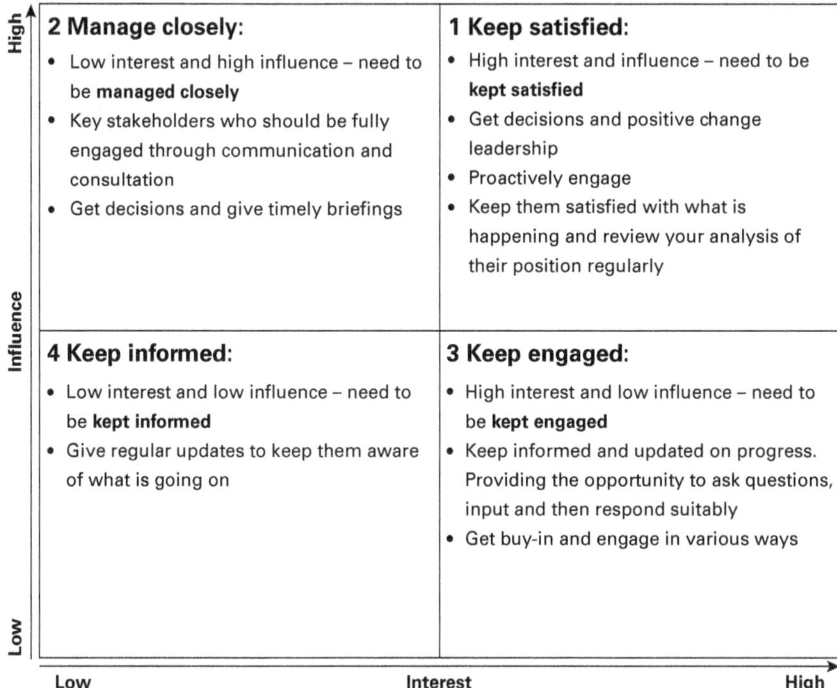

Cultural influencers

One of the most important stakeholder groups comprises those who are most ready to change – the so-called authentic informal leaders.[4] This group can be found at any level of an organization and they are willing to acquire new skills, use all the tools and opportunities available and demonstrate the value of the business transformation by example. These informal authentic leaders are influential not because of their position but because of their capability, energy and commitment. They are change accelerators, in that they volunteer to rapidly deepen their skills, help to support learning among their peers, tend to have social acumen and influence, have a passion for helping others succeed and can assist with understanding how employees feel and how to engage them. It is, therefore, important to identify who the authentic informal leaders are so that they can help to engage others in the transformation.

Power and politics

The process of building relationships and engaging stakeholders with transformations usually involves the enactment of power and politics, so to effectively engage stakeholders with change there is a need to understand those dynamics, especially as transformations provide excellent opportunities for gaining, keeping or increasing power – or losing it. How power is used by an individual can have an impact on a transformation, either positively or negatively. It is important to note that power is not just a matter of an individual's formal position in the organization but also of their personal characteristics and experience. People are more likely to enthusiastically accept and commit to an individual whom they admire or whose expertise they respect, such as informal authentic leaders, than someone who solely relies on their position for power. Managers who use their expertise, knowledge, skills and capabilities positively to influence people during transformations are, therefore, more likely to gain their commitment rather than someone who wields their power to coerce and threaten people.

A business transformation can also trigger and intensify political behaviour because it can create a diversity of opinion, values, beliefs and interpretations. For instance, stakeholders who believe that they will lose out in some way or who feel that there are better ways to achieve the same results or better results, might oppose planned transformational changes. This highlights the need for managers to be able to intervene in the political system of the organization in order to legitimize the rationale for change, particularly when faced with opposition to it, but importantly also to be able to ensure that the voices, whether of dissent or support, are listened to and acknowledged (see Chapter 4 on engaging opposing voices). This entails being able to understand the expectations and needs of stakeholders and influence the political dynamics that can come into play during transformations. This can be done in several ways, including:

- ensuring the support of key stakeholder groups
- generating enthusiasm in support of a transformation, in order to build commitment, which can help manage destructive political behaviour
- using communications to create energy and commitment for the transformation (see Chapter 5 on communication of change)
- building in sources of stability by identifying and articulating which elements of the status quo will remain the same, because people need to know what will remain stable and what is likely to change
- mapping the political landscape of who will be affected by the transformation

- identifying the key influencers, within each stakeholder group, that is, those who have the influence and interest to convince others of the benefits of transformation
- assessing the readiness for change (see Chapter 11 for how to assess readiness)
- mobilizing influential sponsors and promoters – those authentic informal leaders who have the skills, connections and insights to influence others and increase engagement
- engaging influential and postive stakeholders as well as negative sceptics

People-centric change means overcoming not only powerful vested interests but also the powerlessness that people may feel, which can impede any organizational change. This can occur when stakeholders feel that they lack the power to make decisions which, in turn, can lead to a lack of commitment. It can also impact negatively on wellbeing and motivation. It is, therefore, vital to identify ways to proactively engage stakeholders in a transformation.

Ways to engage stakeholders

Top-down vs burning platform

People-centric change is about giving people more autonomy to choose how they can help to tackle critical business problems and/or opportunities. This is important, because amongst many employees there is a sense that they are not included in decisions about organizational changes, which is not surprising given the traditional ways of engaging people with business transformations. In general, there are two traditional ways of engaging stakeholders with a transformation: i) top-down; and ii) the burning platform scenario. The top-down strategy is set out in advance and is an attempt to impose transformation as an initiative, usually by the senior executive team. This way of driving a transformation tends to centralize decision-making at leadership levels and excludes frontline staff, even when they are directly impacted by the change. It also provides few opportunities for gathering information about stakeholder expectations or asking for their feedback; instead, the goals and the direction of the transformation, such as 'you will become more customer-focused', are decided by the senior executive team and cascaded down to everyone else. Admittedly, this does have the advantage of clarity, a unity of purpose (there is only one message) and the speed of communication (from one to everyone). However, while it appears to have benefits of speed and unity, these are rarely achieved in practice because employees are unlikely to readily accept the change if they have not been engaged in the decisions about it. They may well hear the message but that does not mean that they support it or will act on it, and even if they do there may well be a lot of passive opposition for a number of reasons, such as: they do not understand how the message translates into their everyday work; they are not clear on what they are supposed to do that is different; and/or they feel that they do not have the capabilities or capacity to implement the proposed changes. These reasons, and others, can create frustration and dissatisfaction because individuals feel that they have been ignored and/or undervalued and that the transformation is being done *to* them rather than *with* them.

The other traditional route to engage people with a transformation is the use of the 'burning platform' scenario, which some leaders and managers persist in using in order to scare their staff out of their comfortable complacency, by implying that their organization is standing on a burning platform and everyone must jump or perish. The implication that the burning platform is a matter of life or death was taken from interviews with a survivor of the 1988 Piper Alpha disaster that killed 167 oil rig workers in the North Sea (about 120 miles north-east of Aberdeen in Scotland), and was included in Daryl Connor's book *Managing at the Speed of Change* and has gone on to be part of the lexicon of managing organizational change.[5] Surely, it is now time to recognize that this cliché is no longer appropriate as a way of motivating staff, but instead is counterproductive as research suggests. For example, an initial survey by Constantinos Markides found that 74 per cent of CEOs thought that the following statement was true: 'To create a sense of urgency, you have to make your people appreciate the imminent threat of disruption and the mortal danger the company is facing', whereas a similar survey conducted a couple of years later found that nothing could be further from the truth.[6] Similar conclusions were drawn by Christina Gravert, a behavioural economist at the University of Copenhagen, who stressed that getting people to fear something in order to change behaviour can only work in the very short term because it is an emotion and so, longer term, it is going to be very exhausting to maintain.[7] The main drawback to using fear as a tool for transformation is that although it might break habits it can also extend anxiety. Instead of creating fear, the need for change should be made positive and personal and individuals encouraged to feel emotionally committed to the necessary transformation. This is a more appropriate and realistic approach than the burning platform scenario, especially because transformational change inevitably requires people to stop doing something that is known to them and to do something that is often unknown to them. So, while the top-down strategy to business transformations provides a one-way, centralized approach and the burning platform creates a sense of urgency, neither of these strategies engages people effectively. Instead, a people-centric change strategy acknowledges that the leadership of the company has views and a strategy but also focuses on bringing into the mix the ideas, insights and energy of stakeholders to co-create change.

Co-creation of transformations

Rather than seeing change as a top-down, hierarchical process or an urgent burning platform, an alternative way is to see it as a people-centric process of co-creation involving the facilitation of a collaborative partnership with stakeholders in the development of a business transformation. This focuses on encouraging multi-stakeholders to engage in the discussion about what needs to change and to use their insights, experience and energy so that they feel accountable and have a sense of ownership over the transformation. In this way, a transformation is constructed and/or negotiated *with* rather than *for* stakeholders. This means that power is more widely distributed across the organization and amongst stakeholders, which is in contrast to leaders monopolizing the creation of change and keeping a tight rein on its content and process because they believe that it will be more efficient and quicker if fewer people are involved in it.

The co-creation of a transformation involves harnessing the collective intelligence of stakeholders and seeing from a pragmatic perspective where things are working well and not so well. This necessitates going beyond the usual suspects and involving people from all levels and parts of the organization to contribute to ideas for improvement and change, which is a real gesture of inclusion (see Chapter 9 on equality, diversity and inclusion). Co-creation also means actively asking employees for their insights and opinions and, crucially, managers acting on what they hear.

Bringing people from across the organization together to discuss ideas and improvements can help to break down silos and encourage cross-functional working. There are thus significant advantages to co-creation.

Despite the benefits of co-creation, there are also some risks involved, one of which is the danger of being paralyzed by opinion overload. To avoid this, the right, highly diverse, group of people from inside and outside the organization need to be brought together in online and/or in-person settings that are intentionally designed and facilitated to encourage challenges to conventional wisdom and to generate the emergence of new ideas through meaningful conversations. This can be done by identifying the right stakeholders to involve and then asking tough questions and listening to the responses. To entice people to have the confidence and courage to speak up, phrases can be used such as, 'Tell me more about this' or 'That sounds interesting, do you have an example of how this worked for you?' In addition, scenarios can be suggested such as: What if X happens? How will we handle Y? Is it worth giving up A to get B? Individuals and team members should also be encouraged to initiate such conversations themselves, especially online, in order to help to include their colleagues in discussions and to create a virtual community around the transformation where ideas, views, hopes and concerns can be shared. Through such conversations, individuals will have space to share their ideas as well as express their concerns and frustrations.

Engaging people directly in conversations about a transformation means that those who get involved will have a better idea of what others feel, the choices and trade-offs they face and how this measures up to their own thinking and experience.

An example of how this can be done is the approach taken by a global insurance company. The IT function of the company had noticed an increase in quality issues, delays and dissatisfaction about software development projects. In response to these issues, the chief technology officer (CTO) decided to adopt a standard software development methodology and replicable project management practices in order to improve the quality and reliability of new software. There were, however, some significant concerns about this approach amongst project managers because they felt that they would no longer have the licence to customize processes and standards, would need to give up their independence and innovation, and faced increased oversight from management. To address these concerns, the CTO brought together the project managers and various other stakeholders and asked them to consider two questions: If the new framework was adopted, what would the company gain? And, equally important, what would it lose? Participants were invited to consider the benefits of the proposed changes for themselves as well as the reasons why the initiative might not work and how potential roadblocks could be addressed. These discussions helped to diminish the concerns raised by the project managers and to build support for the changes. The new project methodology and practices were eventually adopted in half the expected time and were recognized for their contributions to customer satisfaction and the improved quality of projects. The success of the transformation was largely due to the people-centric approach taken of engaging stakeholders in discussions and identifying solutions which were then implemented. This reflects a departure from many of the current norms of change management, where leaders start with the belief that the change that they have launched is the right one and its merits are not questioned because they believe that, at most, the change might need minor fine-tuning. With this stance, the work of leaders becomes convincing people about the proposed change and overcoming any resistance, which all too often becomes a checklist activity without any attempt to engage stakeholders. To avoid this happening, there has to be opportunities for open and honest conversations to take place with no blaming or defensiveness, in that management actually listen and do something in response. Beer proposes the Strategic Fitness Process as one way of doing this.[8] The following outline is an adaptation of the Strategic Fitness Process to meet the needs of conversations about business transformations:

- The conversation must be open, honest and build trust and commitment. It must also focus on something about the transformation that matters and that participants can identify with, for instance, enhancing customer service or improving the number of widgets produced each year.
- The process must be facilitated by a senior manager and not HR or consultants, since it is the willingness of these with positional power to make themselves vulnerable and listen that begins the process of building the trust and commitment that is required for participants to be open and honest.
- The facilitator must create a structure – a container/space – that ensures the establishment of psychological and career safety for truth to speak to power. In other words, participants need to feel confident that they will not be castigated or told off if they are open and honest.
- The facilitator must listen and reflect on what participants say and identify the actions which can be used to develop a systemic action plan for change based on what they have heard.
- The facilitator and members of the leadership team must make themselves accountable to the participants who have provided the feedback;

FIGURE 3.2 Action research

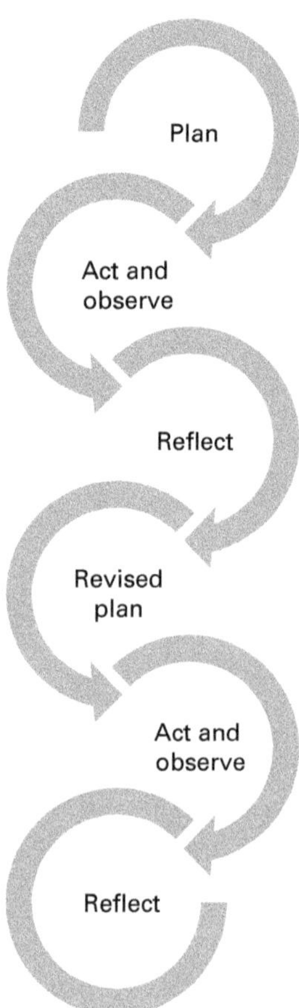

that is, accountable for having listened accurately and for the transformative actions in response to what they have heard.

- Having heard the unvarnished truth and knowing that the whole organization knows they have, the leadership team will then need to act to ensure that trust is not broken.

This process is one approach to encouraging conversations about what needs to change and how; other ways to co-create change include using methods such as action research, a World or Knowledge Café, the four walls approach and passion projects.

Action research

Action research is an emergent inquiry process in which applied behavioural science knowledge is integrated with existing organizational knowledge and employed to solve real organizational problems. It is commonly used to improve conditions and practices in a range of organizational environments and involves employees conducting systematic inquiries to help them improve their own working practices, which in turn can enhance the overall working environment. In practice, action research proceeds in a spiral of steps composed of planning, acting, observing and reflection (see Figure 3.2). The objective is to develop a participative and inclusive process where individuals and teams jointly explore problems, initiate action and evaluate outcomes, and where the overall purpose is organizational change. For change to be effective, action research stresses that it must take place at the team level and must be a participative and collaborative process which involves all of those concerned. To be successful there also has to be a felt need that change is necessary. Although it is often characterized as a diagnostic process, action research is about creating a dialogue that enables individuals to reach a common understanding of what needs to change and how. Its strength is its focus on generating solutions to practical problems and its ability to empower employees by getting them to engage with research and idea generation and the subsequent development and implementation of change activities through co-creation.

World or Knowledge Café

A World or Knowledge Café is designed to bring together large groups of people to discuss issues that are important to them, based on the assumption that people already have within them the wisdom and creativity to confront even the most difficult challenges.[9] This method aims to provide an environment to stimulate an open and creative conversation on a topic of common interest in order to identify collective knowledge, share ideas and insights, and gain a deeper understanding of specific issues and about what changes might be necessary. It makes use of the principle that in everyday conversations (in cafés) individuals self-organize, bring new people into conversations, debate ideas, share knowledge, challenge thinking, ask questions and persuade others. It takes seriously the idea that an organization is an evolving web of conversations and encourages groups to foster networks as they explore a common issue or concern.

FIGURE 3.3 Key themes of a World Café

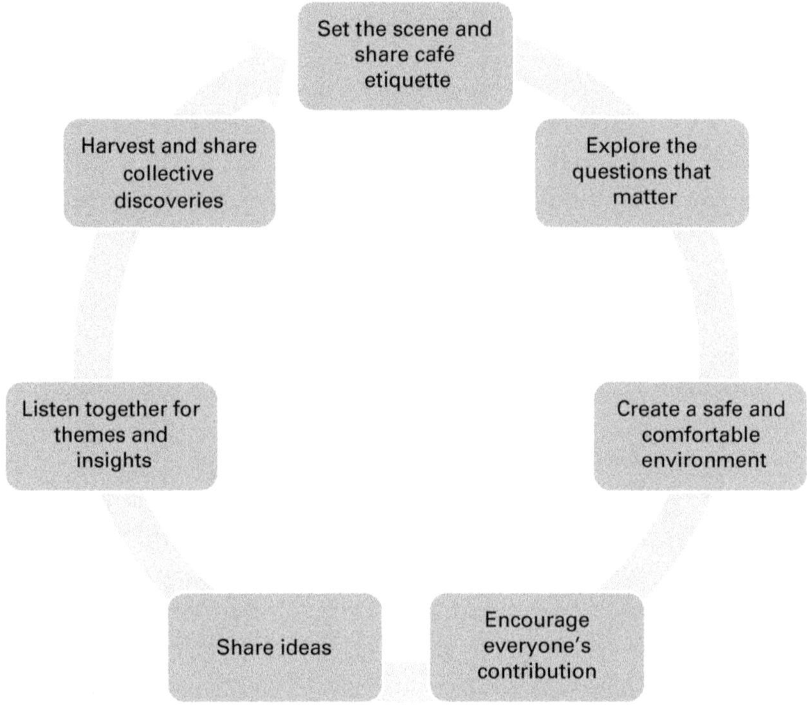

The main principles of a World Café (see also Figure 3.3) are:

1 ***Setting.*** An environment is created, with small round tables, paper and pens, with an optional 'talking stick' which is held by the individual who is talking. This is then passed to another individual when they want to talk.

2 ***Welcome and introduction.*** The facilitator begins with a welcome and an introduction to the World Café process, setting the scene and sharing the café etiquette.

3 ***Small-group conversation rounds.*** The process begins with the first of three or more rounds of conversation for each small-table group. The discussion focuses on a question that matters and guides the group's conversation, such as: 'What opportunities can we see in this situation?' or 'What assumptions do we need to test or challenge in our thinking?' Everyone's contribution should be encouraged. After a 20- to 30-minute conversation,

most of the participants rotate to new tables to begin new conversations with new table members, leaving one table member as the host to explain the previous conversation to the new participants.

4 ***Questions.*** Each round is prefaced with a question designed for the specific context and desired purpose of the event. The same questions can either be used for more than one round or be built upon to guide the direction of the conversation with everyone listening actively for themes and insights.
5 ***Harvest.*** At the end of the event, and/or between rounds, individuals are invited to share the main themes and discoveries from their conversations with the rest of the plenary group.

In this way, the World Café method can be used to identify issues and solutions as part of the co-creation of a business transformation.

Four walls method

The four walls method – proposed by McKinsey[10] – provides an approach for people, with different backgrounds and experience, to focus on a specific issue/threat or opportunity. It involves setting up a room and bringing together people from across the organization, such as from design, engineering, IT, operations and project management, depending on the issue to be explored. Each group gets its own wall, which functions as a working surface dedicated to key issues to be explored, such as customer journeys, technology or business operations. Participants discuss what issues they confront and how they might address them. Each wall becomes an ordered mosaic of Post-It notes capturing ideas, actions, challenges and ideas, visible for all to see. In this way, cross-functional teams can work in the same room simultaneously, using each wall to track a specific focus.

Passion projects

Another way to enhance co-creation and to give people more agency and choice in business transformations is through encouraging individuals and teams to get involved with change projects that match their capabilities, passions and capacity. Such passion projects give individuals and teams new development experiences and opportunities to learn in the flow of change as well as enhancing their skills, knowledge and experience. These opportunities benefit organizations and employees in several ways. First, by giving people the chance to volunteer for transformation initiatives that they prefer and value, they provide valuable information about individuals' interests, passions, and capabilities that might otherwise not be disclosed. Second, they enable the right individuals to be more quickly identified and redeployed in critical business transformations. And third, individuals who are able to do what matters to them become more motivated and more engaged. In this way, passion projects enable individuals to become involved with co-creating change that they are enthusiastic about.

Co-creation is thus an opportunity to create space for people to share what they think needs to be improved or done differently, and to be involved in making it happen. It means involving stakeholders at all levels so that they can: identify what needs to change and why; appreciate the need for, and importance of, making the transformation work; understand how they can contribute; and be more confident that their contribution will be valued. Generating the co-creation of change is, however, a gradual but by no means straightforward practice since it means offering opportunities for stakeholders to be positively involved, but not forcing them to be. In sum, co-creation is how people-centric change gets done, whenever feasible to do so, because co-creation is more likely to deliver an energizing and engaging experience, especially as it enables stakeholders to have more autonomy in the change process and to shape the transformation.

Autonomy

Having a sense of autonomy can help employees feel more motivated and lead to stronger engagement and greater commitment to a transformation. To enable autonomy involves managers working proactively with their staff to find ways to create more freedom for them to be involved in business transformations. This is done in different ways by various companies; for example, Spotify, a digital music service, groups its employees into agile teams called 'squads' that are self-organizing, cross-functional and co-located with no single appointed leader. The mantra of the squads is that alignment enables autonomy, in that the greater the alignment, the more autonomy is granted. The manager's job is to identify the right problem and communicate it, so squads can collaborate to find the best solution. Whereas Valve, a gaming software company, has a flat organizational structure in which no one has a boss and employees are provided with desks on wheels, which they are encouraged to push around the building to join projects that seem interesting to them and that they are held accountable for. When they join a new project team, employees are given clear expectations of what their role is, and when the project ends they have to complete a 360-degree evaluation to gain feedback on their individual contribution.

The importance of autonomy, created by companies such as Spotify and Valve, is highlighted in a study which examined a transformation within the frontline units of a healthcare organization where the autonomy of nursing staff was critically important to its implementation.[11] The study found that autonomy was encouraged by some unit managers by involving staff in the early planning activities. For example, one manager surveyed staff to ask for their opinions about the proposed changes while other managers initiated face-to-face conversations with staff about the changes. These conversations provided staff with an opportunity to talk about what they knew about the changes and what they felt about them. As a result of the conversations, staff perceived managers' genuine interest in involving them, listening to them and incorporating feedback into preparatory work for the transformation. They felt that managers really listened to their ideas rather than just ticking the box on staff consultation. Surveys were used to engage staff in the hospital units where shift and casual work was common, which allowed early involvement of more staff. These activities were not unidirectional but provided opportunities for managers and staff to identify how to pursue and identify critical change activities, instead of managers dictating what had to be done. Planning together with the managers potentially allowed staff to incorporate their insights into implementation activities and helped them to retain a sense of autonomy in the change process. In turn, this strengthened the staff's commitment to the change.

People need to be given autonomy to contribute to, and own, the transformation, that is, they need to be empowered to take personal ownership for those aspects of the change that they can control or influence, which is often best created by involving employees in identifying problems and co-creating solutions. This then needs to be reinforced by incentives and rewards, which can be tangible (for example, financial compensation) or psychological (such as camaraderie and a sense of shared achievement). It is critical that there are not only incentives but also processes that help people to build the commitment and capability to own the change. If this does not happen, it is likely that the transformation will either be ignored by the key stakeholders impacted or there will be minimal engagement with it.

How to give autonomy without losing control

Co-creation approaches such as a World Café give people the canvas and paint, and it is then up to them to decide what they paint and how. In other words, people are given autonomy, but within certain parameters or boundaries. These parameters help to guide people about what decisons they can influence and changes they can suggest and make decisions about. As well as the decisions about changes which they will have to ask permission or advice from senior management about.

To ensure transparency, there needs to be clarity on what the parameters are and what the difference is between parameters that guide decision-making and autonomy versus initiative-killing rules and regulations. This requires two types of parameters to be put in place: the first is the organization's strategy needs to be clearly communicated; and the second is the organization's values and purpose also need to be clear and understood. As long as these are ingrained in the organization's DNA, they will help employees decide what changes will support the company's strategy, purpose and values and what changes will not support them. There is, however, evidence that suggests that employees in many organizations do not know what these are. According to a survey of high-performing companies, only 29 percent of employees knew what strategy was.[12] To ensure autonomy is given without control being lost, employees need to know the strategic choices that the organization has made since this will help them to identify what they can decide to do themselves and what they need to defer to senior management to decide. In other words, this may mean that employees are given autonomy to act on changes that will improve what they are already doing, but not on the strategic choices that the organization has made that define its strategic direction.

Giving workers a voice in what they do helps organizations act more dynamically and in real time. The challenge is to put protective guard rails in place that channel workers' interests and abilities toward the good of the organization, allowing choice not for its own sake but because what is chosen helps the organization and its employees to grow and thrive. If people are clear on what the parameters are within which they can act, then they are likely to exercise autonomy when the decision falls within these parameters and to ask for guidance and permission for any decisions that fall outside these parameters.

The importance of autonomy and engagement is illustrated in the following business insight of a transformation in the airline industry, written by Carlos Pullen-Ferreira, Vice President, Business Transformation at Sage. The case highlights that engagement involves people having the opportunity to be proactive in mobilizing change and to be active agents in its co-creation.

CASE STUDY

Business Insight: An agile approach to transformation in the airline industry

While I was working as the Head of Project and Change Management at a global airline company, one of the most significant transformations in the organization's history was undertaken. It was an ambitious 12-month programme that was implemented to revolutionize the back office, front office, colleague and customer experience. The change included transforming processes, governance, communications, the operating model and technology. The transformation was a catalyst for the future success of the company and was essential to making it more efficient. The transformation started with a vision to simplify the platforms by modernizing and providing the best experience for colleagues and customers. However, with this drive for modernization also came a need to reduce cost, improve security and reduce maintenance.

A modified Scaled agile Framework was adopted for this transformation because it enabled an alignment to the strategy while providing a portfolio structure which allowed the delivery teams to be empowered, and provided the leadership with visibility into the progress of the transformation. Furthermore, this framework focused on an iterative approach to managing change.

With over 15,000 colleagues globally, the airline company flew out of major UK airports, including Heathrow and Gatwick, to destinations across the globe, including North America, the Caribbean, Africa and Asia. Over half of the colleagues were cabin crew and pilots, with their work location being approximately 10,000 feet above the ground. This provided challenges when trying to train, coordinate and communicate a transformation of this scale. Of the 7,000 colleagues that weren't cabin crew and pilots, the majority were UK-based, with smaller hubs in Atlanta,

New York, South Africa, Asia and several other locations. Managing change across all time zones and landscapes wasn't easy, especially with a mobile workforce.

There is always a catalyst for change, and this transformation was no different. The view of a new leadership team and existing shareholders (part owners) was that the company should take on the world and venture into the future brighter and better. On reflection, they were right that the end destination would be fantastic. However, the journey to get there wasn't straightforward.

We started the programme with high levels of energy, and it seemed easy, especially as we were getting alignment on areas where we had previously struggled with transformations, for example when dealing with 15 languages and stakeholders in 25 countries. This time we implemented face-to-face discussions and workshops, which made it much more effective to engage multi-stakeholder groups across the globe and to reach consensus on key decisions. Within weeks we had a high level of understanding of the new processes and technology required, which was followed by a lot of planning and prioritization of requirements.

However, when we entered the next phase, things started to get more challenging. After many failed sprints (sprints are a time-boxed period, usually two weeks, where work is delivered), which helped the team learn what worked and what didn't, we changed how we approached the initial deployments. We began by enlisting several members of the leadership team, including the CEO, in crafting a clear message from the CEO that this was a must-do for the organization and, therefore, a priority. This prioritization was needed so that all colleagues focused on the transformation with a sense of urgency and determination. As we continued, the iterative approach meant that a lot of rework was needed as further requirements were uncovered.

After several months of setbacks, but also, importantly, of learning, a breakthrough resulted in the project team understanding the technical feasibility, which substantially reduced the amount of rework. From my viewpoint, this was due to the resilience of teamwork and how the delivery teams, cabin crew and teams in each location came together to achieve the priority tasks. Finally, after 12 months of iterative development and change, we had a 'go live' date. Overall, it was a bumpy landing that required hyper-care and embedding in each location, but it was eventually a success when all the new processes, systems and ways of working were deployed. This led to significant learning for the teams and for me.

There were an abundant number of techniques that we used during the transformation, from change plans to stakeholder maps and from journey maps to requirements workshops. However, from my perspective, the following five techniques were the hidden gems that allowed the transformation teams and colleagues to create a path through a highly complex transformation:

1 impact mapping
2 what's in it for me (WIIFM)
3 personas
4 for each persona, make it real by bringing training, communication and engagement to life with gamification, rewards and tools that promote in-application learning and reinforcement
5 measuring sentiment

The first technique, impact mapping (see Figure 3.4), was used to plan and visualize the potential effects of the transformation. It helped the project team identify: the key stakeholders (actors) who were affected by the transformation; the outcomes that were desired (goal); and the impacts and deliverables that needed to be undertaken to achieve those outcomes.

Furthermore, impact mapping was also helpful because it ensured that the transformation was aligned with the overall goals and objectives of the organization and that all relevant stakeholders were considered. To document the impact map, we used MindMup – a mind mapping application. By visualizing the potential impact of the transformation, it was easier to identify any potential risks or challenges that might arise and to plan how to mitigate them. I found that impact mapping helped improve communications and collaboration and provided a clear and visual representation of the transformation. It was also a valuable tool for monitoring and evaluating the progress of the transformation, as it allowed for a clear framework for tracking progress and measuring success. Additionally, impact mapping was fundamental for identifying and articulating the 'why' of the transformation, which was required to understand each WIIFM. During this transformation, we had a WIIFM for each stakeholder or persona.

The second technique, WIIFM, is often used to refer to the idea that people are more likely to be motivated by and engaged in something if they perceive that it will

FIGURE 3.4 Impact mapping

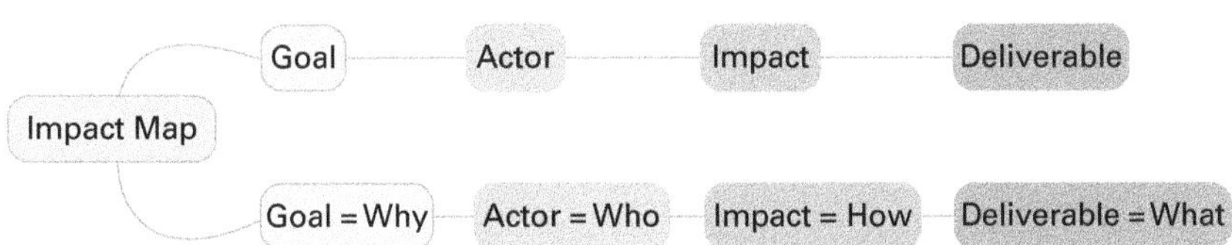

benefit them personally (the 'why' of the change that is personalized to them). In the context of this transformation, WIIFM was used to consider how the change would impact different stakeholders in different countries and to communicate in a way that highlighted the benefits to them. Understanding the WIIFM for each stakeholder group made it easier to build buy-in and support for the change.

The third technique we used was personas – which is the categorization of the different user types affected by the transformation. Having a clear understanding of the various user types, e.g. sales agent for economy sales, helped to create an appreciation of what the persona did on a day-to-day basis and what they needed in terms of training and support. In addition, utilizing personas made it easier to understand how to engage with specific groups (e.g. pilots and cabin crew) and then link their needs to WIIFM. This also helped to build trust because we weren't treating each group precisely the same.

The fourth technique combines training, communication and embedding into a single mechanism focused on each persona. By tailoring these three fundamental techniques, each persona feels more engaged with the training, as it is specific to their role, and they are not wasting time reviewing communication that isn't specific to them. While this might sound simple and logical, I have been on many transformations over the past 20 years where we have sent mass communications to hundreds of colleagues, and the read rates were less than 10 per cent. In addition, we leveraged technology to the fullest by using contextual in-application learning, which meant that colleagues didn't have to leave the system to read training material or watch a video. We found that this contextual help, driven by each persona, meant that the hyper-care and the embedding of the change were easier.

The last technique, measuring sentiment, provides consistent feedback by asking questions frequently (for example, how many stakeholders has the new process or system been deployed to, and who is using it from the deployed group). Using technology (such as Microsoft Forms) to capture data allowed the teams to create trends over time and understand where additional support was needed to improve adoption.

While the start of any transformation is challenging, starting with a clear vision and plan is critical to success. While this sounds simple, it's crucial to clearly understand 'why' the change is needed and what the organization hopes to achieve, but more importantly, how this relates to each colleague and/or customer. Being able to co-create transformational outcomes means that each colleague feels invested and can buy into the change more quickly. Moreover, this buy-in can lead to greater ownership of outputs and deliverables. For me, this helps to guide the change process and ensure that it is aligned with the organization's overall goals or objectives and key results.

Before going into specifics about the lessons learnt from the transformation of the airline company outlined above, I'm going to start with the lessons we had already captured from previous business changes at the company (outlined below) and those aspects we knew we needed to do differently before starting another major transformation. I would recommend that if you don't already capture lessons and have an iterative process for fixing them, start with that. Whether you have retrospectives that unearth lessons which become stories for the next sprint, or are delivering in a waterfall manner (all change is delivered to stakeholders at one time) and lessons learnt are conducted at the end of a project, it is fundamental to track these centrally and use them as a knowledge bank for things to consider before tackling the next transformation.

The list below is distilled and can apply not only to this case but to any transformation.

- *Communicate effectively.* Transformational change can be difficult, and it's essential to keep all relevant stakeholders (colleagues and/or customers) informed about what is happening and why – even if it is terrible news. During the transformation discussed above, we had a mantra to ensure we communicated clearly and transparently and were open to feedback and questions. We also picked the relevant channel to communicate to different stakeholder groups.
- *Involve all relevant stakeholders.* There is always a temptation to exclude some stakeholders because they might disrupt the change. However, change impacts many different people and groups, so it's crucial to involve key stakeholders in the process. This helps to build buy-in, create coalitions and ensure that the change is successful.
- *Manage resistance.* When starting a transformation, it is important to be mindful of resistance as it can make or break a transformation. It is natural for people to resist change, especially if it means adapting to new ways of doing things. I find that resistance can also drive innovation and be positive. So, it's essential to be aware of and manage resistance proactively and constructively and to take time to listen to people's concerns and issues.
- *Monitor and evaluate the change.* Before starting any transformation, I always identify how we will know that we are successful or, at least, moving in the right direction. It is vital to monitor progress and evaluate the effectiveness of a transformation since this will help to identify any issues and allow for adjustments to be made as needed.

- *Be prepared for the unexpected.* Change can be unpredictable, and it's important to be prepared for the possibility that things may not go as planned. Being flexible and adaptable, as well as willing to make adjustments as needed, is vital.

In addition, the key lessons learnt from the airline transformation outlined in this case study are as follows:

- *Plan:* A change management plan was essential since this provided guidance about what needed to be done, by when and by whom. It also enabled the progress to be tracked, and any issues to be quickly identified and dealt with.
- *Rationale:* Start with the 'why'. Using the WIIFM framework helped with this since it is such a powerful technique. When it was hard to articulate the WIIFM, honesty and transparency were the best approach.
- *Iterative:* Transformation is iterative and breaking the transformation into logical bite-sized chunks helps to ensure that the benefits are delivered. This made it easier to train and communicate with the cabin crew, pilots, airport agents, sales staff and support colleagues.
- *Visibility:* To build momentum, we needed to showcase to stakeholders what could be achieved by using journey maps (a step-by-step visual representation of the user experience) or opportunity statements (brief statements of what the solution could be by taking into account the problem) and prototypes which brought ideas to life by turning the conceptual thinking in the opportunity statement into the creation of a visual experience (such as pictures).
- *Agility:* The last lesson, and my favourite one, is that change management for transformations can be agile. In my view, I believe that change management should always be agile in transformations. This is because it reduces the amount of change colleagues need to digest at a single point in time, and by iterating through the change curve, the adoption of the overall transformation will be increased. Moreover, I believe that agile approaches to change management should involve frequent reassessment and flexibility in response to new information or changing circumstances. In the case of the airline transformation, some regulatory changes needed to be included midway through the transformation. We could include these in future iterations and other functionality that makes the WIIFM more digestible to stakeholders.

Here are a few methods that I found during the transformation to incorporate agile principles:

1. Identify and prioritize the most critical aspects of the transformation. This helps to focus efforts and ensure that the most impactful changes are addressed first.

2. Break the transformation down into smaller, more manageable chunks. This makes it easier to implement changes incrementally and make adjustments as needed.
3. Monitor and evaluate progress regularly. This helps to identify any issues or challenges that arise and allows for adjustments as required.
4. Be flexible and adaptable. Transformation is often unpredictable, and it's essential to adjust plans as new information becomes available and/or circumstances change.

Transformational change is challenging, and fraught with tension and resistance. However, it is important to engage with colleagues and stakeholders in a way that enables an effective adoption of the changes. It is not always necessarily the case that agile/iterative delivery is the best method for change management for all transformations. The best approach to change management will depend on the specific needs and goals of the transformation, as well as the resources and constraints of the organization. That being said, I believe that agile approaches to change management can be particularly well-suited for complex and dynamic transformations. In addition, the flexibility and adaptability of agile practices make them ideal for handling the unpredictability that often accompanies transformations.

Questions

1. What were the benefits of using the Scaled agile Framework for the transformation in the airline company?
2. A number of techniques were used to engage stakeholders in the transformation. How might you apply those in a change you are working on, or one you are familiar with?
3. What are the challenges of an agile approach? How might those be addressed?

SUMMARY

Engaging stakeholders as integral participants within and throughout a business transformation is a key element of people-centric change. As outlined in this chapter, there are numerous factors which influence whether or not an individual and/or team will engage with change, including the history of change and the culture of the organization. Identifying the factors that influence engagement is vital and addressing them even more important in order to be able to effectively engage stakeholders with a transformation. There are several ways to engage stakeholders, including top-down or via a burning platform scenario; both of these have limitations, as discussed in this chapter. An alternative approach is to encourage the co-creation of change, whenever feasible, which means constructing change *with* rather than *for* stakeholders. This can be done for instance, with Action Research, a World Café, or the Four Walls method. Co-creation will help to engage stakeholders in shaping a transformation and give them agency and autonomy.

Although leadership and management have the primary responsibility for creating engagement, employees also have their part to play as engagement flows up, down and across an organization. This is contrary to the belief that pervades some organizations that employees are not responsible adults and need to be managed into engagement with change. Instead of aligning people to the organization by shaping them to organizational requirements while treating them as expendable resources, there should be a shift to inclusivity and equality with change so that people have the autonomy to engage in business transformations through co-creation in an inclusive and equal way (see Chapter 9). This will help to ensure that engagement is distributed and collaborative across the organization.

PRACTICAL IMPLICATIONS

The practical implications that can be drawn from this chapter are:

- *Ensure that the relevant voices are engaged and heard.*
  Employees on different schedules or with different personal or professional demands need to be given the opportunity to participate and not miss out on engaging with change. For instance, employees could be engaged in the process using a combination of surveys, personas and interviews in order to understand what they really want and need. This will differ significantly from company to company, so approaches will need to be adapted to fit your local context.
- *Develop a sense of ownership.*
  For co-creation to be successful it is not just a matter of stating that stakeholders can be more involved or participate in decisions but it involves building a sense of ownership and trust. This means ensuring that there are clear owners, responsibilities and accountabilities for actions and that stakeholders are clear on the guard rails.

- *Involve employees in decision-making.*
  Finding ways to include the voice of relevant people into idea generation, planning and implementation shifts business transformations towards being meritocratic, where the best ideas and inputs are included in decision-making. To encourage people to engage in ideas about what needs to improve, ask questions such as:
  - If it was your business, what would make it better for you?
  - What do you think could be improved/done differently?
  - What are the issues?
  - What needs to change or be done differently?
  - What will be the benefits to the organization of this change?
  - What matters most to you with regard to...?
- *Understand customer/client experiences.*
  To engage external stakeholders in a business transformation there is a need to understand the customer/client experience and journey. This involves finding out what works for clients/customers, what they find frustrating and what they would like to change.
- *Tap into existing networks.*
  People-centric change involves gaining support and momentum from stakeholders by tapping into existing organizational networks, both internally and externally, to explore ideas and seek people's experience and advice. This can be done by leveraging the expertise of stakeholders in the co-creation of change through methods such as a World Café.

Notes

1 J Hodges (2019) *Employee Engagement for Organizational Change: The theory and practice of stakeholder engagement*, Routledge, London

2 K Edwards, T Prætorius and A P Nielsen. A model of cascading change: Orchestrating planned and emergent change to ensure employee participation, *Journal of Change Management*, 2020, 20 (4), 342–68. www.researchgate.net/publication/340892189 (archived at https://perma.cc/STR3-VBD5)

3 R E Freeman. A stakeholder theory of the modern corporation, *Perspectives in Business Ethics Sie*, 2001, 3 (144), 38–48

4 J Katzenbach, J Thomas and G Anderson (2019) *The Critical Few: Energize your company's culture by choosing what really matters*, Berrett-Koehler Publishers, Oakland, CA

5 D Connor (1993) *Managing at the Speed of Change: How resilient managers succeed and prosper where others fail*, Villard Books, New York

6 C C Markides (2021) *Organizing for the New Normal: Prepare your company for the journey of continuous disruption*, Kogan Page, London

7 A Hill. It's time to extinguish the 'burning platform' for good, *Financial Times*, 27 June 2021. www.ft.com/content/6a448798-e12c-454d-8378-360ad245dd51 (archived at https://perma.cc/7LM8-C8DJ)

8 M Beer. Reflections: Towards a normative and actionable theory of planned organizational change and development, *Journal of Change Management*, 14 January 2021, 21 (1), 14–29. www.tandfonline.com/doi/full/10.1080/14697017.2021.1861699 (archived at https://perma.cc/LUJ4-W3J9)

9 S Tan and J Brown. The World Café in Singapore: Creating a learning culture through dialogue, *The Journal of Applied Behavioral Science*, 2005, 41 (1), 83–90. journals.sagepub.com/doi/10.1177/0021886304272851 (archived at https://perma.cc/EL2Q-HLCL)

10 J Kilian, H Sarrazin and H Yeon. Building a design-driven culture, McKinsey, 1 September 2015. www.mckinsey.com/capabilities/growth-marketing-and-sales/our-insights/building-a-design-driven-culture (archived at https://perma.cc/Q3V8-H7H2)

11 J Woiceshyn, J L Huq, K Blades and S R Pendharkar. Microdynamics of implementing planned change on organizations front line, *Journal of Change Management*, 2020, 20 (1), 59–80. www.tandfonline.com/doi/abs/10.1080/14697017.2019.1602553 (archived at https://perma.cc/J859-H42D)

12 T Devinney. When CEOs talk strategy, is anyone listening? *Harvard Business Review*, June 2013. hbr.org/2013/06/when-ceos-talk-strategy-is-anyone-listening (archived at https://perma.cc/T5CK-Z4CC)

04

Engaging opposing voices

Introduction

Change, especially transformational change, can cause a multitude of reactions, some of which can be emotionally messy. As Dale Carnegie first said in 1936, 'When dealing with people, let us remember, we are not dealing with creatures of logic. We are dealing with creatures of emotion, creatures bristling with prejudices and who are motivated by pride and vanity'.[1] Many of us have had the experience of a business transformation being unveiled and the response being less than positive. Sometimes such a reaction will be subtle such as a sigh, silence, lowered eyes or tightened lips; at other times there might be questions about whether the change is really necessary, complaints about 'yet another thing to do', a chorus of 'here we go again' or lots of reasons why it is just not the right time for another big change. The natural tendency is to side-line those objectives in an effort to drive a transformation forward. Yet individuals who oppose the change often have valid reasons for doing so and/or have ideas on what can be done better but too often they are dismissed as complainers who should be ignored. This has led to intense debates in the literature around whether opposition to change should be overcome or embraced. Ignoring opposition can, however, result in valid ideas and concerns not being considered, which can cost time, money and potentially the entire transformation. Instead of dismissing opposition outright, people-centric change involves listening to dissenting voices and respecting and empathising with their concerns.

This chapter explores why people oppose change, with particular attention paid to how to address opposition by making change meaningful, giving people a voice (even if it is one we would prefer not to hear) and understanding different perspectives. Emphasis is given to the importance of listening to dissenting voices, especially when there is a need to drive the transformation through to a programme deadline. The chapter concludes with a business insight written by Zoleka Mashiyi which describes the challenges of implementing a transformation within a public sector department in South Africa where there was opposition and apathy to changing the culture of the department. The case stresses the need to embrace diverse and emerging views.

Opposition to change

Anyone attempting to engage stakeholders with a business transformation knows to expect some opposition, because change is not always seen as rational, and it is therefore natural for people to struggle with it, especially when it is imposed upon them. Individuals will react differently because they interpret the information they receive about a transformation in different ways. While some will see it as having benefits for the organization and the potential for personal gain and development, others will perceive it as interfering with the way that they do their work and a disruption to the status quo. As part of their appraisal individuals will evaluate whether the impact of the transformation is positive (enhances their job), neutral (does not impact their job) or negative (threatens to make their job worse or more difficult). Research indicates that employees who assess change as positive are more motivated to react favourably by increasing their commitment to the organization.[2] They may also be more willing to invest their time and energy in their job and in their own growth and development which can, in turn, be a source of personal resilience. The opposite is also true in that the more people feel that the transformation is being pushed and forced onto them without them being involved in the decision process, then the more likely they are to react negatively. This was the case in the Italian subsidiary of a European multinational food producing company where employees reported that changes within the organization were frequently imposed from above and were not communicated effectively with neither explanations nor objectives given for them.[3] The employees also felt that they were not adequately involved in the decision-making processes nor did they feel that they were sufficiently prepared for the practical impact that changes would have on their daily work routines and roles. Hence, they responded negatively to any imposed changes. What the Italian workers wanted to know – which is often what we all want to know when faced with a change – is 'What's in it for me?' Will it make me better at my job? Will it help me get a pay rise? Will it make me enjoy my job more? If the answer to any of these questions is 'yes' then we may be more likely to adopt the proposed changes. Individuals will therefore become engaged with a business transformation because they feel positive about it and about their ability to take on a new challenge, but if they don't feel positive then, like the Italians working in the food producing company, they may well oppose it.

Opposition to change can manifest itself in three ways: cognitive, affective and behavioural. Cognitive is the way someone thinks about change, affective conveys the emotional and psychological reactions to change and behavioural is how an individual responds and is the result of both the cognitive and affective manifestations. These responses can be conveyed in various ways, ranging from arguing and making critical or negative comments, to being destructive and intentionally sabotaging the change. Most of these responses are visible, but there are also some that are more covert, such as reluctant compliance, which is more difficult to manage. Ultimately, such reactions, whether overt or covert, have the potential to slow and/or obstruct a business transformation.

Opposition as a positive reaction

Opposition is usually perceived as a negative response and a barrier to a transformation frequently manifesting itself through counterproductive behaviours. Literature about organizational change often reflects this negativity, stressing how crucial it is to overcome the problem of resistance. Opposition to change is, however, a natural occurrence and the prevalent negative view of overcoming or resisting opposition needs to be reconsidered by taking into consideration what drives people to behave in this way. In other words, the reasons why people oppose a business transformation need to be uncovered and opposition seen as having positive aspects which should not be ignored. One way that opposition can be positive is that it can keep conversations about a transformation and the ensuing changes going rather than discussions dying from a lack of interest. This is important, as ongoing debate and discussion are essential and valuable, especially if employees are struggling with what the change means for them and how they feel about it. Furthermore, opposition can provide additional data about how individuals feel about previous transformations which may be expressed in comments such as 'We have tried that before and it failed' or

'Why should we trust you this time?' Opposition can also play a crucial role in drawing attention to elements of a proposed transformation that may actually be flawed or inappropriate. It can, therefore, provide an opportunity to identify weaknesses in a proposed transformation, including the purpose, approach and suggested ways of implementation. Moreover, people may have competing commitments which means that those who are opposing change usually have some good reason even if their rationale for doing so is not evident. Understanding why individuals object to a business transformation is, therefore, vital.

Opposition is not something to ignore. Understanding a difference of opinion can often be constructive as it exposes the positive and negative aspects of a proposed transformation. So, rather than assuming that those who raise objections to change are 'resisters' it may be better to consider them as people who see what needs to be protected or done differently and are mindful of the impact that the wrong change initiative can have on the organization and its employees. When we consider those opposing change as responsible, thinking adults, rather than seeing them as purely 'resisters' this demonstrates a genuine respect for their views. This demands a need to listen to opposing views in order to understand what the issues are that can provide valuable input about what will work and not work. Opposition, therefore, needs to be reframed so that it is seen as a natural part of people-centric change and a potential source of energy and feedback. In other words, the power of opposition can be used to build support for a business transformation, improve the chances of identifying change initiatives that will be effective, and alleviate some of the discomfort that people may be feeling about yet more change.

Although it is not always feasible to make people feel comfortable with change, managers can minimize discomfort by identifying the root causes of individuals' concerns and opposition and where possible work with them to eradicate or lessen them. If the personal concerns of individuals are ignored and their engagement is lost, the negative impact of them withdrawing their support, either openly or covertly, can be highly damaging. So, instead of interpreting opposition as something negative, it is more valuable to recognize and appreciate the benefits of opposition, because it may well be a sign that people care enough to criticize and that they have not given in to apathy and inertia. It shows that they are taking the transformation seriously and that it is important to them.

Understanding opposition

If opposition is viewed as a natural and expected part of a business transformation, then it is important to understand why individuals are reacting in that way and encourage them to discuss why they are responding as they are. To do this firstly involves understanding how opposition might manifest itself, from apathy to aggregation, from subtle acts of non-cooperation to industrial sabotage, and from verbal protest to destructive opposition. To predict what form opposition might take requires being aware of the reasons why people may oppose a transformation at both an organizational and/or personal level. Some of the factors that can influence an individual's response to a transformation include the following: fear of loss of control and autonomy; wanting to retain the status quo; fear of a lack of the relevant capabilities; a lack of high quality communication about the change; and a limited capacity to absorb change. Each of these is discussed briefly below.

FEAR OF LOSS OF CONTROL AND AUTONOMY

Even if a transformation is likely to improve the working experience of employees, they may still oppose it due to loss aversion bias, which means that they are generally more worried about losing what they have than they are excited about getting something new that may be even better. For example, consider for a moment an organization where there is a move towards a technology enabled flexible working environment using hot-desking. Before adopting this way of working, some individuals who use the same desk every day might be concerned about what they are giving up, which is a place of their own with their name on it. Attached to this desk may be their sense of privacy or feelings about their status within the organization and so letting go of this will be hard to do, especially if they think that their autonomy is being threatened; consequently they may well oppose the change. Conversely, individuals may be less likely to oppose the change if they think that they can freely determine where they perform their jobs (at their own desk at home or a hot desk). Having the autonomy and control to choose can enhance an individual's confidence in accepting changes to their job and their willingness to adapt to new ways of working and to move forward from the status quo.

WANTING TO RETAIN THE STATUS QUO

In their classic article on decision-making, Samuelson and Zeckhauser found that decision-makers exhibit a significant bias towards the status quo due to factors such as: convenience, habit or inertia, fear of the costs to them of the transition, and loss aversion.[4] Status quo bias explains, at least in part, and at certain times, individuals' preference to maintain their current situation. In other words, we prefer what we have already experienced, in other words, what is known. We also tend to prefer the certainty of the status quo and what we perceive to be the current state of affairs. This means that most people are reluctant to change their habits and to move away from or give up their status quo at work because they are committed to aspects of what they know, what they have, and what they do now. Through the lens of status quo bias, research indicates that opposition to change in the form of reluctance or unwillingness to embrace change can be appreciated as a predictable human response.[5] Individuals will often exhibit feelings of loss associated with giving up part or all of what exists as opposition.[6] So, some elements of opposition to a transformation can potentially be linked to the inescapability of status quo bias and a reluctance to lose what we have.

Many employees desire certainty, and this can be found in the known and the now. That results in a bias towards the status quo. As such, business transformations are likely to benefit from the identification and communication of elements of the current state that will be retained in the transformation effort, rather than proclaiming that the status quo is dangerous.[7] This will help individuals to feel more confident about certain elements remaining the same and reduce their fear of loss and anxiety relating to the unknowns which should, in turn, lessen potential opposition. So, if changes to the status quo bring uncertainty and fear, then highlighting elements of the status quo that will stay the same will help to alleviate concerns and may reduce opposition to the transformation process.

FEAR OF A LACK OF RELEVANT CAPABILITIES

A business transformation is often opposed when it makes people question whether or not they have the right capabilities (skills, knowledge, experience and attitudes) to be able to change how they work and behave. Employees might, for example, express scepticism about whether the new online system will work or whether the introduction of digital marketing is really an improvement, when what they are really worried about is whether their current skills will be obsolete, whether they have the knowledge to effectively work the new systems and if they will be able to understand the new processes. To overcome such concerns, there is a need to have practices for identifying and addressing capability gaps for people and teams in order to ensure that they have the competences to adapt positively to the changes.

A LACK OF COMMUNICATION ABOUT THE CHANGE

Opposition can stem from a lack of effective communication about the rationale – that is the legitimization for the transformation, its potential benefits and what it will mean for people's jobs. Effective messaging is, therefore, essential for reducing opposition and enabling employee readiness for change. If there is a lack of communication about the change and how it will affect people then they may well become concerned and might engage in disruptive behaviours aimed at delaying or derailing the change. Communications about change, therefore, must be effective and of a high quality in order to reduce uncertainty and anxiety (see Chapter 5 for further discussion on the communication of change).

LIMITED CAPACITY TO ABSORB CHANGE

Business transformations can inadvertently require people to have to change too much and too quickly. People might, therefore, oppose a transformation if they are unable to change their ways of working and behaviours as rapidly as required by the organization. Even when individuals intellectually understand the rationale for the change, they might not be ready to make the transition due to a lack of capacity to take on more work. They may also be suffering from transformation saturation due to too much change and might not have the energy to focus on yet more change/s (see Chapter 8 on wellbeing). How much capacity employees have to take on more change-related work, therefore, has to be considered.

Addressing opposition to change

Rather than demolishing opposition completely, there is a need to address it through various means, such as: ensuring the transformation has a clear purpose; shifting mental models; giving people a voice; providing psychological safety; identifying pain points; and discouraging unproductive views. Each of these is considered in this section.

ENSURING THE TRANSFORMATION HAS A CLEAR PURPOSE

To feel comfortable about a transformation and to carry it out with enthusiasm, people must understand their role in the transformation process and believe that it is worthwhile for them to play a part in it. It is not enough to tell employees that they will have to do things differently. Instead, anyone leading a business transformation must take the time to think through its narrative and what makes it worth undertaking, and to explain that narrative to all of the people involved in making the transformation happen as well as those impacted by it, so that it makes sense to them as individuals and relates to the work that they do.

This can be illustrated by the following scenario, which took place in a global sales company where the senior executive team was keen to make the company culture less process orientated and more performance driven. In response to this, some staff spent every lunchtime and coffee break complaining, asking 'Why do we have to change? We are never told the reasons for such changes.' These individuals are unlikely to change their behaviour because they have not been informed about the rationale for the change. This scenario highlights that an awareness of the business need for change is a critical component to overcoming opposition. Stakeholders must be able to understand the need for change, to feel that it will make a difference, and that it is important for their work and the workplace. Having a perception that a transformation has a clear rationale, purpose and meaning enables an individual to appreciate why the change is necessary and to feel a part of it. If stakeholders are unable to understand why there is a need to change and if that reason is not clear then they are more likely to oppose it. A clear sense of the purpose is, therefore, crucial, as is evident in the work of Victor Frankl.

In 1946 Victor Frankl narrated his experiences as a prisoner in Nazi concentration camps in his book *Man's Search for Meaning*.[8] Wondering why some prisoners survived and others did not in an atmosphere of hopelessness and despair, he concluded that those who survived lived with a greater sense of purpose. Frankl's book highlights that having a sense of purpose is essential for surviving and thriving in the world. This is also important in business transformations in that people need to be clear on the purpose of the transformation and be able to find meaning in it. Getting employees to understand the purpose of a transformation requires helping them to develop an understanding about the rationale for the change, their role in making it happen and what the impact of the change will be for them. Of course, it also means ensuring that change is aligned to the defined organizational strategy and purpose and is in line with organizational values. A relevant purpose can explain the reasons behind a transformation, and why it is initiated. This includes having clarity on the relevance, justification, urgency, destination, scope and explicit goals of a transformation. While each of these attributes are important on their own, they also build on, and are antecedents to, each other. Thus, it is important to understand the system interactions between each of these attributes when defining the purpose of a transformation.[9]

A clear purpose is not enough on its own. There must also be a focus on individual and organizational readiness and communication of the purpose. Communication is important not only to make sure the different stakeholders receive and understand the purpose and the need for change but also for them to accept the transformation. The purpose must also be supported and prioritized by senior management both in terms of resources and other decisions. Furthermore, there must be alignment between the purpose of the transformation and organizational strategy, which requires that the organizational strategy is clearly formulated and communicated. The purpose of the business transformation should, therefore, be clear and effectively communicated to all stakeholders.

SHIFTING MENTAL MINDSETS

Mindset is often regarded as a firmly established set of thoughts, attitudes and beliefs held by a person or group. It is a lens through which individuals perceive the world and thus drives actions and behaviours, and is a key factor in how they interpret a transformation. This interpretation involves firstly how an individual perceives the transformation itself, and secondly how they interpret the transformation. The combination of these two factors will impact on shaping an individual's mental mindset, which is based on a person's knowledge, experience, values, beliefs and aspirations, and represents how individuals structure and organize concepts cognitively, selectively filter and interpret information, make sense of this information, make decisions and, ultimately, behave. A mindset is, therefore, the frame of reference through which an individual views a transformation, provides guidance for their action and determines how they will react and behave.

Those who covertly or overtly oppose a transformation tend to hold what Stanford University Professor Carol Dweck calls a fixed mindset, that is, the belief that the intelligence and capabilities of adults are essentially stable.[10] In contrast, people with what Dweck calls a growth mindset enjoy challenges, strive to learn and consistently see the potential to develop new skills. They see transformation as a learning outcome and approach change as 'We are learning how to do things differently', instead of 'This is what we will do differently.' When carrying out transformational changes, people with a growth mindset act with humility, often saying, 'I don't know the answer.' They are also open to feedback and will update their knowledge, actions and behaviours in response to it. This disposition promotes individuals acting in ways that foster their own learning and also learning environments. The growth mindset thus embraces change and learning and can help to navigate the uncertainty of a transformation. So can mindsets be changed, and if so, how?

Bounded rationality theory argues that an individual's ability to act is constrained by the information they have, the cognitive limitations of their minds, and the finite amount of time and resources they have to make a decision.[11] So mindsets or mental models become the bounded rationality of an individual shaping how they acquire and process incoming information. Therefore, for a person to change their mental model the information they have has to be unsettled in a way that offers new possibilities. For any shift in a mental model there must be some form of new information, or other stimuli, that leads an individual to experience uncertainty, discrepancies or inconsistencies that trigger conscious examination of their implicit beliefs and the mental models they hold.[12] There also has to be a perception of difference that an individual chooses to consider. The individual then needs to reflect on the change, considering what will be different based on what they know. If the individual makes no connection within their mental model to the new ideas, they are unlikely to adopt them. Alternatively, if the new ideas can be connected to ideas already within their mental model in some way, an internalization of new information will occur, and an adjustment made. This new model then becomes the accepted view and the frame of reference for future decisions and behaviours. The question then becomes, how can amendments to mindsets be triggered?

Although an individual's mindset is firmly established, it can still change. Human brains have high levels of neuroplasticity, meaning they are able to develop new neural pathways allowing individuals over time, and with application, to develop new habitual ways of thinking. In simple terms, the connections between brain cells have the ability to reorganize in response to our changing needs. There are two ways to drive the change required, and both are based on the work of Leon Festinger.[13] His theory is that when an individual experiences conflict between their attitudes, beliefs and/or behaviour, they feel an emotional discomfort called 'cognitive dissonance'. To restore the balance necessitates either taking action to experience something different, which in turn affects an individual's mindset, or alternatively reflecting on a different way of thinking which then changes a person's beliefs, which in turn affects their behaviour.

A key mechanism for changing mindsets can be conversations that enable increased understanding of the desired outcomes of the transformation by discussing related information with employees, thus minimizing uncertainty and anxiety through the reduction of changed related stressors.[14] These new understandings can shift employees' mindsets so that they interpret stimuli in different ways, resulting in changes to their behaviour that support the business transformation. This requires recognizing and accepting the potential impact of ongoing conversations and using that knowledge to purposefully plan for and engage in different forms of conversation rather than simply holding more of the same type of conversation. For instance, planned conversations about transformations can provide opportunities to encourage the incorporation of new ideas into an individual's reality and, thereby, form the basis of future decisions, actions and change.[15] However, people will only begin to be open to accepting, embracing and making a change when their mindset starts to shift from 'This transformation is going to be difficult and stressful' to 'This transformation will be rewarding and beneficial.' Once someone starts to believe a transformation will be achievable, that the rewards of making the change will outweigh the costs and that the change could be the way we do things, then that individual will start to be willing to operate in the new ways that the changes require and to learn and enact the new behaviours so that the change can occur. So giving people the opportunity to voice their views, and to be listened to, is essential in helping to shifting mindsets.

GIVING PEOPLE A VOICE

Opposition may occur when individuals operating under conditions of uncertainty and ambiguity feel anxious and want to know what is happening and, importantly, why it is happening. This puts an emphasis on engaging stakeholders across the organization (and even externally) in conversations about what is happening and how they are feeling. Understanding why stakeholders react negatively to proposed changes does not have to involve guesswork but can instead be done by asking relevant questions to help to gain an understanding. To do this effectively, space has to be created where ideas, issues, concerns, hopes and fears about business transformations can be raised and listened to. This does not mean that such conversations always have to be conducted in a formal meeting. Instead, informal coffee conversations can be just as valuable and be done in-person, in small groups or one-to-one. Such informal conversations can also be conducted online, especially for people who no longer sit in one space, are dispersed across many offices or are working from home.

PROVIDING PSYCHOLOGICAL SAFETY

To be able to feel confident to raise a dissenting point or even an idea requires individuals to feel confident that it is safe to do so, whether online or in-person. The belief that it is safe to take risks, express ideas and concerns, speak up with questions, and admit mistakes – all without fear of negative consequences is termed psychological safety and is best summarized as a sense of permission for candour.[16] Elements of this are present in industries such as music for example, members of Warner music's artist and repertoire (A&R) teams are encouraged to offer frank feedback about each other's hits and flops, a process known as 'retrospectives' or 'retroing'. However, this is not about creating a comfort zone, since it can become a lot less comfortable when people are actually talking to each other directly about how they feel and are making observations and providing feedback that others may not like. Psychological safety is not just a 'nice to have' but can make a critical difference to whether or not people actively engage with business transformations, because they may be more likely to do so when they feel safe enough to address underlying issues and to contribute to challenging the status quo.

Despite awareness of the concept of psychological safety, there are still misunderstandings about it which inhibit many organizations from undertaking the effort needed to create a safe space for conversations about transformations. For instance, some managers worry that creating psychological safety will result in too much cross-talk or unleash endless chatter, taking up valuable time, slowing progress or create confusion. Or worse, they fear that people might speak up in unproductive ways, complain endlessly and expect someone else to fix the problems they raise. When psychological safety is low and employees hold back in meetings, the quality of both conversations and results is diminished, diversity of thought is reduced, excellent ideas may not come to light and plans will not benefit from thoughtful debate.[17] At worst, crucial information or critiques remain unshared, resulting in what might have been a preventable failure; and, at best, precious time is wasted by holding a meeting that adds little value.

Nevertheless, it can be difficult and unproductive to have a meeting where everyone speaks up energetically without self-discipline, talking past each other, adding irrelevant points, or even getting into heated arguments that turn personal. Recognizing these possibilities, Edmondson and Smith map out four archetypes of participation modes in a conversation based on two dimensions: speaking up or remaining silent, and productive or unproductive contributions.[18] The resulting four archetypes are called: withholding; disrupting; contributing; and processing. To facilitate productive voice (contributing) and productive silence (processing) requires understanding the forces that contribute to each of them. Strategies can be employed to help minimize unproductive silence (withholding) and unproductive voice (disrupting). The aspiration should be to ensure that everyone's knowledge and experience are engaged so that their diverse experiences and expertise can be integrated effectively. In short, good meetings happen when all participants are contributing with minimal withholding or disrupting, whether they are formally organized, or informal and ad hoc, virtual or in-person. For productive conversations to occur, they may need to be facilitated with gentle nudges or overt direction-setting because if left to unfold spontaneously sometimes conversations can meander off topic, silence crucial voices and/or fail to agree a solution. To avoid this, the use of simple guidelines or principles can be of help. For example, two crucial principles for effective conversations about transformations are: (i) to ask questions; and (ii) to listen (see below) which can help to raise and understand pain points.

UNDERSTANDING PAIN POINTS

It is important to create a psychologically safe space for people to be able to share their pain points, which are specific problems and issues that they are facing with regard to their role and responsibilities in relation to a business transformation. Pain points can be diverse and vary between individuals and team, and include a lack of clarity in communications, lack of engagement with management, lack of investment and unreliable technology, and a lack of involvement in key decision-making. If ignored or not allowed to be raised, such pain points can become chronic and undermine commitment and engagement. To avoid this happening, relevant practices need to be developed and implemented, including effective communication, and the creation of space for dialogue and opportunities for individual expression of voice. Such practices need to be a core feature of the transformation, which is what Matti Lievonen, the former CEO of Neste – a Finnish oil company – did when the organization decided to become more sustainable by using more renewable feedstock to make its fuel. Progress to achieve this aim was slow, and Greenpeace activists began to demonstrate against Neste's use of palm oil as a feedstock for refining. Hence, Lievonen knew that, despite the company having done all it could to ensure sustainability in everything related to palm oil, he had to listen to and address the concerns of the activists, because of the impact that they could have on the operations and reputation of the company. Lievonen, therefore, invited the protestors to a meeting to discuss their pain points, and although the company did not have answers for all the concerns raised, Lievonen and his colleagues did listen. They viewed the criticism as an opportunity to improve the company and to do things differently, and ultimately won the trust of the activists.[19] This case illustrates the importance of understanding pain points.

Another way to entice people to share their pain points is to encourage edge rather than centre conversations. The centre is the area where everybody knows what is going on and is where conversations are safe and predictable such as the weather, current markets, customers and what the competition is up to. If the conversation stays in the centre, an organization will achieve incremental change at best. In contrast, edge conversations go into uncharted territory and are risky, but they provide the opportunity to explore challenges and opportunities that the organization is facing. For example, consider the following question a manager may pose in a meeting: 'Does everyone agree?' The unintended signals this question is sending is that everyone should agree. So, even if the manager is genuinely open to challenge, members of the team may not feel comfortable speaking up. A better question may be, 'Who would like to share why this bad idea will not work?' It is, therefore, important to create an environment where individuals are comfortable in raising pain points; for example, asking everyone to share three reasons why an idea will not work is better than asking an open, generic question inviting anyone to share an opposing view. Moreover, it can be helpful to invite people to share pain points anonymously online such as via Padlet. Creating space for open and constructive discussions about pain points is integral to the success of a business transformation because it can identify what might get in the way of a transformation being successful and what needs to be addressed, and how. When organizations encourage employees to engage in the tough edge conversations, they create a culture of greater transparency where people are not holding back and feel able to share what is not working as well as what is.

Ultimately, providing a safe space for employees to share pain points will contribute positively to individual and organizational wellbeing (see Chapter 8 for further discussion on wellbeing).

DISCOURAGING UNPRODUCTIVE VIEWS

Productive voice comprises: speaking up constructively with relevant information, ideas or opinions; actively contributing to a conversation; building on a concept, asking questions; and constructive disagreement or dissent. This occurs when people make comments and give feedback in a way that reinforces the norm that candour is welcome and when an organization actively nurtures a climate of psychological safety and helps to move the conversation forward. In contrast, unproductive voice ranges from wandering off-topic to making rude or unprofessional comments. All of these consume time and diminish candour and only lead to a contagion of destructive opposition. To discourage unproductive voice that wastes time and inhibits others' subsequent participation takes discipline and self-awareness. Simple techniques such as agreeing ground rules, adhering to organizational values and providing empathic feedback can help.

Understanding the perspective of others

QUESTIONING

One of the most important ways to address opposition is through enquiry which means asking open-ended questions and valuing the answers that ensue. Frequently asking questions can unlock new insights and open up space for people to do their best thinking. Hal Gregersen in his book *Questions Are the Answer* proposes that by getting better at questioning we can raise the chances of unlocking better answers.[20] For Gregersen, the best questions are catalytic in that they knock down barriers to thinking and channel energy down more productive pathways. Questions such as the following can be useful for generating views about a transformation: What would you like to see changed at work, so that you could be more effective or so that work would be more satisfying? What is getting in the way of you supporting the change? What is keeping you from being more fully committed to the transformation? As Ernest Hemingway said, questions need a clean, well-lighted place to unfold in. To achieve this requires places and times where different approaches can be tried. For instance, Mark Zuckerberg, the CEO of Meta, has instituted a weekly question time with his employees during which they are encouraged not only to seek information but also to bring up challenging issues which they think the company's leadership might be missing or might not be addressing actively enough.

Such an approach could also be done in facilitated online or onsite sessions which are devoted to forward-thinking questions such as 'Why are we doing this in this way?' This can help to challenge the rigidity and complacency of the status quo. It was creating space for such questions to be asked that led Pixar – the film making company that made films such as *Finding Nemo* and *The Incredibles* – to launch Notes Day. This concept, which focuses on inquiry and asking questions, was inspired by the tradition in film-making of senior executives sporadically asking for a screening of a film in progress, so that they can provide feedback about it in the form of notes. Pixar's Notes Day has taken this practice further and extended it to the task of assessing whether the studio itself, rather than one of its films, could benefit from some significant improvements. The key to the success of events such as Notes Day is in developing the conditions that: signal that asking questions is a valuable activity worth focusing on; encourage people to linger in a questioning frame of mind before diving into their search for answers; and give permission for people to broaden their perspective on a problem and to view it from different angles. This involves creating purposeful spaces where it is OK to speak up and people will not be embarrassed, rejected or punished for doing so. Questioning cannot, however, survive on its own – it needs the support of active listening.

ACTIVE LISTENING

Actively listening means taking the time to really listen, which involves clearing our mind of any expectations about what others are saying or about to say. In other words, it is about listening to understand rather than listening to defend. This type of listening comprises: asking people for their ideas; taking them seriously; responding with concrete, continuing support; and ultimately transferring leadership of a business transformation to them. This can be done in-person or online in different ways, for example through listening tours which involve managers meeting with colleagues across the organization in either in-person or virtual focus groups and creating a space for employees to share how they are really feeling by actively listening to them. During these sessions, managers might start by showing vulnerability themselves, since this can send a powerful signal that it is OK to not be OK.

This can be illustrated by the example of a technology company that sent its senior executives on a listening tour to understand the challenges faced with the company's transition to remote working. The executives began by opening up about the personal issues that they were facing with working remotely, then in response to thoughtful questions from the executives, employees began to open up. They expressed their growing self-doubts as valued team members and their dwindling sense of belonging to the organization due to remote working, whereas in the office they said that they felt that their informal encounters with peers and even gossip at the water cooler gave them a sense of connection. Employees also shared how they felt that the back-to-back nature of video calls had left them feeling more disconnected than ever, especially from their managers, with whom most touchpoints were seen as transactional. In response to what they heard, the senior executives created space in-person and online for informal connections and conversations which were agenda-free and spontaneous.

Another approach that can be used to listen to people's views and to generate a rich set of insights from a large group dispersed across different locations is technology-based crowdsourcing tools. For example, a global pharmaceutical company brought together hundreds of its employees from across the globe for an hour using crowdsourcing tools as part of a rapid listening session on wellbeing and hybrid working, and consequently found that the lack of work boundaries was one of the strongest contributors to poor wellbeing. Employees raised concerns that working from home meant that their hours had increased since they were struggling to set their own boundaries, partly due to worries about their job security and also concerns about being seen as irrelevant. In response to this feedback, employees were encouraged to raise ideas for what could be done differently, and working groups were set up to implement the recommendations. Overall, the session and follow-up actions made employees feel listened to, valued and respected.

LISTEN AND RESPOND IN NEW WAYS

Listening deeply to people's concerns and questions without being dismissive is vital in order to ensure that people feel heard and supported. In contrast, not being listened to can have detrimental effects on how people react to change. In his TED, talk Ernesto Sirolli suggests the pervasiveness of not listening.[21] He describes a mission to Africa, in which 'We Italians decided to teach Zambian people how to grow food.' The tomato seeds that the team planted flourished so well that they were very proud of their demonstration, but they were baffled at the local people's apparent indifference to the success. The answer to this puzzle came when the tomatoes ripened. Overnight, some 200 hippos came out from the river and ate everything. The Italian team said to the Zambians, 'My God, the hippos!' And the

Zambians said, 'Yes, that is why we have no agriculture here.' In response to this, the team asked, 'Why didn't you tell us?' And the Zambians answered, 'You never asked.' Sirolli says he felt foolish until he saw how many other Western nations were making the same mistake. They came to Africa and saw glitches that seemed to require straightforward interventions which may have performed well in their home environments, but not in the local context which they knew very little about. The title of Sirolli's talk, and the main point he makes, is: 'You want to help someone? Shut up and listen!' What Sirolli and his colleagues had not done was to enact active listening.

When we listen, show curiosity, and model emotional inspiration, we encourage individuals to express themselves. Dan Cable, Professor of Organizational Behaviour at London Business School, calls this emotions projection, and points out that it emphasizes adapting, learning and empowering people with creativity. In his book *Alive at Work*, Cable points out that this needs space and a place for people to experiment in order to be their best selves at work.[22] He goes on to say that giving people this freedom unleashes their seeking systems, that is, their urges to explore and understand, and shows them that they are valued not just for the results they achieve, but also for their creativity and initiative. In other words, it is making enough space so that people can learn and share, rather than creating procedures that they have to follow.

Opposing views often have clear, important messages that are worth listening to. The people who hold these views may be the ones who most vividly see the potential losses or risks associated with a proposed transformation. Listening actively with curiosity, without judgement, and seeking to understand is very important for appreciating opposing views. Of course, the easy bit is listening to what people voice and their ideas, whereas the hard bit is what is done with them; this requires being willing to respond and give arguments for retaining the status quo or not.

The following business insight, written by Zoleka Mashiyi, an independent consultant based in South Africa, outlines the challenges of implementing a transformation within a public sector department in South Africa where there was opposition and apathy to changing the culture of the department so that it was more service orientated.

CASE STUDY

Business Insight: An organizational change journey

A public sector department in the Eastern Cape, South Africa, hired me as a consultant to help them implement a transformational change programme due to the opposition to the change. Many consultants before me had failed to do this successfully and I was tasked with picking up the reins of transforming the department into a service-oriented one. When I first joined the department, I was astounded by the level of apathy towards providing a high level of service to the public, and the poor relations between staff and leaders. I had to quickly find out why the department had such a toxic culture. I began by checking the employee satisfaction surveys and other organizational surveys conducted by my predecessors. These surveys covered topics ranging from the corporate culture to diversity and climate. One important feature I noticed was that each time the surveys were distributed there were fewer and fewer employees responding, with the latest survey achieving only a 40 per cent response rate. From the few employees who had responded, it was clear that they were unhappy about the work environment and did not feel listened to. Consequently, employees felt disengaged because their feedback was never listened to, nor was it acted upon. There also appeared to be an underlying conflict between the employees, leadership and labour unions, with none of these critical stakeholders being able to see eye-to-eye.

I took up where my predecessor had left off with firstly aiming to achieve the goal of improving the working environment and then transforming it into a more service-oriented department. While culture change was not the only change required, for the purposes of this case I will concentrate on the culture renovation since changing the culture was the foundation for all other changes and would impact on elements such as the work environment, leadership, interpersonal interactions, physical environment and union relationships. The preliminary findings from my diagnosis of the data, from the employee surveys as well as from the discussions I had with employees, unions, leaders and the human resources unit, indicated a number of areas, as shown in Table 4.1, which needed to be addressed to achieve the goals of the transformation.

The future state was also so dramatically different from the existing one that people had to change for it to be successfully implemented. To achieve this required fresh perspectives and new behaviours; in reality, leaders and employees had to adjust their behaviours in order to operate in the required new culture (as outlined in Table 4.2).

TABLE 4.1 Current situation

Ineffective leadership practices
Lack of communication and feedback
Lack of ownership and accountability of change
Unconducive work environment
No sense of urgency/deadlines missed
Lack of sponsorship and championing of change
Lack of teamwork (working in silos)
Limited collaboration
Lack of transparency
Lack of trust/trust levels were low across the department
Commitment and accountability lacking in some areas
Employees disengaged
Strained relations (unions and leadership)
Quality of performance management leading to performance challenges and mistrust
Nurturing and growing of talent left to chance

TABLE 4.2 Future state perspective

Improved leadership skills and practices
Integration and collaboration
Focused employee development and training
Review reward and recognition incentives
Creation of a change enabling environment (all to assume their change roles)
Visibility and participation of leaders (active sponsorship)
Improved emotional intelligence levels amongst leadership
Communication and feedback mechanisms established
Post implementation plans (in response and to sustain changes)
Engaged and committed employees
Frequent and periodic performance feedback sessions
Change management specialist to be invited to programme and departmental meetings (leadership and staff sessions)
Change management a measure on leadership score cards – people value

I started by creating a change management roadmap based on the key issues that needed to be addressed. The roadmap proposed a three-year journey, with a fourth year dedicated to reinforcing the new way of doing things and thereby sustaining the change. The roadmap focused on the need for culture renovation, employee engagement and a talent management strategy, and it included the following initiatives: a review of the organizational structure; a leadership development programme focusing on senior and middle management; 360° assessments; and intense development of change management capabilities at all levels throughout the organization. A transformation approach was adopted of inclusivity, engagement and participation; this was supported by feedback, measurement and communication in which success was celebrated. This implementation approach required several levers to be pulled, including: designing activities; planning various engagements; facilitating the adoption of new processes and practices; and reinforcing a mindset change, desired attitudes and behaviours.

When I began this work, where we would eventually end up was uncertain, and the transformation would evolve by trial and error based on the impact of the interventions. This made managing the transition with predetermined, time-bound and linear project plans impossible. We needed to have a grand strategy for change, but the actual change process evolved as we progressed. This meant that leaders, managers and frontline workers all had to function in a state of the unknown, which was a frightening and unpredictable place to be where tension and emotions ran high.

In the middle of our transformation journey we were hit by Covid-19, but despite the effects of the pandemic we were able to stay on schedule with our four-year strategy. To help us to navigate the uncharted waters of the pandemic and ensure that productivity remained at an acceptable level I created a Covid-19 business resilience survey. This enabled the organization to self-assess and comprehend its level of 'disruption readiness'. This provided information which helped to validate the current situation (see Table 4.3 from some of the responses received), keep the transformation on track and to address any issues.

TABLE 4.3 What did not go well in the department in response to Covid-19

Provisioning of working tools/tools of trade (data, laptops, IT capabilities, remote accessing of certain critical systems)
Approval and sign-off processes not making employee lives easy during this time
Compassion, empathy, fairness and understanding from leaders

(*continued*)

TABLE 4.3 (Continued)

Availability and strategic placement of PPE
Employee health and safety vs productivity not made a priority
Cognisance of the 'business unusual' period not at the forefront in business operations
Proper planning and consultation on work rotation schedules
No flexibility on set measurements (adjusting deadlines, review of performance targets)
Transparency and communication, and frequency of communication
Communication from senior leadership and visibility thereof
Reactive in response to the pandemic/disaster
Lack of sense of urgency in making decisions from senior leadership/lack of quick decision-making
Active involvement of senior leadership
'Us and them' practices on WFH application (by some leaders)
Lack of uniformity/consistency across programmes/units in application of WFH process and practice
No direction given by executive management
No consistency in observing of safety protocols

The transformation is now in its final year and to date the lessons I have learnt from it include the following:

- *Adopt and apply a beyond change management approach.* It is not about the now. What matters is that the entire organization is culturally aligned to become a responsive organization over the course of the transformation journey, thus always learning and on a change trajectory to better itself.
- *One size fits all... does not apply.* Being an experienced practitioner and consultant who has worked with various organizations in both the private and public sectors does not mean you can apply a similar approach from one organization to the next. Organizations are living organisms and thus they are all different, and solutions implemented need to be fit for purpose.
- *Build a coalition with all relevant stakeholders.* Everyone needs to feel that they are part of the transformation – this allows them to participate wholeheartedly and play their respective roles effectively. I had to ensure that all stakeholders (employees, unions, leaders at all levels, various teams/groups) had a voice.
- *Enlist leadership support.* Organizational leaders need to be the face and voice of the change. They need to be committed to a transformation throughout its journey.

- *Ensure sponsorship.* Senior leaders have to be the sponsors of change. Their visibility and active engagement are vital. One of my winning cards with this transformation was spending time coaching sponsors to enable them to play their roles effectively.
- *Embrace diversity and emerging views.* Training, developing and engaging change champions helped to ensure that there were advocates of the change throughout the organization. They also provided information and feedback which was critical to the success of transformation. I listened to their feedback, and in some instances I had to review the implementation plan in line with it.
- *Strive to take everyone along.* Change can be positive and exciting for some people, but it can also generate a feeling of uncertainty and resistance in others. Although the aim was to have everyone on board, there was some background noise and cynicism from a pocket of employees who did not trust the transformation, due to the department's history of failed changes. This scepticism could have derailed the programme; however, to help address it we ensured that there was transparency, constant engagement with stakeholders at each level of the organization and effective sponsorship and change champions in place.
- *Don't lose sight of the bigger picture.* Keeping my eye on the ball was the motto that helped me in the most challenging and exhausting times of implementing this transformation. I had to constantly remember why we started the journey but importantly remind everyone involved 'why we are changing' and what the proposed benefits would be.
- *Build flexibility into your journey map.* A transformation requires constant activity and engagement to keep up the energy and vigour, especially during the pandemic. Conducting a resilience survey helped to identify the areas that needed to be addressed to keep the momentum and engagement alive. Flexibility is critical during a transformation as it allows for adjustment when unexpected circumstances call for a change in the plan.
- *Develop resilience and tenacity.* Introducing transformation in an organization of any size is not for the faint-hearted. It needs patience, understanding and staying power, because no two days are the same. You have to be resilient to deal with challenges and setbacks.
- *Emotional intelligence is critical.* Emotional intelligence is vital. Being self-aware and being able to self-reflect as well as appreciate the reactions of others enabled me to keep my emotions in check at the most trying of times.

Questions

1. What were the key challenges that Zoleka faced at the start of taking over the transformation? How did she address them?
2. What are the benefits of creating a transformation roadmap? How might stakeholders be involved in this process?
3. Which of the lessons learnt are most applicable to transformations in the organization in which you work, or one you are familiar with?

SUMMARY

Business transformations can evoke a variety of emotional responses from individuals, including opposition. This is often viewed as a burden that must be endured and, in some cases, even ignored. Ignoring opposition is, however, a misguided response, especially since opposition is a natural part of any transformation process in that it not only shows how someone feels but also affects an individual's behaviour, engagement and commitment to change. This can, in turn, have an impact on how effectively changes are implemented and sustained. It is, therefore, important to have an appreciation of opposition to change and understand how it can be addressed. Understanding the complexities of people's behaviour by asking them questions to bring their concerns and competing commitments to the surface can help to identify aspects of a proposed change that may actually be inappropriate, not well thought through, or just wrong. So, rather than demolishing opposition there is a need to consider ways of reducing it by ensuring that change is meaningful and has a clear purpose, and that people are given space to raise their voice. Ultimately, the approach that is taken in response to opposition has the potential to counteract its potentially negative consequences, since individuals are more likely to commit to a business transformation if they are properly prepared for it and given the opportunity to be involved in making decisions about it, as well as being able to share their own ideas about what needs to change and why. It is, therefore, important to recognize that opposition can be a valid response from engaged and committed people who want a voice in something that is important to them.

PRACTICAL IMPLICATIONS

There are several practical implications which can be drawn from this chapter:

- *Appreciate why people might oppose a transformation.*
  Recognize that individuals will differ in the way that they react to a transformation and that this will impact on the emotions they demonstrate. In a virtual world it is harder to see emotional reactions and appreciate the reasons for them, so to understand why people may be opposing a transformation ask the following questions:
    - How are people reacting to the transformation and the potential implications it will have for them?
    - What do they feel they are losing and what might they gain?
    - How clear is it to them what will change and when?
    - How clear is it to them what will not change?
- *Shift implementation planning to employees.*
  Leaving employees out of implementation planning can increase opposition and failure. Instead, the most relevant stakeholders should be engaged as early as possible in decisions about the implementation.
- *Create a safe environment for opposing views.*
  To foster psychological safety, start by making it clear why you need to hear from your team members, why their viewpoint and input matters, and how what they share will affect the outcomes of the transformation. Actively invite input, asking open-ended questions like: What are you seeing? What are your thoughts on this? Where do you stand on this idea? Be prepared to respond with appreciation and positivity, even if someone's idea is flawed. Finally, don't be afraid to admit your own fallibility. If you can own up to your mistakes and confidently demonstrate how you have learnt from them, you will pave the way for others to do the same and will encourage productive rather than unproductive voices.
- *Create a positive understanding of the need for change.*
  Be careful not to denigrate the status quo; instead, celebrate and honour the journey that got the organization to where it is today. Remember, employees have invested time and energy in developing, sustaining and operating the current environment. Having what they currently do perceived as wrong or defective will create negative reactions. The rationale for change, therefore,

needs to focus on the changing environment, the competitive landscape, customer and employee requirements, societal demands and/or improving service and products.

- *Work to shift employee mindsets*
  Employees will only alter their mental models if they understand the reason for the change and agree with it. Processes for reward and recognition must be adapted to support the required new behaviours and ways of working, and individuals must have the opportunity to develop any new skills that are required. Moreover, they must see people they respect actively modelling the required behaviours. Together these conditions can help to change the mindsets of people by changing their beliefs and attitudes about what can and should change in the workplace.
- *Have regular team meetings.*
  Having regular team meetings, even if they are quick check-ins, where people are able to raise any issues or concerns is vital. This means ensuring that all members of a team are included in those meetings and in the discussions, whether they are working onsite, remotely or on shifts. Since some employees may prefer to check-in or ask questions outside of a formal meeting, it is also worth providing alternative options for them.
- *Share what will not change.*
  Highlight elements of the status quo that will stay the same. This will help to alleviate concerns and reduce the fear of loss and anxiety relating to the unknowns of the transformation, which should, in turn, lessen potential employee opposition.
- *Provide support.*
  It is important that strategies are considered for addressing opposition that is likely to emerge during a transformation. Examples of strategies include: providing support and developing resources that employees can access during the transformation; and setting up support groups, counselling services or employee assistance programmes. These can help employees in dealing with their uncertainty, anxiety and other negative emotions that may emerge in response to a business transformation.

Notes

1 D Carnegie (2006) *How to Develop Self-Confidence and Influence People by Public Speaking*, Simon and Schuster, London, 13

2 K L Cullen-Lester, B D Webster, B D Edwards and P W Braddy. The effect of multiple negative, neutral, and positive organizational changes, *European Journal of Work and Organizational Psychology*, 2019, 28 (1), 124–35. www.tandfonline.com/doi/abs/10.1080/1359432X.2018.1544896 (archived at https://perma.cc/G52H-2ULM)

3 C Bernuzzi, V Sommovigo, M Maffoni, I Setti and P Argentero. A mixed-method study on the bright side of organizational change: Role clarity and supervisor support as resources for employees' resilience, *Journal of Change Management*, 2023, 23 (2), 143–76. www.tandfonline.com/doi/full/10.1080/14697017.2023.2172057 (archived at https://perma.cc/D4VR-MHHR)

4 W Samuelson and R Zeckhauser. Status quo bias in decision making, *Journal of Risk and Uncertainty*, 1988, 1, 7–59. scholar.harvard.edu/files/rzeckhauser/files/status_quo_bias_in_decision_making.pdf (archived at https://perma.cc/DZ2U-zzzz)

5 T A McLaren, B van der Hoorn and E C Fein. Why vilifying the status quo can derail a change effort: Kotter's contradiction, and theory adaptation, *Journal of Change Management*, 2023, 23(1), 93–111. www.tandfonline.com/doi/full/10.1080/14697017.2022.2137835 (archived at https://perma.cc/DZ2U-D4NJ)

6 S Oreg. Resistance to change and performance: Toward a more even-handed view of dispositional resistance, *The Journal of Applied Behavioral Science*, 2018, 54 (1), 88–107. journals.sagepub.com/doi/abs/10.1177/0021886317741867 (archived at https://perma.cc/G3JQ-W6Z7)

7 T A McLaren, B van der Hoorn and E C Fein. Why vilifying the status quo can derail a change effort: Kotter's contradiction, and theory adaptation, *Journal of Change Management*, 2023, 23(1), 93–111. www.tandfonline.com/doi/full/10.1080/14697017.2022.2137835 (archived at https://perma.cc/H7WK-ZCWW)

8 V Frankl (1946) *Man's Search for Meaning*, Penguin, London

9 D Naslund and A Norrman. A conceptual framework for understanding the purpose of change initiatives, *Journal of Change Management*, 2022, 22 (3), 292–320. www.tandfonline.com/doi/full/10.1080/14697017.2022.2040571 (archived at https://perma.cc/GFT2-7VAL)

10 C Dweck. What having a 'growth mindset' actually means, *Harvard Business Review*, 2016, 13 (2), 2–5. hbr.org/2016/01/what-having-a-growth-mindset-actually-means (archived at https://perma.cc/FJ2X-UY22)

11 H A Simon. Bounded rationality in social science: Today and tomorrow, *Mind & Society*, 2000, 1, 25–39. link.springer.com/article/10.1007/BF02512227 (archived at https://perma.cc/BP2H-WUXG)

12 A L Hemmelgarn and C Glisson (2018) *Building Cultures and Climates for Effective Human Services: Understanding and improving organizational social contexts with the ARC model*, Oxford University Press, Oxford

13 L Festinger. A theory of social comparison processes, *Human Relations*, 1954, 7 (2), 117–40. journals.sagepub.com/doi/10.1177/001872675400700202 (archived at https://perma.cc/RP9R-8EM3)

14 C Schmidt, T Kude, A Heinzl and S Mithas (2014) How agile practices influence the performance of software development teams: The role of shared mental models and backup, Thirty Fifth International Conference on Information Systems, Auckland.core.ac.uk/download/pdf /301363318.pdf (archived at https://perma.cc/49XL-5E8H)

15 D A Blackman, F Buick, M E O'Donnell and N Ilahee. Changing the conversation to create organizational change, *Journal of Change Management*, 2022, 22 (3), 252–72. www.researchgate.net/publication/358697039_Changing_the_Conversation_to_Create_Organizational_Change (archived at https://perma.cc/2E84-FW82)

16 A Edmondson. The role of psychological safety: Maximizing employee input and commitment, *Leader to Leader*, 2019, 92, 13–19. onlinelibrary.wiley.com/doi/abs/10.1002/ltl.20419 (archived at https://perma.cc/KY6T-PEZJ)

17 B H Bradley, B E Postlethwaite, A C Klotz, M R Hamdani and K G Brown. Reaping the benefits of task conflict in teams: The critical role of team psychological safety climate, *Journal of Applied Psychology*, 2012, 97 (1), 151. psycnet.apa.org/doi/10.1037/a0024200 (archived at https://perma.cc/Q8T4-QH6T)

18 A C Edmondson and D M Smith. Too hot to handle? How to manage relationship conflict, *California Management Review*, 2006, 49 (1), 6–31. cmr.berkeley.edu/search/articleDetail.aspx?article=5422 (archived at https://perma.cc/3EQX-5727)

19 IMD. Neste & IMD: Partnering for renewal, IMD, nd. www.imd.org/research-knowledge/organizational-transformation/reports/neste-imd-partnering-for-renewal (archived at https://perma.cc/W3QB-UUMW)

20 H Gregersen and E Catmull (2018) *Questions Are the Answer: A breakthrough approach to your most vexing problems at work and in life*, Harper, New York

21 E Sirolli. Want to help someone? Shut up and listen! TED, September 2012. www.ted.com/talks/ernesto_sirolli_want_to_help_someone_shut_up_and_listen (archived at https://perma.cc/B3QH-JBT8)

22 D Cable (2018) *Alive at Work: The neuroscience of helping your people love what they do*, Harvard Business Review Press, Boston

05

Communication of change

Introduction

Communications play a pivotal role in people-centric change before, during and after a transformation. Delivering key messages at the appropriate time, via the right channel and for the right audience is a vital component of all successful change. Yet despite this, communication is often done badly and change too often fails simply because of a lack of proper or sufficient communication. As Bernard Shaw supposedly said, 'The single biggest problem in communications is the illusion that it has taken place.' This is often the case when it comes to the communication of change.

The challenge is that communication, although viewed as an important part of the transformation process, is often done badly and considered as the mono-directional transfer of instructions or explanations, typically from senior executives down the organizational hierarchy until it eventually reaches frontline staff. For example, when a CEO says, 'I want everyone back in the office five days a week' this message has a finality about it and conveys top-down, imposed change. As soon as something like this is said, people try to make sense of it and what it means for them. While some individuals may respond by agreeing to the message, others will openly oppose it. Instead of sending out a dictate, an alternative approach might be for the CEO to use the opportunity to engage people in a conversation about the number of days spent in the office and invite individuals and teams to contribute their views and ideas. This would create an opportunity to widen the channels of communication and decision-making about the best way forward.

This chapter considers the role of communication during a business transformation, including the importance of how the change is described, the words used, the stories told and the pictures created in individuals' minds.

Channels for communicating are examined and there is an exploration of how effective communication and feedback should occur up, down and laterally in the organization so that information is not only provided from the top down but frontline workers are also able to provide valuable information that can help to clarify the need for change and to develop and implement plans. Specifically, the chapter focuses on the need for different types of communications at different levels and for diverse audiences. For instance, how dialogue can help to ensure meaningful change is considered along with email communications. Particular attention is paid to the communication of change in hybrid and remote working environments and as well as how the challenges of online communication can be addressed through techniques such as giving people encouragement and confidence to speak up online as well as creating impromptu conversations. The importance of having flexible multi-level communications is illustrated in the business insight written by Laura de Ruiter, Associate Director in the Behavioural Science Consortium, and Laurence Scates, the former Executive Director and Head of the Transformation from Astellas Pharma Inc. The chapter concludes with some practical suggestions for the effective communication of change.

Communication as a change practice

The quality of communications can have a significant impact on the outcomes of a business transformation. Empirical research has consistently demonstrated that effectively managed communication during transformational change is related to a range of positive employee outcomes. For example, studies show a direct link between high-quality communication about change and reduced anxiety and uncertainty as well as enhanced self-efficacy to cope with impending changes.[1] Communicating about what the transformation means for individuals and teams can help to reduce employees' anxiety about what the change means for them and their job. Effective communication is important for generating transparency and reducing uncertainty about a business transformation, and for encouraging engagement with it.[2] A study of teams in 195 countries found that engagement improved when line managers had some form of daily communication with their staff.[3] High-quality communication is crucial for ensuring that different stakeholders understand and appreciate the purpose and rationale for the change but also for overcoming ingrained cultural barriers and preferences for the status quo. Insufficient and ineffective communication can result in a lack of knowledge and understanding, giving rise to negative and opposing sentiments and uncertainty about the transformation which can trigger fear and anxiety, such as, 'What does this mean for my company, my job and my future?' It is, therefore, vital that high-quality, effective communication is in place from even before the start of a transformation.

Management are often reluctant to communicate too early about a transformation due to too many unknowns and a risk that people will become concerned about potential issues before any answers or reassurances can be given. But people need to be informed and educated about the necessity for change, the progress and challenges associated with it, and the outcomes. Providing relevant information can minimize misinformation, where employees fill in the blanks of missing information for themselves and reduce pessimism and cynicism. Furthermore, it can help to address questions such as: Why is the transformation necessary? Who will the transformation affect? What is going to change and when? How will I be affected by the change? If these questions are not thoroughly answered then people will fill in the gaps with rumour and conjecture, which can have a negative impact and merely increase the uncertainty and anxiety that typically accompanies a business transformation.

The rationale for the business transformation needs to be communicated as early as possible to people so that they can say: 'I know what the reason for this change is.' This may sound easy to do, but it should not be underestimated, especially because there is evidence that suggests that people always overestimate their ability to communicate clearly. For example, in an experiment undertaken by Elizabeth Newton at Stanford University, participants were asked to tap a song to a group of listeners.[4] The tappers were asked to guess what percentage of their listeners would understand what song they were tapping. On average, they expected 50 per cent to understand. In reality, only 2.5 per cent did, which suggests that we consider ourselves better communicators than we really are. Care must, therefore, be taken to make sure that the communication is clear and people really understand the reason and the who, what, when and how of the transformation.

Framing and rhetorical crafting

The way an organization communicates about change and the words and images it chooses to represent a transformation are important. What is said about a transformation is vital, but to whom and how it is said is just as important. Central to this is framing and rhetorical crafting. Framing involves aligning the meaning of messages with the needs and interests of stakeholders and can be done in various ways such as: linking the message with the benefits for stakeholders and reflecting their values and beliefs; moving from 'I' statements to 'we' statements; and expressing confidence in people's ability to engage with and achieve change. A key element of communication is framing the message for everyone to understand it. This was done effectively by Indra Nooyi, the former Chairperson and CEO of Pepsi who led the company through a massive transformation known as Performance with Purpose that aimed to diversify the company's offerings. Nooyi described in straightforward terms why the shift was so necessary and in every possible forum repeated the reasons by saying, 'Society and consumers are changing, and we can't be left behind... This is how we make money, not about how we spend the money we make... This is essential for our employees and their families. This is our route to thriving together.' Nooyi threw her heart and head into such speeches and wanted everyone to sense her deep commitment to the transformation. For Nooyi it worked as she said, 'you could hear a pin drop as I spoke. They were electrified. No shuffling in the seats. And, when I finished, the group stood up and cheered'.[5]

Similarly, Jacinda Ardern, a former Prime Minister of New Zealand, used an effective and passionate approach to communication during the Covid-19 pandemic. After the Covid virus made its way to New Zealand, Ardern declared the country's Alert System as being: prepare; reduce; restrict; lockdown. When announcing this system on TV she began by saying, 'I'm speaking to all New Zealanders today, to give you as much certainty and clarity as we can as we fight Covid-19.' Ardern went on to assure New Zealanders of access to essential services, supermarkets and pharmacies, which helped to lessen the severity of panic buying and concluded her speech with the exhortation, 'Be strong, be kind, and unite against Covid-19.' By explaining the reasons for the government's actions and its objectives, along with the Alert System, Ardern brought New Zealanders into her confidence, made it clear what was expected of them and acknowledged the sacrifice that they would have to make, while also establishing the basis for a united national effort.[6]

Ardern did not stick just to formal communication channels. During her daily walks between Premier House and the Parliament building, she gained insights through informal chats with New Zealanders about their fear of the disease, and consequently realized that she had to enhance her communication so that she took people with her. Clarity was key to Ardern's communication strategy, as was her open acknowledgement of the toll the lockdown would exact on Kiwis, as is evident in the following press statement: 'I do not underestimate what I'm asking New Zealanders to do, I know it's huge.' Ardern spoke logically of the danger of the virus and informed people of the threat that they collectively faced, but also explained the reasons for the measures that she enacted. She acknowledged the sacrifice that the population collectively would have to make and asked for their cooperation, thus reaching out to them on a personal level. During the pandemic, Ardern also held daily press conferences and regular informal live streams where there was no attempt to withhold information or manipulate data or facts. Her messages were sensible, direct and reassuring, while at the same time acknowledging the anxiety and uncertainty created by the pandemic.

As Ardern demonstrated, it is important to consider not just 'what' but also 'how' information is communicated. Research suggests that the communication of change influences employees' psychological outcomes.[7] In other words, 'how' something is said may have equal if not greater importance than 'what' is said. Ardern's language revealed a lot and conveyed a great deal. 'We', 'our' and 'us' were the regular pronouns used in her communications. She spoke in an empathetic way of 'living in a lockdown bubble' and her informal chats managed to make communicating government restrictions and pandemic information more palatable. Furthermore, she would answer questions in a frank and engaging manner with an optimistic mood.

Ardern's communication strategy illustrates that change is a time to be clear and concise with what is said and to avoid creating the wrong impression or misleading people. Often, when doing this, there is a tendency for leaders to default to language with a lot of caveats, conditionals and caution, such as 'we hope…', 'we intend…' or 'we expect…'. This is careful talk, but it is not confident talk and it can create uncertainty at a time when people want and need answers. Instead, it is vital to use confident language such as 'we will…', which is clear, direct, deliberate and active. The power of positive language can help people to overcome their natural fear and anxiety and become more open to engaging with a business transformation.

Even if the right language and approach are used, communications can become hollow rhetoric unless they are supported by everyday actions. In order to get a sense of whether narratives are rhetoric or reality, employees look to the everyday behaviours of those who are communicating about a transformation such as leaders and managers, and whether they acknowledge the challenges they are facing and attempt to engage employees in how these challenges might be approached, or if they listen to others and if so who they listen to. Such moments of truth illustrate that communicators are viewed with a great deal of interest during a transformation and the credibility of their words and narratives is constantly tested against their actual behaviour by those listening. The framing and rhetoric, therefore, has to be supported with the right method of communication.

Methods of communication

To reach people not only working onsite but also those working offsite and in flexible ways, there is a need to consider different and innovative methods of communication, using multiple channels which allow people to understand what is happening, why it is happening, and how it is happening and to provide opportunities for feedback. More creative ways of communicating emerged during the Covid-19 pandemic due to the restrictions and different ways of working that were imposed. For example, organizations turned to using private messaging software such as WhatsApp, blogs, vlogs, podcasts, videoconferencing, shared drives and remote desktop applications. These methods, which have become part of the standard communication toolkit, are now used alongside newsletters, in-person meetings and display screens to ensure that the messages about organizational change are widely disseminated. More creative methods also provide alternatives to the increasing use of email which, although it does have its benefits, has disadvantages too.

A key benefit of email communication is its reach, since it is possible to convey information to many employees at different locations at the same time. In addition, the information is available immediately and at any time, which is important because individuals and teams want information on demand, not just when it suits the deliverer to send it, and they also want to know that they have access to certain information when needed. A further benefit is the speed at which information by email can be conveyed to large audiences, which is vital, especially during times of uncertainty when getting a message out quickly can help to alleviate anxiety. Despite such advantages, there are several disadvantages to using email communications. A key limitation is that it rarely provides an opportunity for the feedback and discussion that may be necessary for increasing the understanding and acceptance of changes. Email also tends to be designed for consumption by a broad audience and hence is rarely tailored to specific stakeholder groups. Furthermore, communications about a transformation that has serious implications for employees can be alienating when delivered via email and can be perceived as impersonal and distant. There is also a tendency to overuse emails, which springs from the assumption that if the case for a transformation is presented as logically as possible then people, being rational, will buy into it and take the appropriate actions. This is, however, rarely effective, and instead there is a need to create space for other forms of communication in-person and online, in one-to-one or in small groups and through online discussion groups.

Another key communication method is the use of online platforms, which can be used to facilitate communication among different stakeholders connected in a virtual world but also in a direct way. For instance, Zoom can be used to facilitate conversations by creating a sense of community and transparency amongst stakeholders located across various sites and countries and for conducting facilitated online feedback sessions. Social media is another way of communicating with a large, highly dispersed group of people and can be used to deliver personalized messages related to business transformations. For example, user-generated content platforms such as YouTube enable short videos or audio segments to be shared. Furthermore, social media can provide a platform for immediate survey-based feedback. For organizations operating virtually, internal social media and collaboration platforms are a fast and effective way to communicate about transformations and to engage people in online discussions. For instance, instant messaging apps are synchronous, in the sense of simultaneous participation, and are primarily text driven, making them ideal for basic collaboration, whilst chat, either in-person or via video, is synchronous and rich, so more suited for complex collaborations and negotiation. Online forums can also be used to connect people and enable them to ask questions and quickly obtain information, leading to increased collaboration and information transfer. Moreover, knowledge networks can be formed using, for instance, MS Teams to share innovative practices, post questions and receive answers in a timely manner.

With the increase in remote working, virtual meetings have emerged as a key source for connecting and decision-making, although research indicates that they are subject to the same productive and unproductive forms of participation as in-person meetings and, therefore, call for real-time facilitation in order to agree the format of the meeting, think about who really needs to be there and especially to keep meetings as small as possible and to reduce the risk of social loafing, when people attend but don't participate. When using online communication channels for calls and meetings it is important to ensure that participants do not talk over each other, that all participants have the opportunity to contribute – chatbox discussions and polls can help with this – and that the nuances of body language are picked up, which is challenging in an online environment.

Although there have been, and continue to be, advances in online communication channels it is vital not to forget in-person communication, which is still the richest method of communication because it has the capacity for direct interaction, multiple information cues, immediate feedback and better personal focus. However, as with email and other forms of communication, there is a need to ensure that any face-to-face communication has a purpose and is timely. Ultimately, the challenge is to use appropriate channels and methods of communication to convey relevant information. The choice of the most appropriate method of communication is important, because different methods can differ markedly in their capacity to convey information, stimulate dialogue and enhance feedback. The method of communication can enhance or distort the intended message, so it is, therefore, important to select the most appropriate method to fit the content and complexity of the message that needs to be communicated and the feedback required.

Messaging

Messages about business transformations must be clear and consistent. The content of the message should focus on what information needs to be conveyed to stakeholders before, during and after the transformation initiative, as well as what information is sought from them. The types of information that affect stakeholders during a business transformation comprise:

- what stakeholders *must* know, including job-specific information
- what stakeholders *should* know, including desirable information about the organization
- what stakeholders *could* know, such as relatively unimportant gossip and rumours

As well as messages about what will change, stakeholders also need to know what will stay the same. The elements that are remaining the same should be clearly articulated, as outlined, for example, in the following message:

> Today we are announcing a restructure that will be implemented by the end of this financial year and that will impact on our customer support teams. The restructure is due to a growth in our customer business. The customer support teams have been engaged fully in discussions about the restructure and have been consulted and they agree on the changes to their remit. This means that, although the responsibilities of some of the teams will change, there will be no change to the number of staff who work in the teams and no roles will be made redundant. To support the change in responsibilities there will be a training and development programme for all team members and an enhanced bonus structure.

This message outlines the change, the reason for it, as well as what will and what will not change. For such messages to make sense, they must resonate with the receivers' perspectives of the change, be considered open and transparent and be delivered with authenticity and sincerity. In addition, there is a need to take into account the length of the message, since few people want to read a ten-page document; instead they want concise, clear information that is accessible anytime and anywhere.

To ensure communications are clear it is better to have short, crisp messages, because if a message is too long, the main point can get lost and lead to confusion. For example, consider how a redundancy programme might be communicated to employees whose roles will be affected. What would be the impact and the response if a generic email or even a text message was sent to them rather than the news being delivered in-person? When there is a difficult message such as this to deliver the kindest and most skilful way is to present it preferably in-person and as directly as possible, in a simple and plain way. When delivering tough messages, it is important to choose the words carefully to avoid miscommunication and misunderstanding by telling people what they need to be told, then focusing on the reasons, details and next steps. This requires candour – something that should be at the centre of all communications. To enable open and honest communication about uncomfortable topics, EY have created a programme called Everyday Candor, which is a team-based toolkit that helps teams to raise specific obstacles and to agree on how to address the obstacles. It involves team members asking each other, 'Could I be candid with you?' and 'May I have your candid perspective?' and has created a new common language that enables employees to raise issues and solve them in real time. So, even if uncomfortable, candour can help to establish trust and credibility.

Catering for different needs

The different needs of stakeholders must be catered for when designing and implementing communications. Although many people clamour to hear the view of leaders and managers, this does not mean that they will be prepared to accept whatever message is delivered. The message needs to make sense to them in order to encourage engagement and energy for the transformation, and must be repeated several times. Repetition is vital since individuals differ in their ability to understand written and spoken communications and repeating messages can thus help to increase the likelihood that everyone will hear the main points. Repeating key messages was what Jeffrey Immelt, formerly the CEO of GE, did when the company was embarking on a major transformation.[8] Immelt kept repeating:

> There's no Plan B. There's no other way to get there. Who's coming with me? What's in your way? What do we need to be doing differently?

Immelt reiterated this message in several forums, such as: at the yearly meeting to 200 senior executives; to over 600 officers and senior executives; to the quarterly corporate executive council attended by top 40 leaders; and at town hall sessions in Beijing and Shanghai. He also did webcasts and wrote about the transformations in internal blogs and the company's annual report. Such repetition and clarity of key messages are important because employees have so many things going on in the operation of their daily working lives that they do not always have, nor take, the time to stop, think and internalize what is being communicated. There is a need to be systematic and intentional in tailoring the message to the audience, since different groups of stakeholders are likely to have different needs, partly because they will be affected by a transformation in different ways and at different times. So the message and the choice of media can be customized to meet the needs and interests of specific stakeholder groups.

Knowledge about the audience is an important prerequisite for effective communication. Without knowledge about the target groups, it can be difficult to provide the information that individuals and teams need to fully understand the transformation and to provide the meaning and justification they are seeking. Effective communication of change, therefore, involves paying attention to the needs and interests of different audiences to ensure that the messages are targeted effectively and feedback encouraged.

Feedback

A key part of communications for change is feedback. This means creating feedback mechanisms to ensure that what is being communicated is clearly understood and that people have the opportunity to respond to the messages. As Alan Greenspan, former Chair of the Federal Reserve of the United States, said, 'I know you think you understand what you thought I said, but I'm not sure you realize that what you heard is not what I meant.' This is why feedback is vital because it provides real-time data on the effectiveness and impact of the communications by gauging:

- Timeliness: Were the communications conducted in a timely manner?
- Usefulness: Did the communications address questions or issues that were meaningful to the stakeholder/group?
- Understandability: Did the audience/s understand the intended message?
- Believability: Did the audience/s believe what was being communicated?

Feedback can provide information about which messages have been delivered most clearly, which methods are most effective, individuals' understanding of the messages conveyed as well as providing an opportunity to address issues, concerns and questions. Proactively eliciting feedback can also help to eradicate silence about what employees think and feel about the transformation, which can prevent individuals seeking information through informal channels such as rumours. It is, therefore, critical that there are feedback loops (see Figure 5.1) as part of the communications strategy and that feedback is gathered regularly, analysed to identify key themes, issues and concerns, and, importantly, then acted upon and followed

FIGURE 5.1 Feedback loop

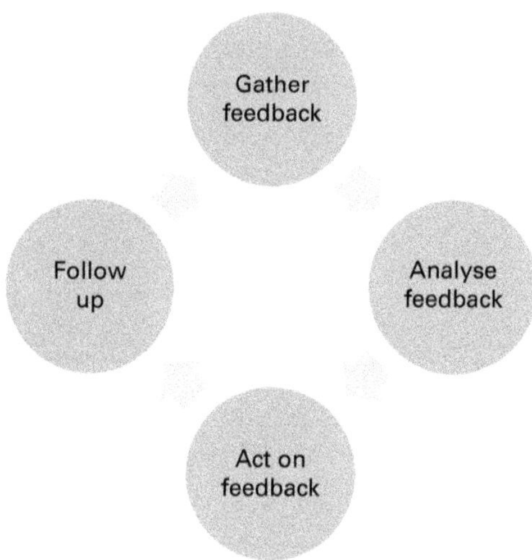

up on, since this will enhance confidence and trust that people's voices are being listened to and are respected.

Silence as a killer of communication

Silence can kill communication. An environment that discourages feedback and upward communication can foster a climate of silence, which can have disastrous outcomes for employees, with knock-on effects for the organization. Amongst employees there may be a fear of speaking truth to power; in other words, they might withhold their opinions and concerns when they believe that speaking up about issues is not worth the effort or that voicing their problems and concerns is too risky and even dangerous. This can result in employees feeling undervalued and affect their commitment and engagement with the transformation, leading to lower motivation, anxiety, stress, psychological withdrawal or even the decision to leave the company. When discouraged from speaking up, employees may feel that they lack sufficient control over their working environment. This lack of autonomy can lead to low satisfaction and even attempts to regain some control through acting in ways that are destructive to the process of a business transformation, such as sabotage.

Not only can there be silence from employees such as frontline staff but there can also be silence from managers. For instance, managers may ignore or remain silent about feedback or queries they receive from their team members about a business transformation. Such silence signals that the issue or person raising the query does not merit the courtesy of a timely reply and the individual awaiting a response may feel annoyance, frustration or even anger that may increase with the length of the delay. This silence can also undermine trust, lead to the withdrawal of support for a transformation and create conflict. In contrast, timely, cooperative and relevant responses can create positive reactions and engagement from employees and other key stakeholders. This was shown in a study which found that the factors that matter when communicating with stakeholders are: the speed of a response (timeliness); the tone of that response (valence); the depth of engagement (richness); and the degree of responsiveness to the specific issues raised (topicality).[9] This suggests that there is a need for greater promptness, openness of tone, depth of response and relevance in responses to feedback and queries about a business transformation. One way that this can be achieved and silence eradicated is by actively encouraging conversations about the transformation process and individuals' experience of it.

Focus on talking, not telling

Conversations are the engines of business transformations. Whether they take place at formal meetings or are informal, such as at the coffee machine or in the corridor, conversations are a crucial determinant of the effective decision-making and implementation of a transformation. However, the inverse is also true, that is, ineffective conversations almost certainly preclude effective change.[10] In remote and hybrid teams, conversations can be complicated by the fact that some people are more comfortable speaking up on screen than others, which can be exacerbated by the power, status and language differences that create barriers to communication online (and in-person). Conversations, therefore, need to be created that are constructive and authentic and enable stakeholders to contribute to decisions as well as share views, concerns and ideas in an honest and open way. One way of doing this is by orchestrating conversations in a way that resembles an ordinary person-to-person conversation rather than a series of commands from above. This involves initiating practices and fostering cultural norms that instil a conversational sensibility throughout the organization by: encouraging conversations with stakeholders rather than just talking at them; ensuring that conversations are open and fluid rather than closed and directive; avoiding the simplicity of monologue and instead embracing the unpredictable vitality of conversations. To make this happen requires creating a welcoming safe space for conversations.

Creating space for conversations, whether online or in-person, can be challenging and requires energy and effort, but it can be done. Online media, for example, can be used to facilitate space for conversations and to create a sense of community and transparency amongst people who are dispersed across different sites or working remotely. Online forums and webinars, for instance, can be used to connect people and enable them to ask questions and share ideas, concerns and/or issues. It is only through creating spaces and networks for conversations that people are able to share what they are thinking and feeling, which in turn enables managers and others to be more informed about stakeholders' perspectives, ideas and concerns.

To orchestrate a conversation so that it is a rich and rewarding experience, participants need to have some sense of what they hope to achieve from it. In the absence of such intent, a conversation will either meander or come to a stop. Having a clear purpose helps to provide order and meaning on even the loosest and most digressive forms of conversations. It is also vital that conversations provide the opportunity for people to move out of their comfort zones, because often when people talk to one another about a business transformation, they tend to avoid unpleasant topics and keep the conversation in the comfort zone, and avoid talking about the unknown, the untried, the unimaginable. This can be severely limiting and work against creating meaningful change, especially since to effectively implement a transformation there is a need to be able to talk about the 'elephant in the room', i.e. the important issues that are outside everyone's comfort zone. Steve Jobs – the ex-CEO of Apple – was famous for pushing people to think outside their comfort zones, which enabled the company to stay ahead in innovation. Although, when Jobs first learnt that his engineers wanted to build an iPhone, that conversation made him uncomfortable, and he had to be reminded that if you can't talk about the new, the unknown, the scary ideas, you will never think outside the box. Such zone of uncomfortable debate (ZOUD) conversations enable deeper and more effective stakeholder engagement, as well as fairness, reciprocity and trust.[11] Through ZOUD conversations, individuals can also understand each other's mindsets, which links their experiences, data, meaning, assumptions, conclusions, beliefs and actions. This can help to develop an understanding of the issues of mutual concern and to identify strategies for addressing them.

Engaging in conversations about a transformation does, however, bring challenges, including: time and resource costs; the creation of often unattainable expectations; and even conflict, which can occur when bringing diverse groups and individuals together. However, in a world of increasing online communication and emails, effective conversations have never been a more important part of a business transformation, especially because they help to advance understanding, learning and progress.

Storytelling

Stories are a powerful form of communication. From pictures on the walls of caves and tales by the campfire to graffiti and comic books, people love stories. Rarely is a list of bullet points on a PowerPoint slide as memorable as a story. The most compelling stories engage and capture hearts as well as heads by using images that create concrete visualization which enable people to imagine themselves in the future.[12] Stories are a critical mechanism for: inspiring stakeholders; creating a shared sense of purpose; and translating the transformation into something more tangible that sticks in people's minds and creates a common expectation and retention of what it is all about.

Storytellers who take time to personalize the story of a business transformation can unlock significantly more energy for it as well as sharing in an innovative way with others the answers to such questions as: Why are we changing? How will we get there? What will be different? How does this relate to me? This means that storytelling needs to include experiences and anecdotes from the lives of the storyteller in order to answer these questions and also to underline their determination and belief, and to demonstrate that obstacles can be overcome. This is why Indra Nooyi, the former Chairperson and CEO of Pepsi, used stories as her primary tool for the communication of change. Nooyi told stories about her personal experience growing up with water and electricity shortages, including examples of health and wellness that were very personal to her, in order to create emotional engagement for transforming PepsiCo and to inspire and evoke purpose and meaning.[13] A storyteller's passion, such as that of Nooyi, and connection to the change story are essential for building momentum for a transformation. However, stories don't just have to come from senior leaders. By involving a broader group of people in the process of crafting a change narrative, organizations can create a coalition of advocates and storytellers that can communicate and amplify the transformation story at scale. To help with the creation of impactful stories, the following principles should be considered:

- ***Keep it simple.*** Including too many details or making the story longer than it needs to be can lead listeners to lose interest.
- ***Be authentic.*** Honesty and authenticity will help the audience connect with the story.
- ***Have a clear outcome.*** Stories should have a clear outcome and provide a hopeful, thought-provoking message with actionable points that compel the audience to connect with it.
- ***Make it entertaining.*** Entertaining stories have the ability to hold the attention of the audience longer.
- ***Make it universal.*** Stories that are universal are able to reach a wider audience base.
- ***Make it emotional.*** The storyteller should talk about how the transformation affects them and consider ways to involve the audience in the story – this can help to strike an emotional connection with stakeholders.

Non-verbal communication

Non-verbal communication is as important as verbal communication. When telling a story, or using other forms of communication, in order to be perceived as credible and trustworthy it is crucial to align what is being said with non-verbal communication such as body language. This can be a challenge online, which means that more emphasis on non-verbal communication is required. When non-verbal messages conflict with verbal messages, the audience and levels of trust can be affected. Hence it is vital to support what is being said with actions, because nothing can be more persuasive than seeing communicators behave in ways that support what they are proclaiming. Verbal and non-verbal communication are, therefore, both crucial and need to be in sync.

The importance of different forms of communication and having flexible multi-level communication plans is illustrated in the following business insight written by Laura de Ruiter, an Associate Director in the Behavioral Science Consortium at Astellas and Laurence Scates, the former Executive Director and Head of the Transformation Office at Astellas.

CASE STUDY

Business Insight: Communication at Astellas Pharma Inc.

Astellas Pharma Inc., based in Tokyo, is a pharmaceutical business that works in more than 70 countries. Astellas stands on the forefront of healthcare change to turn innovative science into value for patients. Keeping our focus on addressing unmet medical needs and conducting our business with ethics and integrity enables us to improve the health of people around the world. Over recent decades, Astellas has grown organically into a global company, however, its commercial organization had largely remained regional. The structure was both inefficient and expensive to maintain. In 2019, senior leadership therefore initiated a project to optimize the organizational structure and operating model. The aim was to streamline regional operational processes and realize efficiencies through standardization and centralization of certain capabilities into a global support model for the commercial organization. The project happened in two main phases: the design phase, which was restricted to a small team of mainly senior leaders, and the implementation phase, which involved everyone in the commercial organization. The implementation happened very quickly: the change was announced in May 2021, and the new operating model went live fully in March 2022. Notably, 40 other change initiatives were going on in the commercial organization at that time.

The project used a hub-and-spoke model to manage change and communications during implementation: a core team (the hub), supporting and supported by leads in each commercial division (the spokes). The core team consisted of a small group of people who were working on the project full time, and others who were 'seconded' (i.e., they also continued to work in their regular role). This setup was intended to strike a balance between having dedicated project/change managers and having employees who knew the operations on the ground well.

Communication during the implementation was designed to avoid email fatigue. Specifically, it involved micro-level messaging, which meant targeted messages that specified what the changes meant for individual teams, instead of only cascading down messages from the top. Regional communicators met regularly with the core team to ensure that everyone was informed about ongoing and upcoming activities. Overall, this communication approach was received positively by managers and employees. The project sponsors were very engaged throughout the process. They provided strategic direction but were also engaged in the details, which allowed for quick decision-making. At the same time, there were aspects to this project that could have been handled differently. A key challenge was that the heads of the new, to-be-created global units had to be appointed ahead of time so that they could be involved in the design. In this liminal space, roles and responsibilities were not always clear. It also made it more difficult for senior leaders to fully align on the approach, which in turn lessened their buy-in and advocacy during implementation. Another challenge was that the commercial organization needed to develop and implement a new operating model quickly, given commercial's importance for the entire company. The decision to limit the design phase to the senior team meant that other stakeholders – the newly created global team, subject matter experts and the affiliates in the regions who had to implement the change – did not have the opportunity to participate early on. As a consequence, some issues and trade-offs were missed that could have been identified and mitigated earlier if there had been a wider design group.

Going through this large project produced several key learnings for Astellas:

- *Engage key stakeholders early.* Key stakeholders, specifically the people who do the 'work on the ground' and who have to build and implement new capabilities, need to be brought in early. This is important for two reasons. First, their expertise and input are needed to fully understand all trade-offs, which is necessary to make informed decisions when designing the solution. Having more information early on reduces the need to course-correct later. It also helps to move more quickly from relatively abstract, high-level conversations to implementation. Second, early participation leads to more buy-in from those that will be affected by the change. However, early involvement means also that the change needs to be announced earlier, resulting in a longer period of uncertainty for the teams.
- *Second high-performing employees.* The secondment of employees into change projects has two advantages: it fosters talent, and it allows the organization to gain and retain knowledge. While working on a change project on top of day-to-day business certainly adds to an employee's workload, it also provides an opportunity for high-performing talent to prove themselves. In addition, working with internal staff instead of predominantly relying on external consultants not only provides better 'insider' insights (see above), but also helps the organization learn and retain valuable institutional knowledge. An approach used was to develop internal talent by providing temporary experienced external support.
- *Have a flexible, multi-level communications plan.* Consistent messaging from top leadership is an important component in change communications, but affected employees

also need to receive communication that is designed specifically for them. Change brings a lot of uncertainty, and people want to know precisely what is changing and why, how it will affect their work and when the changes are happening. These targeted communications can only be developed by people who are familiar with the specific structures and processes. A set-up like a hub-and-spoke model furthermore allows information to flow bottom up, which enables the core team to adjust their plan when necessary.

The commercial globalization project was one of numerous recent changes at Astellas. Among other things, these change projects pointed to the limitations of off-the-shelf change management models that are not fully articulated in the experience of the organization. This realization foreshadowed a process that the organization needed to engage in, which is to understand how it experiences change generally, which will be different from other organizations.

Questions

1 What was the key approach used for communication during the transformation? How successful was it?

2 What were the key challenges faced with communication? How were they addressed?

3 How might you apply the lessons learnt to a transformation you are engaged with?

SUMMARY

The communication of change is a continuous activity which involves providing accurate and useful information and messages using the right channel for the purpose of different audiences in a timely and appropriate way. Effective high-quality communications must: have clear and consistent messages; motivate stakeholder support for the transformation; encourage engagement and commitment; limit misunderstandings and rumours; and align stakeholders behind the overall purpose of the transformation. The choice of language, tone, structure and content needs be appropriate to the context and the audience. Communication of change is not, however, just about providing timely information but is also about creating opportunities for conversations and feedback, up, down and across the organization. As outlined in this chapter, this also involves giving people time to think and reflect, and space to have their voices heard. Furthermore, it means listening and sharing stories that provide a narrative about the change so that people can understand it more deeply. If done correctly, communication can help provide clarity, facilitate the development of trust and assist the sustainability of the benefits expected from a transformation.

PRACTICAL IMPLICATIONS

The are several practical implications which can be drawn from this chapter:

- *Engage in and encourage dialogue throughout the transformation process.* Communications, particularly conversations, are a key way to surface employee concerns, hopes and fears. Holding regular, honest conversations about the transformation will enable individuals and teams to share their questions and opinions, which will drive understanding and make them feel like they are part of the commitment to change.
- *Know your audience.*
  Have a firm understanding of the audience's perspective, what information they already know and what questions or concerns they have. Based on the audience, craft the message's content to align with what they want and need to learn and ensure that the message has the appropriate context for the audience.
- *Focus on visualization.*
  Things that people see are more likely to evoke emotions than things they hear or read. For example, instead of simply telling them, 'We need to become customer-centric because that will make our customers happy,' it is better to show them a video of happy customers complimenting the company on its customer responsiveness. Similarly, instead of telling them, 'We need to become more innovative because that would save people's lives,' it is better to bring patients into the organization to tell the employees how the company's products have saved their lives.

- *Use an appropriate tone and style.*
  Deliver the message with the appropriate tone and style using:
  - *Compassion:* Show the audience that you care about their perspectives. Inform employees as soon as possible about the transformation: why, when and how the process will evolve and within what expected time span. Emphasize the benefits for the organization and for individuals and teams and ensure clarity on the 'why' – the rationale for the change. Remember to repeat and update this message regularly.
  - *Clarity:* Communicate clearly and repeat key messages.
  - *Conciseness:* Ensure that the message is short enough to internalize. Long, complicated sentences can be hard to understand and demand more concentration. Keep communications short, clear and concise.
  - *Connection:* Connect emotionally with the audience and provide opportunities for employees to give feedback by: ensuring appropriate channels for employee voice and that different groups feel able to access them; actively seeking people's ideas; and taking action on feedback.
  - *Candour:* Admit what you don't know. For instance, if an employee asks you whether there will be redundancies, and you are not sure whether they will happen or not your response might be: 'I wish I could tell you exactly what is going to happen. We will give you updates as soon as we know them.'
- *Avoid over-communicating.*
  A word of caution is required because most organizations over-communicate change, which can lead to confusion and disengagement. Rather than overloading people with formal communications, especially email, build in time for conversations.

Notes

1 S L Parker, N L Jimmieson and C E Amiot. Self-determination, control, and reactions to changes in workload: A work simulation, *Journal of Occupational Health Psychology*, 2013, 18 (2), 173. psycnet.apa.org/record/2013-06792-001 (archived at https://perma.cc/2QRB-XLJ2)

2 J Hodges and R Gill (2015) *Sustaining Change in Organizations*, Sage, London

3 P J Zak. The neuroscience of trust. *Harvard Business Review*, 2017, 95 (1), 84–90. hbr.org/2017/01/the-neuroscience-of-trust (archived at https://perma.cc/Z4PH-CQHU)

4 E L Newton (1990) *The Rocky Road From Actions to Intentions*, Stanford University Press, Redwood City, CA
5 I Nooyi (2021) *My Life in Full: Work, family and our future*, Hachette, London
6 S Vani and C A Harte (2021) *Jacinda Ardern: Leading with empathy*, Simon and Schuster, London
7 S Zagelmeyer, R R Sinkovics, N Sinkovics and V Kusstatscher. Exploring the link between management communication and emotions in mergers and acquisitions, *Canadian Journal of Administrative Sciences/Revue Canadienne des Sciences de l'Administration*, 2018, 35 (1), 93–106. dx.doi.org/10.1002/cjas.1382 (archived at https://perma.cc/YFF7-LZTQ)
8 J R Immelt. How I remade GE: And what I learned along the way, *Harvard Business Review*, September–October 2017. hbr.org/2017/09/how-i-remade-ge (archived at https://perma.cc/XW95-ADUZ)
9 L J Nartey, W J Henisz and S Dorobantu. Reciprocity in firm–stakeholder dialog: Timeliness, valence, richness, and topicality, *Journal of Business Ethics*, 2023, 183 (2), 429–51. www.springerprofessional.de/en/reciprocity-in-firm-stakeholder-dialog-timeliness-valence-richne/20143648 (archived at https://perma.cc/6NUN-CRWA)
10 A C Edmondson and T Besieux. Reflections: Voice and silence in workplace conversations, *Journal of Change Management*, 2021, 21 (3), 269–86. www.tandfonline.com/doi/full/10.1080/14697017.2021.1928910 (archived at https://perma.cc/9D9H-BGAL)
11 L J Nartey, W J Henisz and S Dorobantu. Reciprocity in firm–stakeholder dialog: Timeliness, valence, richness, and topicality, *Journal of Business Ethics*, 2023, 183 (2), 429–51. www.springerprofessional.de/en/reciprocity-in-firm-stakeholder-dialog-timeliness-valence-richne/20143648 (archived at https://perma.cc/NCB6-NBWV)
12 S Friedman (2014) *Leading the Life You Want: Integrating work and life*, Harvard Business Review Press, Boston, MA
13 I Nooyi (2021) *My Life in Full: Work, family and our future*, Hachette, London

06

Change as an opportunity, not a threat

Introduction

As John Hagel, author of *The Journey Beyond Fear*, says, it is a world of increasing pressure but it is also a world of expanding opportunity.[1] This is certainly the case with the changes people are facing in organizations and how they are interpreting them. The difficulty is to convince individuals who are surrounded by disruptions to consider them not merely as threats but also as opportunities. At a rational level people will agree with this, but their thinking and feelings will be dominated by the fear of what another transformation might do to them and their jobs. The challenge is to convince people that change can be an opportunity, and to do this again and again.

Imagine the following scenario: you have just been told that your role has been made redundant and you have been offered a generous redundancy package. Imagine, further, that when you get home your partner tries to convince you that even though this is terrible news and will impact on your financial security, it is also a great opportunity for you to move to a different career, or to spend more time with your family, or to start your own company which you have always wanted to do but never found the time for. Of course, you can see the benefits, and you may even feel better about your situation for a short time before you start worrying about your future again and the threat this change poses to you. As this scenario highlights, the challenge is how to convince people that change can be an opportunity when they are exhausted from all the other changes going on around them. This is the challenge explored in this chapter, which begins by discussing why a business transformation should be looked at as an opportunity. The chapter goes on to discuss the different ways of reframing change so that it is seen in a more positive light. It concludes with a business insight written by Zuhair Imran, a digital marketing consultant, which describes how a digital transformation within a pharmaceutical company in Pakistan was repositioned as an opportunity.

The need to consider change as an opportunity

Seeing a transformation as positive is important because change will only be successfully implemented and its benefits realized when it is considered an opportunity rather than a threat. This can be difficult, especially with the tremendous changes occurring in the workplace, including how and where we work, the type of work we do and what we expect from work and employers. These changes, in turn, have led organizations to radically transform how they manage their employees, how they serve their customers, and how they compete with each other. For example, there has been a shift away from hierarchy toward networks; from fixed pricing to dynamic pricing; from mass marketing to customized marketing; from close innovation to open innovation; from traditional strategies to platform strategies. These changes have been dramatic, and organizations have had to transform themselves to not only survive the tsunami of disruption but to exploit it. Yet, no matter how much effort and how many sacrifices have been endured to respond to disruptions, new and more disruptive innovations are occurring, such as generative AI, robotics, machine learning and virtual reality. These disruptive innovations are creating new markets, shaking up existing ones and displacing them, as well as shifting profitability from one business model to another with the same or better value at much lower cost. Companies such as Uber, Amazon and Airbnb have changed their business models in order to quickly adapt to the disruptions. The impact of this is that organizations that rely upon old operating models are losing market share or even being pushed out of business altogether. To cope with such disruptions, organizations need to be on constant alert, ready to respond to whatever disruption comes their way and, if necessary, embark on yet another transformation because the end of one transformation often means the start of another. As Paulo Coelho writes in his novel *The Devil and Miss Prym*: 'When we least expect it, life sets us a challenge to test our courage and willingness to change; at such a moment, there is no point in pretending that nothing has happened or in saying that we are not yet ready. The challenge will not wait.'[2] In other words, having just started or undertaken a tiring transformation, organizations cannot rest but need to be ready to embark on the next one.

To engage stakeholders in this relentless disruption requires reframing the need for even more transformational change from not just a threat but to an opportunity. However, people might be scared about what the change might do to their job which, in turn, can lead to a lack of conviction that the transformation is necessary. Reframing a business transformation as not just a threat but also an opportunity is, therefore, challenging, but not impossible.

Reframing transformations as an opportunity

Convincing people that something is an opportunity when they may feel otherwise can be extremely hard. It requires effective high-quality communications but should not be limited to this, for unless the communicator is as inspirational as Martin Luther King, then the likelihood is that what they say will not be enough to win employees' hearts and minds. Hence the need for additional tactics such as: adapting elements of the organizational culture; making transformations meaningful; focusing on positive narratives; promoting stakeholder-led innovation; and encouraging transformations as a learning experience. Each of these will be considered in turn below.

Adapting elements of the culture

The factors that influence the outcome of any transformation are the why, what, how and when of the transformation. The 'why' is the reason given for undertaking yet another transformation. This needs to be couched in a positive narrative and clearly articulated so that people understand it and are convinced by it. The 'what' is the strategy, which will be specific to the need for a transformation and has to be innovative and clearly communicated so as to win commitment to it. The 'how' refers to the organizational support required to execute the strategy and the roles and responsibilities of key stakeholders in the implementation. Finally, the 'when' outlines the timing and pace of the transformation. To effectively enact the why, what, how and when of a transformation and support the behaviours for this requires the organizational culture to promote seeing change as an opportunity and not merely a threat.

The culture that exists in an organization comprises its: norms; values; assumptions; structures; processes; hierarchy; systems (such as information, recruitment, market research); incentives; and the people who bring with them their own mindsets, attitudes and assumptions. It is the combination of these elements that creates the culture, which in turn produces behaviours. If employees are not demonstrating the behaviours and attitudes associated with seeing change as an opportunity, this may be due to some cultural elements which are preventing them from doing so. This means that to adapt behaviours and attitudes, the underlying cultural elements that produce them must first be changed in order to support what people are being asking to do. Elements of a culture are, however, interconnected so that if there is an attempt to amend one of them, this may cause a change in another one, which can result in a series of unintended consequences. Unfortunately, this is a problem that arises far too frequently in organizations because there is a tendency to address problems through linear thinking, in that once a problem arises, there is a tendency to look for the most obvious reasons for it and address the symptoms, rather than diagnosing the root causes. So to address the cultural factors that will help shift the view of change from one of always being a threat to one of also opportunity there is a need to identify the elements of the culture which need to be improved.

To get people to change their behaviour and see change as an opportunity means creating an organizational culture that supports and promotes the required behaviours. If the existing organizational environment does not produce the desired behaviours, there is a need to change the elements of it which are not supporting the view of change as an opportunity. This may sound like a difficult task but all social systems/cultures seem to have a few sensitive influence points through which the behaviour can be changed.[3] One of the most common ways to change elements of the culture is by a top-down major culture change programme. However, this approach can take time and it can feel as if culture is being imposed upon everyone from above. An alternative way is through the butterfly principle, which proposes that managers and team leaders introduce small changes in their own local environments. The rationale for this is that the right kind of changes, if done properly, can produce big changes in each of these local environments, and if all these local changes are undertaken within an overarching framework and within strategic parameters developed by senior management then the sum of the many local changes will add up to one big change in the organizational culture. This might, for instance, be done by managers adopting small and symbolic changes in their day-to-day behaviour, since employees pay close attention to how their managers behave and what they say, and based on what they see or hear they will form their beliefs, which tend to be reinforced and strengthened over time. In other words, if culture is created through the day-to-day actions of leaders and managers, then the way to change elements of the culture is by changing those behaviours in a visible and symbolic way.

Making transformations meaningful

In his book *Change or Die*, Alan Deutschman writes that, after undergoing a coronary artery bypass, most people try to improve their health by making radical changes to their lifestyle, for example eating a healthier diet, quitting smoking and/or exercising more.[4] But eventually people slowly start to drift back to their old habits and Deutschman points out that within two years 90 per cent of them have resorted to the same lifestyle they had before their operation. This spotlights that change is hard, and that even the fear of death is not enough to convince the majority of people to change for good. It also illustrates that although scare tactics can be used to create an urgency for change – a so-called burning platform (see Chapter 3) – they will only create change that is short-lived. This can be similar in organizations when an urgent reason for a transformation is announced – scare tactics will produce a short-term reaction from people which is rarely sustained.

The following story outlines how it might be done differently. A senior technician was told for years by their doctor that they needed to change their lifestyle because they were suffering from a rare heart disease, but nothing succeeded in getting them to change their behaviour until one day their partner described to them, in detail, what the future wedding day of their 3-year-old son might look like. The partner described how proud the technician would look and how happy they would be at the wedding reception. The story had a big impact on the technician who said that it was as if a light switch had been turned on and they realized that they needed to change. The next day the technician embarked on a programme of personal change. Twenty years later, the technician was fit and healthy as they attended their son's wedding. This simple story highlights that to reframe change as an opportunity and to get people to change permanently, the need for change must be made positive, personal and emotional.

To make the need for change positive does not mean ignoring the tough issues, because people still need to know the consequences of not changing as well as the positive things that will happen if they do change. Making the need for change personal involves aligning the transformation with something that is of value to each stakeholder/group by highlighting what it means for them. This requires explaining what the threats are that the organization is facing and how they are driving the need for change. Stakeholders then have to be given the facts about the transformation and the reality of what will happen if the organization does not change. Framing the threat in this way needs to be complemented with a positive reason why there is a need to change, ensuring that this positive reason is personal to every stakeholder/group. This can be difficult, because different people are motivated by different things, so it means finding a common denominator – something that most people will relate to or find worthwhile. For example, an energy company explained to its employees the need for a radical transformation in its safety procedures in this way: 'We have to make these changes because we want you to finish work every day and go back home every night, safe and sound.' This depicts how the need for change can be made personal by giving people something that they can identify with and aim for. Along with making the reason for change personal, there is also a need to make the change meaningful emotionally. The importance of doing this was shown in a global survey conducted by Harvard Business School researchers, which found that when employees were asked why they had a positive outlook, one of the main reasons they cited was the prospect of more interesting and meaningful work.[5] Both automation and technology, they felt, offered opportunities on these fronts by contributing to the emergence of more flexible and self-directed forms of work and by making it possible to avoid tasks that were dirty, dangerous or dull. There is, therefore, a need to make change meaningful personally and emotionally in order to win people's commitment and to enable them to see the positive impact of it.

Focusing on positive narratives

The fact that, compared with the future benefits that a transformation might bring, people will often put more emphasis on its immediate negative consequences, which they see and feel now, has implications for communicating about a transformation. More time and effort has to be spent explaining to people why the transformation is an opportunity rather than a threat, which in practice means not only providing a clear articulation of the specific challenges facing the organization, along with the choices and trade-offs, supported by the facts, but also ensuring that people appreciate that disruption is an opportunity at an emotional level. This requires a move from communicating only about problems to focusing on positive narratives. According to research, such a shift can have a contagious effect by creating positive emotions, helping people become more resilient and increasing openness, innovation and desire for action.[6] Within business transformations, this can be done with the use of appreciative inquiry, which promotes positive narratives by shifting conversations from 'what is broken' to 'what works'.

APPRECIATIVE INQUIRY

Appreciative inquiry is a collective process of investigation into the best of 'what is' and what the future would be like if the best of 'what is' becomes the norm.[7] This is in contrast to traditional diagnostic approaches where problems of the past are examined through disciplined data gathering and examination, and solutions are implemented and measured. Instead, appreciative inquiry is based on the power of positive narrative and supports the notion that organizations grow and construct their future realities in the direction of what they most persistently, actively and collectively ask questions about. Appreciative inquiry does this by engaging stakeholders through a cyclical process which comprises the following stages: discovery; dream; design; and delivery, which can be used in various situations such as a team, focus group or workshop.

- ***Discovery:*** During this initial stage participants reflect on and discuss the best of 'what is' concerning the subject of investigation. Participants are interviewed by other participants about their own 'best of' stories, and are asked questions, such as 'Tell me about the time the organization most inspired loyalty in you' and 'What works well in this organization/team?'
- ***Dream:*** This involves drawing on the themes identified during discovery and envisioning what the future will look like if the best of 'what is' becomes the norm. Participants are asked to imagine their team and/or organization at its best in relation to the issue being discussed, with common aspirations being identified and symbolized in some way. For example, participants can draw pictures of what they feel about the situation and then explain their drawings to one another. This enables individuals to express their emotions in pictures, which some might find easier to do than trying to put them into words.

- ***Design:*** The next stage is to translate the dream into potential options that are likely to challenge the status quo and current assumptions. The output from this is that participants identify what needs to change and then develop proposals for delivering the proposed change/s.
- ***Delivery:*** This involves identifying the actions for how the organization/team will move towards implementing the changes (the design). Agreement for the proposed options is sought during this stage, and participants are asked to commit to take action to help to implement the changes identified.

Through this cycle, appreciative inquiry promotes a positive narrative, with quality conversations focused on identifying issues and options for addressing them as well as helping to build relationships and trust amongst participants. Moreover, since participants have a vested interest in the positive changes they have identified, this can help to enhance their commitment to making the change happen successfully. As with all such frameworks, there are some limitations to be mindful of. The main concerns that tend to be voiced about appreciative inquiry are whether or not it is any different from other methods of investigation and, since it does not focus on problems, whether this means that it assumes that they do not exist or that the problems have become marginalized. Despite such criticisms, appreciative inquiry is appealing because it provides a proactive and optimistic approach by accentuating the positive and thereby focusing on what the organization is good at and can build upon. It can also create positive and synergistic energy by enabling participants to develop a sense of commitment, confidence and affirmation that they can actively contribute to identifying and implementing transformational change rather than having it imposed upon them.

Promoting stakeholder-led innovation

Creativity and innovation are crucial for shifting the view of a transformation from a threat to an opportunity, and for enabling organizations to be agile and competitive, and adapt to the accelerating pace of change. Creativity is the generation of new and original ideas, associations, methods, approaches and solutions in relation to a problem or need; while innovation is the application of a new idea to initiate or improve, for example, a product, process or service. Companies such as DuPont and Google have found that 'free time' can increase the breadth of the intellectual rigour of ideas and amplify wisdom and insights, although these insights have little impact unless people feel empowered to act on them.

To encourage creativity and innovation requires people across the organization to be involved and given space and time to develop and share innovative ideas. A key group of stakeholders who are often overlooked when it comes to being creative are line managers, who form an important bridge between senior leaders and frontline employees. It is managers who have the power to give employees the time and motivation to be creative and innovative and who can make sure that any ideas generated are refined, filtered and, if worthwhile, brought to the attention of senior leaders. Companies can implement various strategies to help support the crucial role of managers in creativity and innovation. For example, Bayer – a German multinational biotechnology company – has a network of over 800 innovation coaches based in every country in which the company operates. These coaches help managers to coach and motivate their teams to innovate through a range of activities, including co-creation sessions, lunch-and-learns, and small group workshops known as fast sessions. Bayer has also instituted local innovation coordinators who offer assistance by reviewing the ideas generated, providing feedback and connecting innovating teams across the organization. Not only do the coordinators help to remove the pressure on managers to spot good ideas, but they also shut down bad ideas before too much time and energy has been wasted on them. This cross-company innovation framework is supported by WeSolve, a digital platform that enables all employees to post any challenges or problems that they are facing. Issues submitted can range from a frontline worker in Spain trying to help farmers monitor pesticide levels, to a manager in India asking for brand name suggestions for a new product. The crucial element of this method is that any employee from any department, regardless of their job title or training, can visit the forum and post potential solutions to any of the challenges. In this way, all employees are able to be creative and to innovate by sharing and connecting to colleagues across the company. Bayer is not the only company to support a culture of innovation, nor is it the only one to understand the importance of getting managers to champion creativity and innovation. At financial services company Allianz UK, for example, managers are incentivized to get their teams to spend time innovating through an innovation league table.[8] Similarly, Unilever has a start-up hub to keep bright ideas generated by its employees in-house, which is aimed at validating intrapreneurship. Integrating creativity and innovation throughout a company, such as that done by Bayer, Allianz UK and Unilever, is crucial to ensure a continuous flow of creative and actionable ideas. This requires a strategy that enables individuals and teams to share and discuss potential innovations and to experiment and fail, learn from the failure and then put the lessons into practice. In addition, opportunities need to be created to bring together internal and external stakeholders to galvanize their wisdom and generate ideas (such as in a World Café; see Chapter 3). The conditions, therefore, need to be created to inspire, enable and promote stakeholder-led innovation.

Engaging multiple stakeholders in finding innovative solutions and empowering them to implement those solutions is a key element of people-centric change. Frontline employees will often need an invitation to engage in innovation, and a high level of support, particularly within a hybrid environment which has not only changed the nature of innovation but also endangered it. The most obvious type of innovation which has been impacted by hybrid working is collective innovation, where a group of individuals come together to bat around ideas. Although this can be done online via platforms such as Zoom, although scheduled times and formats for generating ideas might not be as productive as the more fluid conversations and unexpected innovation that can occur when a team informally kicks around ideas or works intensively together in-person on solving an issue. Hybrid and remote working also endanger individual creativity, because although quiet time alone can help many people to generate ideas, having to work alone over several days or weeks may not necessarily prove to be a generative environment for some individuals, especially since social interactions and spontaneous conversations are important for creativity and innovation. In hybrid and remote working environments there is, therefore, a need to work harder to create conditions and practices for stakeholder-led innovation.

To encourage the generation and experimentation of ideas various methods can be used, such as idea laboratories where people work together on specific projects like software development, or activities that employees themselves suggest. PwC call this approach citizen-led innovation. It involves leadership setting the direction, and the organization's citizens, that is the empowered employees, taking it forward. Using this technique PwC staff can, for example, select what digital apps to work on, build solutions, test them and post them to PwC's Digital Lab for other employees to download and use. The users then provide feedback and ratings, and the higher-quality ideas are taken forward. Ideas that have emerged from this approach include bots and apps for: conducting rapid high-value analysis; streamlining common tasks such as reserving rooms or entering timesheet data; converting data from spreadsheets to more sophisticated dynamic dashboards; and rearranging work to bring critical issues to the surface. Since implementing citizen-led innovation, PwC has observed an inspiring level of enthusiasm and emotional commitment to it and have generated over a thousand active digital solutions within a few months.[9] Admittedly, to make this happen does require a lot more than simply scheduling brainstorming meetings and whiteboarding sessions. Innovation is, thus, critical for highlighting that change can be an opportunity rather than a threat.

Encouraging transformations as a learning experience

The most enduring business transformations are those that not only realize sustained benefits but also enable stakeholders to take the time to reflect on the lessons learnt and identify how these can be applied to future changes. Learning from business transformations should be a continuous collective process of acquiring and sharing knowledge and experience which leads to changes in how future transformations are enacted. Key to this is creating time and space for learning and reflection in order to enable staff, at all levels, to learn collaboratively and continuously and build and develop further their capabilities for improvement and business transformations. To encourage this within their culture, the Australian retail bank Westpac created a social learning platform called 'Learning Bank' for its employees that tags content to employees' profiles and enables employees to select what they want to learn but also when and where they want to learn it.

During and after a business transformation, learning can be enhanced by the implementation of a process for reflecting on and reviewing the lessons learnt from the successes as well as failures of the transformation. Reflective practices can help to identify what went wrong, how to fix it and what to do differently, as well as what went well and what should be built upon for future transformations. To be effective, reflective practice needs time for reflection-in-action and reflection-on-action.[10] The former, sometimes described as 'thinking on our feet', involves individuals and teams reflecting on what they are experiencing and feeling, and building new understandings to inform their actions in the current situation. This process of 'thinking on our feet' can be linked with reflection-on-action, which enables an individual and/or team to spend time exploring why they acted as they did, and what was happening in the team. In doing this, individuals and teams are able to develop questions and ideas about their activities and practice. As part of a business transformation, this involves encouraging employees and other stakeholders to learn from their experiences and share what they have learnt with others. Encouraging such learning and reflection enables people, at all levels, to learn collaboratively and continuously and to put their learning into practice. It is, therefore, important that the value of learning as a continuous individual and collective process is recognized and that time is given for people to reflect on their learning from both the successes and the failures of the transformations.

LEARNING FROM FAILURE

A business transformation will be seen as a threat when people have experienced change as a failure in the past, especially when this has resulted in blame, punishment and shame. Unfortunately, in too many organizations employees are punished for failures. Such cultures not only reinforce the idea of change as a threat but also reduce risk-taking and innovation because people will only be willing to try new ideas and to take risks when they feel that they will not be penalized. This is a pity, because learning from failure and mistakes can help to create and reinforce learning. As Michael Dell, founder of computer company Dell, once said, 'mistakes are not bad... as long as you are learning from them.... You are going to fail and you are going to experiment and learn and then ultimately find your way to success as a result of that, so don't be afraid to go make some mistakes'.[11] Being open to failing and to learn from it are linked closely to what is commonly known as a growth mindset (see Chapter 4).

Obviously, not all new ideas will work out as hoped, so ideas that lead to dead ends are an inevitable part of the learning process. By adopting a positive disposition towards change as a learning process, individuals are able to respond and adapt their actions and behaviours as new learning occurs. This can also promote a positive perspective on the failure and mistakes of a transformation because of the learning that it generates.

The importance of learning during a business transformation and how to position a transformation as an opportunity rather than a threat is illustrated in the following business insight of a pharmaceutical company in Pakistan, written by Zuhair Imran, a digital consultant.

CASE STUDY

Business Insight: Transformation in a pharmaceutical company in Pakistan

It was at our quarterly brand review meeting when the chief executive of a leading pharmaceutical company in Pakistan mentioned that we needed to increase our sales in a mountainous region of Pakistan where we had little or no coverage. The sales rep only visited this area once in every two months. In comparison, one of our competitors was active in the region and they were developing and increasing their market share.

The pharmaceutical company was a legacy business with stable sales and a footprint across the major cities of Pakistan. There were a total of 764 pharma companies operating in Pakistan and out of those 26 were multinationals.

Since I was in charge of leading the digital transformation of the company, I mentioned at the brand review meeting that I had a potential solution for increasing our market share in the region. The solution was to reach out to the customers via digital channels. For several months, I had been trying to convince the leadership team that digital was the way forward, but due to the nature of the pharmaceutical industry in Pakistan the leadership team was reluctant to move into the digital market. However, the issue with the lack of sales in the mountainous region gave me an opportunity to really showcase the value of reaching out to customers via digital channels. With the increasing threat from competitors, the leadership team was now prepared to listen to me and agreed to accept my proposal that we needed to develop a digital strategy.

With my team, I started working on the digital strategy, focusing on how to penetrate into the mountainous region. Our recommendations included remote detailing,[12] social media, email and SMS marketing, and the development of an app.[13] The digital strategy that I presented to the leadership team included the solutions as well as a road map for the future integration of digital projects within the company. The leadership team liked the idea but said that we didn't have the capability to launch such an initiative and were initially reluctant to go ahead with the recommendations. The concerns which they raised included: 'What if our sales team does not know how to use the remote detailing app?' and, 'If we have a social media crisis, how will we manage if it has a negative effect on our brands and leads to a decline in sales?' Furthermore, they were concerned that the company did not have a proper structure or a mechanism to manage the proposed digital solutions. After my team and I had various conversations with directors and showcased to them the value of digitalization, the strategy was eventually approved by the leadership team and I was tasked with implementing it.

The approved strategy had a direct impact on several stakeholders, including the sales team, IT team, admin team and communications team, who were all a bit scared that, as a result of the digital transformation, they might lose their job or position, or they might get transferred. To alleviate these fears my team and I sat with each of these stakeholder groups and discussed with them the benefits of the digital solution and how it would free up their time on non-essential tasks.

The strategy was implemented over a number of months and focused at first on the launch of remote detailing. This was a digital solution through which the sales team could connect with the doctors via a dedicated iPad application. Once the iPads were procured, the application was developed and new marketing material was developed by the brand team to raise awareness of the digital approach.

I conducted training sessions for the sales reps, and during the workshop the reps kept asking whether the new approach would have an impact on their jobs. I showed them the value of using the iPad and mentioned that if they added this solution to their work plan, they could stay more connected with their customers.

Three months after the digital solution was launched there was a 7 per cent increase in our market share and a 3 per cent increase in the number of doctors being visited. As a result of the initial success of the change, the chief executive decided that we should launch the digital strategy across Pakistan so that we can increase our footprint with minimal carbon emissions.

The key lessons I learnt from this digital transformation are:

- *Training is essential to ensure people have the new skills they need.* Since the remote detailing feature requires a different set of skills compared to traditional face-to-face detailing, medical representatives were trained on how to use the application effectively, how to communicate clearly and professionally during sales calls, and how to build relationships with customers remotely. A nationwide sales training programme was conducted for the medical reps and the doctors.
- *Communication is vital.* The proposed digital transformation was communicated across the organization, and we ensured that medical representatives communicated effectively to potential and existing customers through different channels, such as email, phone and videoconferencing.
- *Need to be flexible.* Implementing the remote detailing was challenging, especially when doctors were geographically disbursed, had varied schedules and poor internet connectivity. We had to be flexible in pace and timing of the implementation of the digital solutions to meet the needs of doctors and our sales representatives.

- *Data analytics is a priority.* A lot of data was generated with the help of remote detailing, such as customer feedback, sales metrics, engagement rates, number of consents, time spent on each interaction with the doctors, etc. This data was used to identify trends, areas of opportunities and improvement.
- *Collaboration with key stakeholders is vital.* Implementing the project required very close collaboration and coordination between multiple stakeholder groups, such as marketing, IT, sales and business continuity teams. All these teams had to be engaged and involved in the transformation and their views and concerns taken into account in order for the implementation to be successful.

Questions

1 What were the benefits of the approach used for the digital strategy?

2 From your experience, what are the challenges of positioning a digital transformation as an opportunity rather than a threat?

3 How might you apply the lessons learnt to ensure that a transformation is seen as an opportunity?

SUMMARY

How a business transformation is framed will act as the lens through which people will look at the challenges they are facing. As outlined in this chapter, it is important to be able to see a transformation as an opportunity and not just a threat, because the change is only likely to be successfully implemented when people are engaged and committed to it in a positive way. Although convincing people that something is an opportunity when they feel otherwise can be extremely hard, it is not impossible. It can be done by reframing the threats first, by giving stakeholders all the facts about the transformation and the reality of what will happen if the organization does not change. Second, this framing needs to be complemented with a positive reason why there is a need to change, ensuring that this positive reason is personal to every stakeholder/group. The challenge is not to tell or communicate to people that the transformation is an opportunity but instead to convince them that this is the case. This requires tactics such as: adapting elements of the organization's culture; making change meaningful; focusing on positive narratives; promoting stakeholder-led creativity and innovation; and encouraging change as a learning experience.

PRACTICAL IMPLICATIONS

The practical implications which can be drawn from this chapter are:

- *Adapt behaviours.*
  The way to change elements of the culture is by changing behaviours in a visible and symbolic way, which can be done by managers adopting small and symbolic changes in their day-to-day behaviours. Employees pay close attention to how their managers behave and what they say. Based on what they see or hear, employees form their own beliefs and decide whether or not to adopt the same behaviours.
- *Foster creativity and innovation.*
  To encourage creativity and innovation, generate lots of ideas, even bad ones. When you want your team to solve a creative problem, try implementing an idea quota, which is a deliberate practice of generating lots of options to solve a problem instead of going back and forth trying to arrive at the right answer. Encouraging people to come up with multiple ideas can unlock some of the less obvious solutions. Consider innovative formats such as:
  - *Creating a sandpit or test bed:* Create a technical space to test ideas. This may entail building a dedicated online site or creating a lab-based test environment that can be used for a various projects or a model office.
  - *Running design sprints:* Assign a team to a design or innovation task with a demonstrable output for a fixed time, such as a month.
  - *Adopting agile approaches:* Consider using agile methology either instead of, or along with traditional Waterfall development approaches to support experimentation and rapid learning.
  - *Building prototypes:* Build a mock-up or demonstration to test the technical feasibility and user reactions, and to highlight potential challenges and problems.
  - *Sharing ideas.* Hold regular hackathons to encourage the sharing of ideas.
- *Recognize the learning from failure.*
  Emphasize that failure is a necessary part of change. Sometimes, discovering what works starts with discovering what does not, so recognizing and

learning from failure is a vital part of reframing change as a positive experience and an opportunity for learning.

- *Protect innovation time.*
  Protect open, unscheduled time on the calendars of your team and emphasize that this is not only permissible but necessary for innovation.

Notes

1 J Hagel (2021) *The Journey Beyond Fear*, McGraw-Hill, New York
2 P Coelho (2000) *The Devil and Miss Prym*, HarperCollins, London
3 J W Forrester. Counterintuitive behavior of social systems, *Theory and Decision*, 1971, 2 (2), 109–40
4 A Deutschman (2007) *Change or Die*, HarperBusiness, London
5 J B Fuller, J K Wallenstein, M Raman and A de Chalendar. Your workforce is more adaptable than you think, *Harvard Business Review*, 2019, 97 (3), 118–26. hbr.org/2019/05/your-workforce-is-more-adaptable-than-you-think (archived at https://perma.cc/4Y8Q-D96Y)
6 B L Fredrickson. The broaden–and–build theory of positive emotions, *Philosophical Transactions of the Royal Society of London, Series B: Biological Sciences*, 2004, 359 (1449), 1367–77. doi.org/10.1098/rstb.2004.1512 (archived at https://perma.cc/99EV-T3QW)
7 D L Cooperrider and D Whitney. A positive revolution in change: Appreciative inquiry, *Public Administration and Public Policy*, 2001, 87, 611–30.
8 B Bensaou and K Weber (2012) *Built to Innovate*, McGraw-Hill, New York
9 D Caglar and C Duarte. 10 principles of workforce transformation, Strategy + Business, 25 September 2019. www.strategy-business.com/article/10-principles-of-workforce-transformation (archived at https://perma.cc/K4M9-SPZ7)
10 E H Schein (1991) *What is Culture?* Sage, Newbury Park, CA
11 E Rosenbaum. Michael Dell on the simple way to tell a good mistake from a bad one, CNBC, 14 October 2021. www.cnbc.com/2021/10/14/michael-dell-on-the-simple-way-to-tell-a-good-mistake-from-a-bad-one.html (archived at https://perma.cc/6W3Y-PKXM)
12 Remote detailing, often referred to as e-detailing, is an online system which enables meetings to be scheduled with the pharmaceutical company medical reps at a time and location most convenient for doctors.
13 The app was a CRM solution which contained various features such as face-to-face detailing, brand-related videos, reps incentives, number of visits a rep did in a day, their bonus, rep trigged emails and SMS, and e-consents of the doctors' remote detailing.

07

Re-imagining the role of managers in change

Introduction

As Indra Nooyi, former Chairperson and CEO of PepsiCo, said, 'Huge change has no shortcuts. It requires honesty, agility, and courage.'[1] This is so true but it is not something that can be done by CEOs in isolation because it requires connection with managers and other stakeholders to effectively identify the need for change and agree the what, when and how in order to implement change effectively. Managers are the threads that connect people and business transformations, yet managers often feel like they are the squeezed middle because they are tasked with carrying out change imposed from above whilst, at the same time, having to motivate the people who they manage to engage with the change. As the frontline to implementing business transformations, managers are having to adapt to managing change in hybrid and remote environments, while also coping with the changing expectations of team members who want more flexibility and autonomy in where and how they work. Being a manager, therefore, brings pressure which research suggests managers are struggling with. According to a study of 20,000 knowledge workers in 11 countries, 53 per cent of managers feel that they are burnt out.[2] Similarly, a study by Gallup, a US polling company, found that managers often face unclear expectations and multiple competing priorities.[3] Such findings, along with the acceleration of change in the workplace, indicate that the traditional command-and-control role of managers is no longer relevant and may, in fact, be counterproductive, especially with business transformations. This raises the issue, which is explored in this chapter, about the need to reframe the role of managers so that they can embrace a people-centric approach to change. The chapter begins by considering the evolving role of managers and goes on to discuss the need for them to pivot to people-centric change. Particular attention is paid to some of the issues facing managers as they grapple with transformations, such as falling into the trap of micromanagement, especially in remote and hybrid work environments, which can ultimately drive down engagement, motivation, productivity and trust. To avoid such risks, the chapter explores the behaviours that are most relevant for managing business transformations. It then goes on to explore the capabilities that managers need in order to reframe their role so that it is people-centric during transformations. Managers cannot make the required shifts in their role alone so consideration is also given to the support that managers will need to pivot their role successfully. The chapter concludes with a business insight written by Kathrin Schrepfer that describes the role of managers in a merger between two international cyber security companies based in France, Germany and the UK. The case highlights the importance of managers fostering ownership, equipping teams to cope with transformations, limiting the pressure on people and using dialogue for effective change.

The evolving role of managers

Historically, the role of managers in organizational change has predominantly been about control and ensuring compliance. In recent years, this function has been diminishing due to the advent of a whole series of process and technical innovations such the development of internal digital platforms, which have seen the direct interactions between managers and employees eroding as leaders and others have been able to interact directly with employees, potentially leaving managers out of the loop. This has been further exacerbated by the introduction of agile working, in some organizations, which has broken down intact teams into fluid projects, all of which has further weakened the role of managers and their daily interactions with their team members. As a result, there has been increasing recognition that the traditional role of managers in organizational change, based on a convention of low trust and high control, is out of date and fits uncomfortably with a paradigm of employees who are expected to be accountable, empowered, and willing and able to engage with organizational change.

Consequently, some of the key areas in which the role of managers with business transformations is evolving include the following:

- ***From being reactive to being proactive.*** In the past, managers were frequently brought in to oversee change projects after they had already started. Managers now have a more proactive role in helping their organizations foresee and get ready for changes in the future rather than just reacting to them as they happen.
- ***From the tactical to the strategic.*** To assist organizations to integrate their transformation activities with their more general company goals and objectives, managers' roles are becoming more and more strategic. Managers are increasingly required to grasp the strategic direction of the organization well and to collaborate closely with senior executives to make sure that changes are in line with that direction.
- ***From a procedure to a person.*** Managers' roles are gradually shifting to become more people-oriented, whereas management has historically been focused on the process of managing change. Managers are increasingly considered as supporters of those affected by change, aiding in its management not merely from a technical and procedural standpoint but also on an emotional and cultural level. In addition, managers are required to be able to manage ambiguity and uncertainty as well as function well in contexts that are complicated and chaotic.
- ***From rigid to flexible.*** The conventional method of managing change has been linear, emphasizing the implementation of a pre-set plan following a set number of steps. However, managers' responsibilities are evolving to be more flexible, with an emphasis on being able to adjust to changing conditions and make rapid decisions in response to evolving and often complex situations.
- ***From siloed thinking to collaboration.*** With a focus on collaborating across functions, communicating effectively with a wide variety of stakeholders and guaranteeing that transformative projects are integrated and coordinated, managers' roles are evolving to become more collaborative which includes developing strong relationships with stakeholders across the organization.

These shifts are putting a tremendous onus on the role of managers with organizational change. In their study of 11 large Finnish companies, Karasvirta and Teerikangas found that companies assume that it is part of the role of managers to make sure that change gets done.[4] This shows a recognition of the importance of effective management in achieving successful business transformations. Overall, managers are increasingly having to be advisers, advocates for people, agile and collaborative, and able to help organizations navigate the dynamic, complex and rapidly changing environment in which they operate.

Pivoting to people-centric management

The view that managers are vital to this poses that organizational change may seem odd, since for years the focus has been on leaders, to the extent that the role of managers has been queried. Indeed managers have been referred to as the permafrost of change, meaning that they are not seen to be at the forefront of organizational change but instead prefer to be at the frozen middle. Unfortunately, as critics point out, some managers prefer to stay within their comfort zone, focusing on tasks rather than people, and are reluctant to hear the truth, so that they often fail to engage stakeholders in transformation initiatives.[5] This stance is, however, no longer feasible, especially with the increase in hybrid and remote workplaces where managers are no longer able to maintain the continual close management of individuals. Instead, as organizations move from structured to fluid teams and away from traditional hierarchies and top-down initiative-driven change focused on short-term surface improvements, managers are having to pivot from behaviours and attitudes such as 'I manage and control a transformation' to supporting people to be engaged and motivated with change and ensure that they have the skills to do so. The challenge that this poses is that, whilst the role of managers is vital in a people-centric approach to change the design, support and development of managers has taken second place to the focus on that of leaders, particularly in the academic and practitioner literature. So, until there is recognition of their important role in the people element of business transformations as well as adequate support and development for doing so, managers may struggle to be in a position to support people-centric change.

If managers are to fulfil their critical role with people-centric change they will need time and resources. For instance, artificial intelligence (AI) can take away many of the managerial transactional tasks and free managers up to do what really makes a difference, such as listening, coaching and supporting the development of skills and knowledge amongst team members. Changing the architecture of the manager's role and investing in AI to automate some of their tasks will help to create space for managers to support people-centric change by ensuring that they have the time to focus on the people elements of transformations. Furthermore, redesigning the role of a manager to give them time for these different activities in organizational change, as well as investing in their development so they can do so, will help to shift their focus from micromanaging the tasks of change in a command-and-control manner to one of micro-understanding.

From micromanagement to microunderstanding

As remote and hybrid work have become the norm, some managers are falling into the trap of micromanaging change, a practice that can ultimately erode engagement, motivation, productivity and trust. Whether they admit it or not, micromanagers usually feel that they cannot trust employees to be part of a business transformation away from the physical workplace environment. Employees who don't feel trusted may lose self-confidence and contribute less, which can also stifle creativity and growth. Managers who are prone to micromanaging change may exhibit the following behaviours:

- limit the autonomy of others to make decisions and contribute ideas
- observe and control the work of their team members
- continually have concerns about or question employees' contribution to a business transformation
- constantly want to be informed about every bit of progress made
- frequently check that someone has actually done what they were asked to do
- limit the authority of others so that they themselves continue to be involved with the transformation at the expense of others
- find it difficult to delegate tasks because they don't trust that others will do them.

Rather than enacting these behaviours and micromanaging a transformation, the role of managers needs to shift to one of microunderstanding. Whereas micromanagement is restrictive, with heavy meddling that undermines trust and manifests itself, amongst other things, in exhaustive reviews of the transformation, innumerable checklists and levels of approval and eventually in dissatisfaction, opposition and even fatigue with change, micro-understanding is about managers integrating themselves more effectively into their team's involvement with the transformation and engaging them with problem-solving and decision-making. Furthermore, it is about trusting team members, helping with unanticipated difficulties, delegating, being there to support individuals, being flexible and also looking out for change adversely affecting wellbeing. To move from micromanaging to microunderstanding so that managers design and create business transformations with others and not just manage them, managers need to reflect and take action on moving away from eroding, to emerging and enduring behaviours.[6] Eroding behaviours are antiquated management patterns such as command-and-control decision-making, relying upon hierarchy for influence, and rigid top-down change strategies. Enduring behaviours are traditional capabilities that focus on ethics, and building and maintaining trust and integrity. Emerging behaviours include engagement and collaboration skills, digital savviness and focusing on wellbeing and change. In addition, managers must be able to manage through chaos, uncertainty and increasing complexity as well as being able to focus on equality, diversity and the inclusion of different perspectives. To effectively make these moves requires enhancing and developing core capabilities for business transformations.

Core capabilities for business transformations

To enact people-centric change effectively, managers need to develop core capabilities that provide them with the skills and abilities to engage in and manage more confidently business transformations and go beyond what is immediately required for satisfactory performance, to enable effective and sustainable change. The crux is the ability to plan, design and implement transformational change with the engagement of key stakeholders, causing minimal negative impact on people and operations, so that benefits can be achieved and embedded into daily operations. To do this effectively requires a number of capabilities, some of which are discussed in other chapters of this book, including: engaging stakeholders with change (see Chapter 3); responding to opposing voices (see Chapter 4); providing high-quality communications (see Chapter 5); demonstrating and encouraging creative agility (see Chapter 6): ensuring positive wellbeing (see Chapter 8); creating an equitable, diverse and inclusive environment (see Chapter 9); fostering collaboration (see Chapter 10); and design thinking (see Chapter 10). To pivot the focus of their role to people-centric change, managers also need to develop and enhance the following capabilities: compassion; adaptability; stakeholder agility; sense-making; resilience; and coaching. Embracing these behaviours and skills will help to fuel the shift that managers need to reframe their role in business transformations. Each of these capabilities is outlined below.

Compassion

Compassion is about caring and having the intention to be of benefit to others. When managers are able to put themselves in the place of another person by listening, acknowledging and understanding their perspective and emotions, then they can take a fresh look at a challenging situation. This also enables them to recognize that they have one view of the situation but that things may, and probably do, look very different from another person's point of view. The importance of this was illustrated by Kiersten Robinson formerly the, Chief People and Employee Experiences Officer of Ford Motor Company when she described how she led efforts to make acknowledging and understanding emotions a core part of the company's culture and leadership DNA. Robinson stressed that, 'When we allow space to talk about how we are feeling and the struggles we are facing, we create a greater sense of compassion and common humanity that in turn fosters a more positive and productive work environment'.[7] A similar approach was taken by Jacinda Ardern, the former Prime Minister of New Zealand, in her first address to the nation about her government's response to the Covid-19 pandemic, when not only did she communicate in a clear and honest manner, but also translated her empathic concern for her fellow citizens in the following message of compassion and unity: 'Please be strong, be kind, and unite against Covid-19.' Ardern adopted a 'go hard and go early' response to the pandemic by imposing a stringent nationwide lockdown and deploying a rigorous national effort for testing, contact tracing, quarantine measures and public education and engagement.[8] She regularly acknowledged the hardships and extraordinary restrictions on people's personal freedoms that these policies inflicted but also simultaneously stressed her determination to prevent the spread of the Covid-19 virus. Ardern's compassionate leadership resulted in high public confidence and adherence to a set of strict pandemic control measures, the effective elimination of the virus in New Zealand, overwhelming voter support and her subsequent victory in the national elections in October 2020.[9] Compassion, such as that shown by Ardern, thus plays a crucial role during a business transformation, particularly when people are looking for guidance, direction and hope.

The characteristics of compassionate behaviour demonstrated by Ardern and others comprise: reading emotional cues in oneself and others and anticipating their effects; empathizing with those who are suffering; listening to them with respect; and acting to alleviate the suffering of others. During a transformation, the competent and disciplined performance of these behaviours need to be a crucial aspect of a manager's role. This was evident in how the former Chancellor of Germany Angela Merkel empathized with the struggles of her German compatriots in her first address to the nation about the pandemic. As Merkel said:

> Our idea of normality, of public life, social togetherness – all of this is being put to the test as never before. We all miss social encounters that we otherwise take for granted. Of course, each of us has many questions and concerns in a situation like this, about the days ahead.[10]

Compassionate managers and leaders like Ardern and Merkel make space for human moments that make a huge difference during a business transformation. Human moments are when a manager is present for, and provides their full attention to stakeholders whether these are people affected by the impact of a transformation or colleagues who show signs of distress. For such moments to happen, managers' attention needs to be both intellectual and emotional, and their presence must be physical. For people working remotely, physical presence may be substituted by virtual presence in that a physical image and voice, even a short five-minute conversation online, can provide a perfectly meaningful human moment. Compassion is, therefore, vital for managers in demonstrating a people-centric approach to business transformations.

Adaptability

Adaptability is the ability to be flexible and aware of, and open to, the need to make changes to a transformation as it progresses and before pressures build to the point where the changes become more difficult, or even futile. Surveys show that adaptability is a critical success factor during business transformations since it allows faster and better decision-making and orients managers towards the opportunities ahead, not just the difficulties.[11] Nevertheless, the same conditions that make adapting so important can also trigger fear, resulting in managers resorting to familiar behaviours or to whatever solutions worked previously. This is known as the adaptability paradox which occurs when managers most need to learn and change but instead stick with what they know, often in a way that stifles learning and innovation. Even positive change, such as receiving a promotion or beginning a new workstream, can turn negative unless an adaptable mindset and a focus on learning is maintained while under pressure. However, managers are often reluctant to apply the time to learn something new unless there is a compelling motivation to do so. When that motivation occurs it is often accompanied by pressure, such as having to avert failure or aiming to attain a reward or incentive. To avoid this trap, managers must work on building adaptability as a skill that benefits themselves, their team members, and their organizations at a deeper level, because being adaptable helps to cope with mistakes and failures as they occur. For example, when faced with a blunder in the implementation of the quarantine regulations in New Zealand during the pandemic, Jacinda Ardern made no attempt to blame anyone. Instead she adapted quickly and took decisive action to correct the deficiencies in the quarantine system, and acknowledged that her team had 'adjusted our settings every step of the way based on what we've learnt, based on what we know is working and based on what needs to be done… we just have to fix it'.[12] In these few sentences, Ardern articulated some of the key reasons for New Zealand's success in containing the pandemic, that is their observing, learning and constantly adapting. High levels of adaptability, such as those shown by Ardern, are associated with greater levels of learning ability and better performance, confidence and creative output.[13] Adaptability is also crucial for psychological and physical wellbeing and is linked to higher levels of social support and overall job satisfaction.[14] Moreover, adaptability incorporates the ability to adapt to ongoing changes in the internal and external environment through the capability to develop, learn, self-empower and grow. This is a practice that has emerged as managers have had to respond to factors such as: unplanned internal and external environmental dynamics; perceived uncertainty due to new role expectations; conflicting messages and priorities set by senior executives; and self-doubt relating to their own capabilities. These factors (and others) make it even more important that managers have the ability to adapt voluntarily and to manage ambiguous, complex and ever-changing circumstances in order to proactively perform their roles and responsibilities in business transformations.

Stakeholder agility

Effective people-centric change involves building and maintaining relationships with internal and external stakeholders. This requires stakeholder agility, which focuses on being able to engage and build rapport and support with stakeholders as well as being able to deal with multiple stakeholder groups in a variety of ways. Furthermore, it requires managers to be able to identify and to get to know stakeholders who will act as enablers during a transformation, in other words the authentic informal managers (see Chapter 3) who are individuals who have a high degree of social connectedness, influence and emotional intuition. Building working relationships with these authentic informal managers is critical in shaping the stakeholder experience and engagement with business transformations. The importance of stakeholder relationships is described by Jeffrey Immelt, the former CEO of GE, who said:

> I enlisted people in the transformation by forging personal relationships. One weekend a month, a GE officer and his or her spouse would have dinner with my wife, Andrea, and me at our home. The next morning, I'd spend four hours talking with him or her. I'd say, 'Tell me what's important in your business. What do you think we should do at GE? What are you working on? What else do you want to do?' Those weekends were a way to hear perspectives I might not get otherwise. In addition, they gave me a chance, person by person, to build deep connections, which are important in driving change.[15]

Building and maintaining constructive relationships between a manager and their team members is more important than ever owing to hybrid and remote working because they will be less likely to be working in the same place, at the same time, on the same transformation. Managers can no longer rely on informal corridor conversations to gauge the emotional temperature or to check out how people are feeling. Consequently, managers have dramatically less visibility into the realities of the day-to-day work of their employees on a transformation, which means that it is important for them to take time to understand the individual worries and stresses about transformations by checking in with their team members online or in-person on a regular basis to discuss and understand the issues. Building relationships also requires managers to help others to make sense of the complexity and uncertainty that transformations bring.

Sense-making

The ambiguity and dynamic nature of a transformation requires individuals to be able to make sense of it by constructing, filtering, framing and rendering the information about the change into something more tangible.[16] This involves using evidence from past events to construct a storyline that makes sense in the present. In other words, individuals will refer to their past experiences of business transformation to make sense of proposed future change initiatives. In this way, an individual's interpretation of a transformation is unique in that it is affected by the way they internally process information about it. This may sometimes be difficult, due to a lack of information, concerns about the impact of the change or worries about moving away from the status quo.

To help people make sense of the complexity and uncertainty of a business transformation and how it will affect them, individuals and teams need the opportunity to express how they feel about what they will lose, keep or gain. The following exercise is useful in helping people to identify the impact of the change and can be used in different situations such as workshops, team meetings, or away days. Participants should be asked to:

1. List all the relationships/roles/work habits/methods/systems/processes/ideas that they have now and will still have after the transformation is implemented. What will they keep?
2. List all the relationships/roles/work habits/methods/systems/processes/ideas they have but will not have after the transformation is implemented. What will they lose?
3. List all the relationships/roles/work habits/methods/systems/processes/ideas they do not have now but will have after the transformation is implemented. What will they gain?
4. Identify what the benefits of the transformation will be to them personally as well as to their team/department/function/organization.

This exercise can be useful in sorting fact from fiction and helping individuals and teams to make sense of the transformation by identifying the positive aspects of it, especially what they will be gaining from it.

Building resilience

Only 57 per cent of managers report having enough capacity in their day-to-day work to support their teams through change.[17] Instead of trying to champion every change, managers should instead act as resilience builders by building their teams' ability to self-navigate through change and ensure their teams learn by doing. This involves managers identifying their employees' strengths and motivations and connecting them to colleagues with the relevant experience who they can learn from. It also means that managers have to ensure that they build and maintain their own resilience and look after their own wellbeing (see Chapter 8 for further discussion on building resilience).

Coaching

The role of managers in people-centric change necessitates a shift from one of control and compliance to one where the focus is on people. For some managers this emphasis on people management will be new, especially if they have been appointed or promoted on the basis of their professional or technical skills and where their performance objectives focus on commercial or similar interests rather than on concern for supporting, developing and engaging team members with business transformations. To enable this shift to happen managers will need to pivot their stance from compliance to coaching. Coaching focuses on improvement and progress, and what individuals are capable of doing and not just what they have done. It involves using enquiry, active listening, asking questions, summarizing, empathy and reframing, to help individuals see new or different possibilities towards which to direct their efforts. When done well, coaching can improve personal effectiveness and wellbeing. A practical framework to use for coaching is the GROW (goal, reality, options, will) model outlined in Figure 7.1.[18]

- *G is for goal.* The coach (manager) and coachee (team member) agree what the coachee would like to achieve in the session and what they want to do differently.
- *R is for reality.* This is an opportunity for the coachee to explore what is happening and to understand what has already been tried.

FIGURE 7.1 GROW coaching model

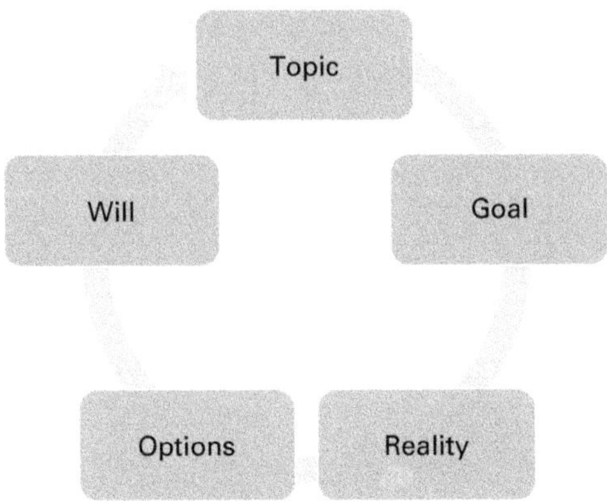

- ***O is for options.*** This focuses on the coachee identifying the options they have available to address the issue being explored. At this stage it can be helpful for the coach to keep asking 'What else?' to assist the coachee in identifying different options. The coachee should then be encouraged by the coach to select the best option to take forward.
- ***W is for will.*** This involves getting the coachee to commit to some actions they will take. To help the coachee identify what they are willing to work on and to do differently the coach should ask, 'What options will you choose?'

At the start of using the GROW model can be added 'T' – topic – which helps to focus on what it is the coachee would like to talk about. In this way, coaching is about the coachee taking responsibility for identifying solutions rather than a manager. The role of the manager (as coach) is to ask questions to help to facilitate the thinking of the coachee. In sum, to enact people-centric change effectively a coaching style is crucial, rather than simply issuing demands. Otherwise, staff who feel under pressure with a business transformation will disengage or may even leave the organization.

Alongside the core capabilities outlined above there is also the need for the following skills and knowledge to effectively plan and implement a transformation:

- ***Analytical skills.*** In order to understand change, interpret the external and internal drivers of change (see Chapter 2), set goals and align objectives and tasks, analytical skills are required to gather, analyse and interpret data.
- ***Programme management.*** For the planning and implementation of a transformation, programme and project management skills are needed, such as planning activities, setting clear, measurable objectives such as key performance indicators; monitoring and measuring progression; and benefits and risks management. Such programme management skills enable the effective delivery and implementation of a transformation through the engagement of various teams and also provide managers with the ability to prioritize workloads and other relevant transformations in order to ensure that there is sufficient capability and capacity.
- ***Systems thinking.*** This is an approach to problem-solving which views complex entities as a series of components, with each part interacting with, and influencing, the rest. The components of the organization are viewed as continually interacting with and affecting each other. Systems

thinking skills will, therefore, help managers to view the organization as a whole system that is sustained by how well its parts are aligned to the overall purpose of the enterprise and to appreciate that a change in one part of the system will impact on other parts.

All the capabilities described above are required not only for managing people-centric change when employees are working in the same time zone and the same place but also when they are working in hybrid and remote environments.

Managing transformations in a hybrid environment

Since operational models are changing, driven by the shift to remote and more flexible patterns and locations of working, managers are having to learn to effectively manage transformational change in hybrid and remote workplaces. There are several practices that are helpful for managers in moving to people-centric change in flexible work environments, including the following:

- ***Shifting to outcome-based performance.***
  Moving to an outcome and impact orientation, while enabling employees to determine how they get to, and take full ownership of achieving change, will create a shift to outcome-based management from input-based management – where teams focus on achieving outcomes by whatever means they think is best. In contrast, outcome-based management is more people-centric, which means that management practices designed for top-down control must shift to practices designed to empower and enable individuals and teams, since the goal is to focus employees on outcomes, not inputs. Prerequisites for this shift include setting clear roles and tangible goals and milestones, then checking in weekly or even daily to hear about any roadblocks to the transformation journey, offering support to clear them, and ensuring that work on the transformation is manageable. Furthermore, it importantly requires individuals to be accountable for achieving the outcomes.
- ***Increasing the capacity to change.***
  One of the goals of managers in people-centric change is not just to manage within certain constraints, but to actually increase the organization's overall capacity to change. To do this, it is important to be able to predict where in a transformation overload and saturation might occur

and then channel resources to those places to help absorb stress and build the capacity for change. This can be done in various ways, such as:

- identifying signs of overload with employees by: gathering feedback to quantify and measure perceptions of the transformation; setting up a network of change advocates to act as listening posts; and responding to feedback on a regular basis
- running sessions designed to explore the changes people will be asked to make and how they will affect them in order to identify what support they will need
- connecting changes across the organization and teams so that people can see the whole picture and the impact across the company (see systems thinking above)

- ***Building trust and togetherness.***
  Without proximity, building and maintaining trust is harder. So, to help build and maintain trusting relationships in remote and hybrid environments there is a need for connection – being attentive, open, curious and credible – ensuring behaviours are ethical and managers do what they say they are going to do.[19] To develop trust, managers will also need to solicit input from employees, acknowledge employee ideas, understand how their decisions influence employees' experiences of transformations and communicate why some ideas are not or cannot be accepted. Asking for input and feedback can help employees to feel heard and valued. Building trust thus rests on employees seeing how managers listen to them and care about the concerns they raise and their wellbeing.

  In hybrid and remote working environments, traditional methods for building trust such as walking around, chatting at the coffee machine or having lunch with team members are less readily available. In an online environment managers will, therefore, need to proactively establish trust by role modelling and encouraging the following characteristics:

  - *Reliability:* This means managers ensuring that they meet their commitments, for instance sticking to regular check-ins online, helping to remove roadblocks to change, ending virtual meetings five minutes before the next one to ensure punctuality throughout the day.
  - *Acceptance:* This involves managers accepting and respecting the perspectives of others for example, deliberately inviting all meeting participants to speak up online, even those with divergent opinions; establishing rules for participative decision-making online; being

familiar with and recognizing the traditions and habits of a diverse set of employees and how they translate online.

- *Openness:* To create an open environment online involves encouraging everyone to share what they think, do and feel, and to be open to giving and receiving feedback, for example starting every morning with a check-in online and/or holding a monthly online team lunch to take a temperature check about the transformation and how it is going.
- *Authenticity:* This requires managers to walk the talk, for example by role modelling required behavioural changes – even online.

- ***Developing team engagement and problem-solving.*** In online settings, various behaviours can erode engagement with transformations, such as failing to be mentally or emotionally present at meetings, turning the camera off and/or checking emails or phone messages. Beyond avoiding these pitfalls, managers should keep meetings short and use interactive tools online, such as the chatbox, polls and breakout sessions to facilitate involvement in discussions. It is also vital to encourage team problem-solving because, particularly when under pressure, managers may resort to making decisions themselves about a transformation. In contrast, people-centric change involves managers adopting a team approach for problem-solving and decision-making. In practice, this means that to tackle the hard issues during a transformation managers will have to engage personally, mobilize resources and link teams up. This will help to involve people in finding a solution that will create commitment and encourage ownership of the transformation.

Adopting these activities, such as fostering outcome-based performance, building and maintaining trust and togetherness and developing team engagement and problem-solving, will help to shift the role of managers from one of command-and-control to a people-centric approach to change, but in order to do this effectively managers will need support.

Support for managers

For managers to effectively shift their role to one that focuses on people-centric change they will need support and development. It is important that managers not only receive the training and development they need to enhance the key capabilities required to manage effectively during a transformation but also essential that they receive clarity, guidance and space to do what is expected of them in enacting people-centric change. Moreover, managers will need help with maintaining and enhancing their own well-being while changing their role.

The challenge and changing role of managers is outlined in the following business insight written by Kathrin Schrepfer, a senior change expert, trainer and business coach based in Germany. Kathrin describes the role of managers during a merger, including the challenges faced and the lessons learnt.

CASE STUDY

Business Insight: The challenge of engaging managers in a merger

In 2022 two medium-sized international cyber security companies based in France, Germany and the UK were undergoing a merger. The driver for the merger was that in the evolving market both companies were about to broaden their scope and move towards similar fields of expertise. To avoid becoming just another one of many smaller competitors, those two companies decided to combine their different strengths and assets in order to develop and grow into a key player in their field. The size of the new company would open up entry to a number of new markets for holistic end-to-end cyber security services and for larger customers.

To raise awareness of the merger amongst staff a general communication was prepared which outlined the short- and long-term benefits of the merger for staff in both companies. Regular online briefings were also held to prepare people for the change and to clarify any outstanding issues. Aware of the critical impact of the merger on employees and knowing that in the cyber business talents are a key success factor, the management team were keen to develop a plan to engage employees in the transition. I was brought in as a Strategic Change Advisor to conduct the impact analysis, build the involvement plan, train internal resources on change management basics and provide advice on how best to implement the merger.

To begin with, I worked on the following key areas: supporting communication with all employees; analysing the impact of the merger with key stakeholders and subject matter experts; and aligning with senior management on the big picture of the new company. Top management defined the vision and values and the way of working they wanted to foster in the new company. This was followed by employee focus groups, where participants discussed the different behaviours and actions they felt would best reflect the new values and ways of working.

While subject matter experts prepared the legal, infrastructural and procedural side of the merger, employees were asked for their opinions on a new company name and slogan. I worked closely with the Change Project Team to get more details about the impact of the changes and to clarify which target groups needed communication and support.

To provide the best possible support, we recruited Change Enablers (volunteers) from across the two companies. The role of the Change Enablers was to ensure proximity to employees by providing space, in a fortnightly forum, for people to discuss their needs and problems and to raise questions; jointly develop support measures for the target groups affected by the change; and to promote ongoing dialogue about the merger. To help managers guide their teams through the transition, we invited participants to a series of four training sessions (90 minutes each) on the change process. Each session focused on: current observations about the merger; the needs behind those observations; and recommended actions for managers to take to support their team during the merger. Following the sessions managers were asked to hold team meetings to address the hopes and fears about the merger, and the Change Enablers were happy to help facilitate these sessions. Since not all of the details of the impact of the merger were clear at this point, we also provided managers with some recommendations for dealing with uncertainty within their team/s. A few weeks before going live with the merger, managers were invited to training sessions on the key new processes and their role in supporting their teams. This was followed by training for users on the new processes.

On the first day of the newly merged company, we had a great moment when employees from the different regions were able to meet in-person (the first time since the Covid-19 pandemic started) and celebrate together. We had posters with the new company's big picture hung up in the hallways to illustrate the vision of the shared strength of the new company and the benefits for employees and customers. The CEO gave a motivational speech about the future and how everyone could work in line with the new values. The Change Project Team was extremely proud of its achievement in bringing the two companies together within a very challenging time frame of only eight months. The good news was that the company already had some potential new customers. Ultimately, it was a great stress relief that the merger appeared to have been a success.

Given the success of the first part of the change plan, the project team then planned the next six months in a similar fashion. We knew that the integration of some processes had not yet been completed and that some harmonization still had to be carried out during ongoing operations. So, we were in close contact with the functional managers and aligned our support activities with their overall plan. We planned three parallel work streams: (i) culture development; (ii) operational change support; and (iii) training internal resources to support the change in the long term. People's involvement and collectively building the new took centre stage, across the work streams. As part of the culture development workstream, focus group members, along with sponsors from top management, planned monthly campaigns to bring the new values and ways of working to life. At the operational level, we worked with the various functions and main departments on identifying their key tasks and how the changes might affect employees. We also identified which people were in need of support for the transition. To address the impact of the changes we focused on communication materials to drive adoption of the new operating model and to ensure that employees understood why the new company had chosen to implement a new process in a specific way. In addition, we scheduled interactive sessions to discuss how teams could define their key contributions and objectives from the company's overall strategy. Furthermore, because some processes still needed to be harmonized, we scheduled workshops where employees considered potential synergies and shared their needs and expectations in relation to the synergies identified. Unfortunately, this plan of scheduled initiatives was not executed due to growing discontent among the workforces.

Two months after the merger, frustration started growing and complaints surfaced owing to two main factors. First, the migration of the different IT platforms proved to be more difficult than expected and colleagues were not able to participate in the projects as needed owing to blocked access rights and/or access to the new processes. Furthermore, the new company faced legal restrictions on collaborating and sharing information online. In the field of cybersecurity, the protection of data and the management of access rights are very strict. Cultural differences and different usage of key terms and titles bred confusion. For example, several project leaders felt that, owing to changes in their role, they had been downgraded, were unappreciated and some even feared a salary loss because their freedom in terms of decision-making and budgets had been curtailed, despite their administrative responsibilities having been increased. For example, whereas bookings, budget development and hours already worked were previously reported on a monthly basis, this was now required on a weekly basis and needed to be much more accurate. Second, processes that were not yet ready were severely hindering day-to-day work. The technical experts who could have helped solve the problems were not available to answer questions because they were busy with other problems. People began to feel that they were spending more time solving internal process problems or manually managing workarounds than adding value based on their expertise. Overall, the transition period left people dissatisfied and unable to work as effectively as they had done prior to the merger and with no short-term improvement in sight some of them decided to leave the company. As a result, the remaining employees were confronted with significantly higher workloads and a lack of technical expertise.

Consequently, employee frustration began to escalate. The collectively built new approach was soon perceived as management incompetence in leading the new company. Several of the previous leaders took advantage of the merger to retire, and the leadership team that took over on the first day of the merger had not had much time to gain the trust of the workforce. There were also differences in the leadership styles of the two companies and in how the change was supported. Some of the top management tried to keep the company as stable as possible and spread the message that not much would change; others maintained an open dialogue with their teams from the start, assuring them that they would listen and work on solutions to the most pressing problems; while others said that it's normal for employees to leave during a transformation, and that it's part of a company's adjustment to the new. This inconsistency of messages from top management and the many unresolved issues were in serious conflict with employees' need for stability, perspective and leadership. The CEO's intention to shape the processes in the new company together with the employees now became synonymous with a lack of concept and of relevant experience.

To address the concerns, a virtual meeting was held by the CEO and the top management team which focused on the strategic next steps, but the meeting was filled with frustrated and angry employees who expressed their annoyance through irate comments in the chat-box about the perceived lack of preparation, anticipation and clarity about the impact of the merger. As a result of the discontent, the focus of the overall transformation project had to shift to trying to pacify angry employees and dealing with IT problems and a lack of process enablement, instead of implementing the initiatives originally agreed upon. By this stage, managers were overwhelmed and felt ill-equipped to handle the negativity and criticism. They completely neglected their role in the change process, ignored emails, refused to participate in any training and barely spoke up in dialogue sessions, but instead just kept escalating issues to the top management team. As a result, top managers wanted more operational change support for their managers with much shorter emails, more sequential content and an increased local presence from the project team. Middle and local managers hoped the increasing pressure from employees would result in an external expert being brought in to quickly implement the change for them. In an attempt to help, the Change Enablers network was asked to deliver coaching to support the local teams and also to provide advice to managers on how they should lead themselves and their teams through the turmoil.

As the Strategic Change Advisor, I was asked if this downwards spiral could have been prevented: Was there anything we missed? Were there any important steps we skipped or something we could have recognized earlier? What should we have done differently? In hindsight the answer is yes, there was something we had missed as we reacted quickly to implement the merger within the short time frame. It had been clear for four months that there was a lack of middle and local management buy-in to the merger. Although we invited managers to attend briefings on the changes, next steps and how to cope with potential employee reactions, and we were also available to attend team meetings to support managers in their change roles, few managers attended the briefing sessions, nor did they ask for our help.

Prior to the merger, we had developed, for managers, a learning journey that consisted of short videos, readings, case studies and online tests explaining how people typically respond to change and what managers can do to support them, as well as recommendations for reducing stress and dealing with uncertainty during the merger. But managers responded that it was too early for them and that they did not see a need for any training or support at that point. We also held four training sessions for the managers, focusing on the current needs related to the merger, recommendations for the managers to cope with the situation, and practical tips. However, we did not follow up to find out whether the materials provided or the advice given were implemented. The majority of managers were not engaging with any of the training provided, as was evident when, just before the merger was completed, less than 20 per cent of all managers had attended a hands-on training session on the tools and procedures of the company's new enterprise resource planning system.

How could we have expected them to work flawlessly with the new system from day one when they had not been trained? Although the poor IT infrastructure was the main cause of frustration, a well-trained and engaged workforce might have coped better with it. So why did most of the middle and local managers not participate in our offerings?

There was a failure to recognize that the two merging companies had completely different leadership styles and to understand the role of managers in the transformation. While managers in one company saw themselves as leaders who felt responsible for their teams in all areas of work, managers in the other company saw themselves as the best subject matter experts in their field. For the latter group, communication and managing change had always been carried out by the communications team and/or HR department, so they did not perceive leading people through change as part of their role or responsibilities. This issue came to the surface only later, after discussions with other project teams from Sales and Strategy who were trying to establish new processes and who were also struggling with engaging the middle and local management in the transformation.

To address these issues, we began by scheduling joint meetings with employees to discuss the current situation and explain the strategic direction, and importantly to actively listen to employees' needs and concerns and discuss expected changes. Each session was led by a subject matter expert and one or two local managers who were asked to put the information, such as strategic direction, into the context that was relevant to their teams. At first, management were reluctant to do this and asked for a more thorough briefing on the topic. Eventually, the open dialogue at the meetings helped to increase awareness and address the concerns raised. Local management began to take an active role in the change and, for the first time in weeks, there was an open dialogue with employees in which they shared their expectations for the coming months with their managers.

My personal take-away from the experience of this merger is that middle and local managers are the key enablers for change in transformations. Their buy-in and ability to lead people in uncertain times dictate the energy for or against change happening in their teams. The specific key lessons I learnt from this experience are that managers leading a transformation need to:

- *Differentiate between the impact of the change on the team and on self.* Managers who were able to separate their own perceptions, potential personal impacts and judgements about change from how they informed their teams about change were more open to the real needs of their teams. They were able to lead their teams more constructively and offer more options for potential benefits from the merger.
- *Give perspective and foster co-ownership.* The managers who engaged their teams in the common goal and fostered ownership throughout the merger gave hope and perspective. The teams that lacked this became disappointed and lost faith when the transition wasn't as smooth as expected, and some even saw greater opportunities elsewhere and moved on.
- *Equip teams for what's next.* The managers who sent their teams to the training sessions and involved them in the process design of the new company enabled them to act with an eye for the bigger picture. Their teams understood better the background and impact of disruptions in the system and were able to defuse the situation when blockages occurred, efficiently and effectively. This enabled them to manage both their tasks and the needs of the business as a whole.
- *Limit pressure and count on dialogue.* The managers who communicated clearly about the situation, how their team might be affected and the different options of dealing with it were the ones who helped their teams to reduce their stress levels. Teams that felt well informed trusted their manager and were more willing to engage and bridge gaps that occurred.

Overall, my experience from this merger has taught me that in future projects I will engage more directly with local management in order to identify specific challenges facing them and their teams. This will make it possible to more easily verify that managers have the skills and mindset they need to confidently manage and support their employees through change. My next change plan will also include a specific part on activating managers for change, in addition to providing training and support materials.

Questions

1 What was the key role of managers in the transformation? How might this role have been reframed so that it focused on people-centric change?

2 How was the failure to recognize the blind spots eventually addressed? What might have been done differently and why?

3 From the lessons learnt, which ones are the most important for you in implementing a people-centric approach to a transformation?

SUMMARY

The approach to the management of transformational change has conventionally been hierarchical, which may have made sense when jobs were fixed, workplaces were physical, information flowed downwards and a change was seen as an isolated project. This is, however, no longer the case, especially since the world of work is becoming increasingly enabled by technology and there is a prioritization on agility, speed, innovation, responsibility and connectivity. Consequently, managers are facing increasing ambiguity in their role as they try to manage change in a hybrid environment with less control and visibility into the processes of change, and fewer opportunities for impromptu conversations, while at the same time trying to recreate the cohesiveness, collaboration and camaraderie of the office through the freedom and flexibility of remote working. Managers are thus having to address intractable, complex problems and to adapt more quickly to the drivers of transformational change – all of which requires them to be flexible and agile. This is contrary to the assumption that change can be managed and controlled, as if in a vacuum. Change management books abound and feed this narrative, but in a rapidly evolving and chaotic world traditional approaches to managing change are no longer sufficient. As business transformations bring greater complexity, the manager's role is more about the ability to tolerate ambiguity and uncertainty rather than offering certainty and clarity. This requires a reframing of the role of managers, as outlined in this chapter, and the development of key capabilities. Managing transformations well requires the focus of the role of managers to be on a people-centric approach, with an agile mindset and capabilities including compassion, adaptability, stakeholder agility, sense-making and coaching. Embracing a people-centric approach will help to fuel the shift that managers need to make in order to reframe their role in business transformations.

PRACTICAL IMPLICATIONS

There are several practical implications which can be drawn from this chapter:

- *Build on being flexible and adaptable.*
  Steps that can be taken to become more flexible and adaptable include: developing an agile mindset; building deeper human connections; and making it safe to learn. It is also vital to welcome changing requirements, even late in the transformation process, and modify the transformation to ensure the work continues to be relevant and will deliver value.
- *Focus on engaging team members who are working remotely, flexibly and/or on shift patterns.*
  Ensure that you check in with team members, especially those working flexibly, remotely or on shift patterns on a regular basis to understand concerns and challenges. Establish ongoing listening mechanisms that enable you to keep a pulse on employee and stakeholder sentiment, particularly with those working in remote and flexible ways. This means listening carefully to what people are asking and saying, and giving reassurance whenever possible to do so. Start online meetings with five minutes in small breakouts of two or three people with no agenda for these breakouts and where the only goal is to catch up with each other for 10 minutes.
- *Build and maintain trust.*
  To develop trust requires soliciting input from employees, acknowledging employee ideas, understanding how their decisions influence their experiences of business transformations and communicating why some ideas are not or cannot be accepted, while others can be. By asking for input and communicating a response you can ensure that employees feel heard and do not feel dismissed, which can help to build and maintain trust.

Notes

1 I Nooyi (2021) *My Life in Full: Work, family and our future*, Hachette, London, 208

2 Microsoft. Hybrid work is just work. Are we doing it wrong? Microsoft, 22 September 2022. www.microsoft.com/en-us/worklab/work-trend-index/hybrid-work-is-just-work (archived at https://perma.cc/8KL8-7BUX)

3 Gallup. People management: Pros, cons and development opportunities, Gallup, nd. www.gallup.com/workplace/321074/perks-and-challenges-of-management.aspx (archived at https://perma.cc/DW4C-LTGB)

4 S Karasvirta and S Teerikangas. Change organizations in planned change: A closer look, *Journal of Change Management*, 2022, 22 (2), 163–201. www.tandfonline.com/doi/full/10.1080/14697017.2021.2018722 (archived at https://perma.cc/KT7B-X6S9)

5 M Beer. Reflections: Towards a normative and actionable theory of planned organizational change and development, *Journal of Change Management*, 14 January 2021, 21 (1), 14–29. www.tandfonline.com/doi/full/10.1080/14697017.2021.1861699 (archived at https://perma.cc/T94J-NMFY)

6 Z Church. Writing a new leadership playbook, MIT Sloan, 3 March 2020. mitsloan.mit.edu/ideas-made-to-matter/writing-a-new-leadership-playbook (archived at https://perma.cc/9ZXP-VSFD)

7 R Hougaard and J Carter (2022) *Compassionate Leadership: How to do hard things in a human way*, Harvard Business Review Press, Boston, MA

8 T Maak, N M Pless and F Wohlgezogen. The fault lines of leadership: Lessons from the global Covid-19 crisis, *Journal of Change Management*, 2021, 21(1), 66–86. www.tandfonline.com/doi/abs/10.1080/14697017.2021.1861724 (archived at https://perma.cc/Q74F-XN22)

9 M G Baker, A Kvalsvig, A J Verrall and N Wellington. New Zealand's Covid-19 elimination strategy, *Medical Journal of Australia*, 2020, 213 (5), 198–200. www.mja.com.au/journal/2020/new-zealands-covid-19-elimination-strategy (archived at https://perma.cc/5VG2-8DGX)

10 A Merkel. Angela Merkel: Address to the nation on the novel coronavirus outbreak [lightly modified English translation transcript provided by the Government of Germany], American Rhetoric, 18 March 2020. www.americanrhetoric.com/speeches/angelamerkelcoronavirusaddresstonation.htm (archived at https://perma.cc/CJM6-B4R2)

11 J Brassey, A De Smet, A Kothari, J Lavoie, M Mugayar-Baldocchi and S Zolley. Future proof: Solving the 'adaptability paradox' for the long term, McKinsey, 2 August 2021. www.mckinsey.com/capabilities/people-and-organizational-performance/our-insights/future-proof-solving-the-adaptability-paradox-for-the-long-term (archived at https://perma.cc/WWV7-GYL6)

12 S Vani and C A Harte (2021) *Jacinda Ardern: Leading with empathy*, Simon and Schuster, London, 312

13 J Brassey, A V Witteloostuijn, C Huszka, T Silberzahn and N V Dam. Emotional flexibility and general self-efficacy: A pilot training intervention study with knowledge workers, *PloS One*, 2020, 15 (10), e0237821. journals.plos.org/plosone/article?id=10.1371/journal.pone.0237821 (archived at https://perma.cc/3Y7L-MDZR)

14 M Zhou and W Lin. Adaptability and life satisfaction: The moderating role of social support, *Frontiers in Psychology*, 2016, 7, 1134. www.frontiersin.org/articles/10.3389/fpsyg.2016.01134/full (archived at https://perma.cc/7WZG-ZX4V)

15 J R Immelt. How I remade GE: And what I learned along the way, *Harvard Business Review*, September–October 2017. hbr.org/2017/09/how-i-remade-ge (archived at https://perma.cc/MXV9-9ZLC)

16 K E Weick (1995) *Sensemaking in Organizations*, vol. 3, Sage, London

17 C O Morain and P Aykens. Employees are losing patience with change initiatives, *Harvard Business Review*, 9 May 2023. hbr.org/2023/05/employees-are-losing-patience-with-change-initiatives (archived at https://perma.cc/H4F2-KAC9)

18 M Landsberg (2015) *The Tao of Coaching: Boost your effectiveness at work by inspiring and developing those around you*, Profile Books, London

19 R Hougaard and J Carter (2022) *Compassionate Leadership: How to do hard things in a human way*, Harvard Business Review Press, Boston, MA

08

Wellbeing during change

Introduction

In August 2020 Jen Fisher, Deloitte US's Chief Wellbeing Officer, posted a LinkedIn message that asked leaders to share the strategies and practices they were piloting to influence wellbeing in their organizations. The post, which received more than 500 reactions and 200 comments in a few days, revealed an expanding organizational focus on wellbeing. Leaders of organizations large and small said that they were tailoring their wellbeing efforts to the needs of various segments of workers rather than taking a one-size-fits-all approach; as well as finding new ways to allow workers to disconnect and recharge; and focusing on equipping workers with the mental, emotional and social skills needed not just to cope, but also to adapt and thrive. What was interesting about this was the examples of organizations designing wellbeing into work itself. This is a positive step, since individuals and teams cannot function effectively let alone adapt, compete and thrive when they are struggling and suffering.

The pandemic reminded us of the dual imperatives of wellbeing, as illustrated in the responses to Fisher's post, but some organizations are still missing the importance of connecting wellbeing and business transformations. This is crucial, since transformations are synonymous with introducing adverse effects on wellbeing, such as increased employee anxiety, stress and, ultimately, burnout. Poor mental and physical health can affect productivity, morale and engagement with transformations, resulting in not only an increase in absenteeism and turnover but also a higher likelihood of the benefits from the transformation not being realized. Organizations that recognize that business transformations and wellbeing are interdependent are more likely to achieve successful change through the engagement of healthier and happier employees especially since integrating wellbeing into the design of transformations is far more likely to build change that is sustainable, with workers feeling and performing at their best. To achieve this, there is a need for practices that help to ameliorate the negative impact of transformation on the health and wellbeing of people.

The aim of this chapter is to discuss and identify practices for ensuring positive wellbeing during business transformations. It begins by stressing the importance of wellbeing and the impact of change, particularly technological, on people's physical and mental health. Since employees feel more productive when they feel happy and healthy, consideration is also given to how wellbeing can be achieved by designing transformations around people while prioritizing their health and achieving a successful work–life balance. The chapter concludes with a business insight of the case of a police service in the Midlands, UK, written by David Howell, the founder of Able and Rush (People Solutions) Ltd, which emphasizes the need for wellbeing and mental health to be an intrinsic part of a business transformation rather than an extrinsic one, in order to increase the likelihood of successful outcomes and to ensure a healthy transformation journey for everyone involved.

The importance of wellbeing

Wellbeing is vital for ensuring the success of a business transformation. This is supported by the findings in Deloitte's Global Human Capital Trends survey, where 80 per cent of respondents identified wellbeing as an important priority for their organization's success.[1] Employees with higher wellbeing are more likely to enjoy their work, recommend their organization to others and report high levels of engagement and adaptability which, in turn, can lead to improvements in organizational performance, higher productivity, customer satisfaction and lower turnover, sickness and absenteeism. Furthermore, research suggests that employees who are engaged are almost three times as likely to experience positive emotions at work, such as enthusiasm, cheerfulness, optimism and contentment, rather than negative emotions, such as feeling miserable, worried, anxious, gloomy, tense or uneasy.[2] People with higher levels of wellbeing are also likely to take a more positive approach to their work and their relationships with colleagues and are less likely to see ambiguous events such as transformations as threatening. So having higher levels of wellbeing can mean that individuals are more likely to engage effectively with a transformation, be more enthusiastic about it, accept the changes it brings more readily, and see it as an opportunity (see Chapter 6 on change as an opportunity rather than just a threat).

Despite the benefits of wellbeing, there is a continuing disconnect between employers and employees when it comes to prioritizing wellbeing in business transformations. In a survey by Deloitte, senior business leaders, HR executives and individual employees were asked to answer the following question: 'What are the most important outcomes you hope to achieve in your work transformation efforts in the next one to three years?'[3] Responses varied between the three groups: employees said that the top three objectives of a transformation should be improving quality, increasing innovation and improving worker wellbeing; senior executives said that improving the customer experience, increasing innovation and reducing costs were the most important priorities; whereas HR executives were slightly more deliberate than non-HR executives about the necessity to focus on wellbeing as an important outcome of a transformation, with 20 per cent of HR executives selecting it as a priority compared to 15 per cent of non-HR executives. Such a variation in responses suggests that there is a need for a more concerted approach to wellbeing in organizations, especially with the acceleration of technological and other disruptions.

Technology and wellbeing

Technology and work are inextricably intertwined, with humans and machines partnering in ways previously unimaginable to accelerate work outputs and achieve new outcomes. As technology becomes ingrained in every aspect of how people work, there is a growing responsibility for organisations to ensure that those technologies, and the workflows and processes that complement them, are designed and executed in a way that promotes worker wellbeing. For example, in France the 'right to disconnect' concept has prompted a law limiting the extent to which workers can be required to answer phone calls and emails during non-work hours, in recognition that 24/7 access to emails and texts encourages an expectation of being always available, which can compromise wellbeing.

To counteract the potential to impact negatively on the wellbeing of individuals, there is an imperative to design technologies to boost workers' health, performance and quality of life. Such as technologies: to help people develop self-awareness; build collaboration and deeper team connections; and to help people maintain and optimize health and cognition to support their general wellbeing. Technologies such as these can help to improve wellbeing by enabling employees to develop and learn faster, eliminate distractions, connect with others across organizational and global boundaries and reduce stress.

Impact of transformations on wellbeing

When major aspects of a workplace are being transformed people may experience a great deal of disruption, and for some this can be experienced as a shock to their system. This is evident in a study of a police organization which found that extensive organizational changes, including downsizing or a change in job tasks, are associated with an increase in work stress, disturbed sleep and incomplete recovery from health complaints for employees.[4] Evidence thus shows that a business transformation has the potential to increase the stress levels of individuals. In fact, research suggests that transformations may pose a risk for the health and wellbeing of individuals because organizational changes usually involve changes in roles, an increase in work overload, and a shift in the skills and knowledge required from individuals to perform their work and also to implement the change.[5] On top of being a stressful experience, an organizational transformation is also linked to reduced motivation, increased uncertainty, doubts, fear and intentions to withdraw from the change.[6] According to a study by Gartner, 45 per cent of HR leaders believe that their employees are fatigued from all the change that they are experiencing.[7] Yet, despite the potential for a transformation to have a negative impact on the wellbeing of individuals, research indicates that employers are failing to consider the importance of it. A study by Gallup suggests that fewer than one in four American employees feel strongly that their employer cares about their wellbeing.[8] Added to this is the impact of working remotely where, due to the weakening of work–life boundaries, resilience may suffer and lead to higher stress and burnout levels. Moreover, less structure and predictability can also reduce the feeling of being in control when working remotely on a business transformation. Individuals may also be less cognizant of the pace and timing needed when they are in their own safe space at home. There is, therefore, a need to be aware of the impact of transformations on wellbeing.

Uncertainty

Change naturally involves some degree of uncertainty regarding its impact and outcomes. Uncertainty, or lack of knowledge or predictability of an individual's circumstances, can lead to feelings of a lack of control, which in turn can lead to stress and ultimately burnout. For better or worse, people are wired to fear uncertainty. Furr and Furr, in their book *The Upside of Uncertainty*, propose that if we can tolerate uncertainty then we can develop uncertainty ability – the skill to navigate unknowns both planned and unplanned.[9] This is vital for business transformations, which are characterized by high levels of perceived uncertainty due to transformations no longer being a single event with a neat and tidy beginning and ending. Furthermore, uncertainty can occur when there is lack of clarity about what is being proposed, such as why there is a need for change, what will change, when and how it will change and what the impact will be on jobs. It is also related to whether or not employees perceive that the organization is capable and has the capacity of implementing the transformation successfully based on their past experiences of business transformations. Although uncertainty can never be completely eradicated, it can be reduced in order to create more positive perceptions and improve wellbeing. This can be done in various ways, such as by: creating a sense of familiarity by showing people how they can use their skills and knowledge to implement the transformation effectively; engaging people in dialogue about what the transformation will mean for them; and highlighting what will stay the same and what will change. For instance, letting people know that they will still be able to use the same skills to do their work, and/or will be remaining in the same work unit or team can help reduce uncertainty, as can on-the-job training and small, digestible communications about the changes in employees' day-to-day operations. Although uncertainty can never be completely alleviated, it is imperative to keep it to a minimum before, during and following a transformation by involving employees in the process and by promoting opportunities for engagement (see Chapter 3) and collaboration (see Chapter 10).

Loss of resources

A key source of stress during a business transformation is the threat of losing tangible and/or intangible resources. At a tangible level, change can lead to the loss of jobs, work roles, status and rewards, as well as an increase in obsolete skills and in workloads. At an intangible level, a transformation can drain psychological resources by causing feelings such as unworthiness, stemming from individuals; perception of their lack of ability to cope and adapt to the impact of the transformation. In order to deal with those stressors, individuals who support the changes and want the transformation to be successful will often work longer hours, deal with an increasing number of problems, attempt to overcome the doubts of others and do everything they can to implement the change. This can result in role strain caused by trying to maintain standards of performance while at the same time implementing changes and having responsibility for people who are uncooperative or have concerns about the transformation. Role strain can be further exacerbated when individuals are not involved in decision-making and have inadequate managerial support. Identifying and reducing the impact of a transformation on wellbeing is, therefore, vital to ensure that individuals are not negatively affected.

Decrease in job control

Changes in employee roles and responsibilities are often a central part of a transformation process, which can increase job demands, such as the amount of work and time demands. It can also lead to a decrease in job control, for instance by affecting the amount of influence an individual has over decisions regarding their daily tasks and interactions between co-workers and clients. Such changes can result in people facing conflicting demands, a lack of resources to complete their additional assigned tasks and/or uncertainty related to the objectives and expectations of their new responsibilities. Furthermore, transformations have the potential to increase an employee's sense of role conflict (that is, conflicting demands and lack of resources) and lower their sense of role clarity (for instance, clarity regarding responsibilities and expectations). Wellbeing can also be affected by the extent to which employees are involved in the decisions that affect their job and role for example, research indicates that employee participation in planning and implementing changes, are linked to reduced mental health complaints and sick leave and by the number and frequency of changes.[10] Eventually, there is a risk that transformation saturation can occur as a result of frequent changes and several transformations happening at once.

Transformation saturation

A barrage of continuous transformations are likely to create a sense that the organization is turbulent and continuously changing which, in turn, can lead to exhaustion and even burnout, where employees become confused, overwhelmed and unable to work effectively due to transformation saturation. Left unaddressed, transformation saturation can reduce people's ability and capacity to implement change, which eventually can reduce the realization of expected benefits and even lead to the failure of the transformation. To prevent this from happening there is a need to appreciate that saturation can constrain a transformation and be mindful of the impact of too much change or mismanaged change. Furthermore, it is critical to look at the collective transformations across the organization, take into account the personal impacts of these changes, and gauge just how much employees are coping with them day-to-day and what can be done to alleviate any pressure. For example, it may be necessary to slow down a transformation or delay the start of another one in order to give people some space to breathe and recuperate. Some of the other key factors that need to be taken into account to address transformation saturation comprise:

- ***Initiation:*** When to initiate a transformation matters. In many countries there are norms around national holidays. Starting a transformation just before holiday season can impact the focus, attention and pace of the initiative.
- ***Rhythm:*** The pace of change is important to people's wellbeing. Transformations that are too fast, too frequent or too slow and drawn out can, and will, impact on health and stress levels.
- ***Duration:*** The length of a transformation is often a result of its complexity, ambition and scale. Transformations that take a long time can sap energy, motivation, enthusiasm and commitment. Where possible, it is beneficial to break it down into chunks with clear interim outcomes and also to provide opportunities to reflect and learn in order to check and validate the progress and direction of the transformation, so that changes can be made along the way, if needed.

- ***Magnitude:*** The intensity of a transformation in terms of workload is an important factor in relation to wellbeing. Although people might have the capacity to work in short bursts at an intensive pace, this can be difficult to sustain over long periods of time without it impacting negatively on their wellbeing. Where there is a need for intensive periods of work on a transformation, this needs to be countered with time for rest, recuperation and reflection in order to rebuild resilience (see below).

Building wellbeing into transformations

Wellbeing practices

Since the start of the Covid-19 pandemic organizations have launched a myriad of wellbeing initiatives, ranging from wellness programmes to video-conference happy hours, to individual one-to-one coaching. While these have been undertaken in earnest, they have often been received by employees as yet another thing to do and have failed to address the levels of stress and drains on staff energy. Such approaches to wellbeing in organizations tend to fall into three categories. The first is the systemic approach, where the organization looks at the processes, policies and practices that have an impact on the wellbeing of their staff. The second is where the organization looks at developing (or protecting) the wellbeing of their staff through workplace interventions, which tend to be delivered through a coordinated range of activities. The third is an approach that signposts individuals to specialist practitioners, such as occupational health and counselling, for bespoke help. The second and third approaches are more prevalent in organizations than the first, which tends to remain in the 'too hard box'. Ideally, during a transformation organizations should apply a mix of these approaches as part of their wellbeing agenda in a number of different ways including:

- talking and listening to people and finding out about the challenges and stresses that they are facing, and ensuring that they have support to cope with them
- creating wellbeing advocates from across the organization to support colleagues and signposting them to relevant sources of help and advice
- tackling wellbeing from the bottom upwards rather than the top down
- encouraging individuals to take responsibility for their own wellbeing

- setting up employee forums, which are used as a conduit for information but also for listening to ideas for shaping the transformation
- running focus groups which enable those involved or impacted by the transformation to come together to share experiences and learning, and identify solutions and support mechanisms

Practices such as those outlined above have been found to create heightened wellbeing and positive work-related attitudes and behaviour through the norm of reciprocity.[11] In other words, practices that promote wellbeing can result in people responding positively, which in turn will be reflected in their performance levels, organizational commitment and engagement, a willingness to collaborate and to engage in transformations, as well as having higher energy levels.[12]

Many of the existing wellbeing efforts tend to focus on the health and wellbeing of individuals, rather than also focusing on the wellbeing of teams/groups and the entire organization. This means that practices that are often primarily enacted at the individual level also need to be applicable at team and organizational levels. At the individual level, employees should take the initiative, and be encouraged to do so, in setting their own boundaries, making their wellbeing needs understood, and be able to influence the prioritization and design of wellbeing initiatives through participating in the development of flexible and responsive practices that balance their own needs with those of their team and organization during transformations. At the team level, members need to be able to understand and respect each other's wellbeing needs in order to create an environment in which the team can perform its best, ensuring that the energy of the team is managed not just by the team leader but also collectively by team members. To complement this, managers must focus on showing appreciation when goals and priorities are completed, since celebrating wins, even small ones, such as 'wins of the week', can have an impact on maintaining motivation and wellbeing during a long-term transformation. At the organizational level, there needs to be not only investment in, and promotion of, wellbeing but also a commitment to designing wellbeing into the transformation process and a recognition that the health of individuals is as important as any other factor that affects the success of the transformation. This may, for instance, include investing in skills development as well as providing support for behavioural changes. Equipping people with the capabilities and capacity to adapt and change quickly as well as providing support and guidance, at an organizational level, can help to reduce stress levels.

To enhance wellbeing, organizations also need to take into account the environments in which they are implementing a transformation, especially as transformations increasingly cross cultures, geographies and functions, as well as physical and virtual workspaces. The suggestions and questions below offer a starting point for thinking through what might be done differently:

- *Cultural:* How might wellbeing be built into social behaviours and norms?
- *Relational:* How can wellbeing be fostered in relationships among colleagues?
- *Operational:* How can wellbeing be included in management policies, processes and programmes?
- *Physical:* How can the physical workspace be redesigned to facilitate wellbeing? What support can be given to ensure home workspaces are fit for purpose?
- *Virtual:* What new technologies and virtual workspaces can be introduced to enhance wellbeing?

In designing wellbeing initiatives to address these factors it is crucial to accommodate the interests of people and adopt a mutual gains approach by engaging employees themselves in designing wellbeing initiatives as part of the transformation process. Microsoft Japan for example, experimented with such a strategy that resulted in the company reducing its working week from five to four days. To be able to enhance people's contributions to wellbeing practices, as was done by Microsoft, requires gaining insights into their needs. This can be done through various tools for collecting workforce wellbeing data. For instance, researchers at the Mayo Clinic in Rochester, Minnesota have developed a Wellbeing Index that assesses dimensions of distress and wellbeing, such as the likelihood of burnout, meaning in work, and work–life integration. This data, as well as input from employees, can be used to understand what changes to practices may have the greatest impact on wellbeing. For instance, in Germany health circles, which are systematic, structured workshops, provide a space where workers can discuss ways to minimize or eliminate health risks and other stress factors. In this way, health circles empower employees to redesign practices for maximizing both wellbeing and performance. Reinforcing wellbeing efforts across individual, team and organizational levels can, therefore, help to improve the physical and mental health of individuals and teams so that they are not negatively affected by changes but instead are able to drive improved outcomes and achieve and sustain the benefits of the transformation. Practices that can help with this include (but are not limited to): prioritizing transformations: chunking change; building resilience and adaptability; and encouraging rest and recuperation.

PRIORITIZING TRANSFORMATIONS

Transformation saturation (as described above) can occur when there is a lack of prioritization. To avoid this happening, support and guidance needs to be provided to show employees where to invest their energy and efforts. Without such guidance, employees might over-commit to each transformation, resulting in an increase of their levels of stress. In addition, consideration should be given to the employee experience when determining the optimal speed for implementing transformations. IT leaders at Sky Cable – a Filipino telecom – recognized the need for this by developing guidelines for minimizing fatigue arising from a constant flow of technology changes. They also created a calendar that was synched with the transformation initiatives across all departments. Consequently, IT leaders were able to identify the best times to launch new initiatives.[13] Prioritizing transformations can also help to identify any that should be stopped altogether because if a transformation is always at the bottom of the backlog list and continually delayed then it is probably not that critical.

CHUNKING CHANGE

Often, the sheer scale of a transformation can impact on wellbeing and stress levels. To address this, a transformation can be broken down into smaller projects (chunking) which can help to reduce the perceived scale and complexity of it and take away the shock of an extensive and far-reaching transformation. Chunking can also encourage small wins over shorter periods of time. To effectively chunk a transformation into smaller incremental changes, it is worth getting the key stakeholders involved in defining the goals and the discrete phases of the transformation. This is what Lockheed Martin, an aerospace and defence contractor, did when it launched LM-21, which was a transformation that aimed to fully integrate the company's corporate acquisitions and to achieve lean operations, continuous improvement and optimum value for customers. The solution and targets for how this aim was achieved were left to workers to decide, which for some managers in the company was equivalent to turning over the asylum to the lunatics. However, it worked, since the approach involving breaking the transformation down into small changes and then testing them. All of LM-21's interim targets were eventually met or exceeded.[14] Chunking can therefore help alleviate concerns and anxieties about long-term transformations and ensure short-term wins. A slight word of caution about chunking is that, paradoxically, it may increase perceptions that change is occurring significantly more often. So there needs to be careful consideration of the amount and frequency of transformations and constant monitoring of their impact on wellbeing.

BUILDING RESILIENCE AND ADAPTABILITY

Resilience and adaptability are vital for wellbeing. To help build them requires an understanding of how a transformation is impacting on people and what will help alleviate any stressors. It can be helpful, for example, to know what the concerns are that individuals are experiencing about the transformation and what is really causing their anxiety. For instance, they may fear losing their job because they are unable to learn new skills fast enough, or they have been put into new jobs where they have not had the chance to adapt to the new ways of working before yet another major change occurs. Although not all fear is about having the right skills, some people might be given training but still be scared and want someone who they trust and in a position of authority to say, 'This may be painful for a few months, but it will be OK.' By having such conversations with individuals and teams so that they are able to identify what the concerns are and what the right thing to do is, managers will be able to help people strengthen their resilience and ensure that individuals are also able to develop adaptability to improve their wellbeing. Building resilience and the energy for adaptability can be done through encouraging rest and recuperation.

ENCOURAGING REST AND RECUPERATION

If people are to thrive and maintain their wellbeing during a transformation, then organizations must ensure that their change practices and processes do not wear employees out. Research has found that 20 per cent of employees with the highest engagement levels also report burnout.[15] These engaged but exhausted employees have mixed feelings about work, in that they report high levels of passion and stress concurrently. Organizations that do not recognize the symptoms of transformation fatigue and saturation may lose some of their most driven and hardworking people when they experience burnout. One approach that can be implemented to address this is to build recovery and self-care into business transformations. For example, during a transformation where employees are anxious about the impact of the changes on their job security, many will not take time off. Yet in times of pressure, people need time off to recharge and recover. For example, a global telecoms company put a stop to new transformations for two months to allow for recovery and also periodically examined which transformations to reduce, and how to intentionally limit the amount of work in progress. To legitimize the importance of recovery time, managers need to actively role model it. This happens in the UK Navy where, after particularly stressful periods, captains navigate ships to calm waters where sailors can rest. In an organizational environment, calmer waters might be managers themselves taking time off to unwind and encouraging their team members to do the same. Organizations that take this seriously have gone as far as mandating that employees take personal time off or have given them an extra paid day or two off. Proactively encouraging recovery time, even short breaks, during the day is a good start to boost resilience, but this is easier said than done. Crowdfunding platform Kickstarter, for instance, started offering unlimited holiday time but retracted the policy a year after its launch because people were not using it. In contrast, The social media management platform Buffer took a different route by introducing financial incentives to encourage employees to take more leave, but when that did not work it implemented a mandatory policy, which helped to increase the number of vacation days that staff took.

To identify the best ways to encourage rest and recuperate, it is worth bearing in mind that people naturally function in what are known as ultradian cycles – periods of high-frequency brain activity (about 90 minutes) followed by lower-frequency brain activity (about 20 minutes). Taking a recharging break every 90 minutes is especially important for people using computer screens, because they make the brain overly active. Ironically, technology can help with rest and recuperation. For instance, there are some apps and software programs that remind and encourage people to take physical and mental breaks regularly throughout the day such as StandApp and Break Time. Another way to encourage rest and breaks is by redesigning onsite workspaces. For example, PwC Netherlands has redesigned its workspaces to reflect the natural rhythm of collaboration. Rows of cubicles have been replaced by communal tables and comfy corners so that people can come together as a group and then spend time apart. The key is to provide employees with a working environment that they want and feel comfortable with, and also recognizing the importance of ensuring that people working remotely and on shift patterns have areas for taking time out for proactive rest. To do this effectively involves considering the characteristics of proactive rest which comprise:

- *Available.* There needs to be a robust set of options for employees to use to rest and stay charged, including no-meeting days, defined working hours, planned down time and all-company days off.
- *Accessible.* Employees should be encouraged to take advantage of the available tools, such as out-of-office responses on email.
- *Appropriate.* Rest tools should meet the individual needs of employees.[16]

Creating available, accessible and appropriate ways for rest and recuperation will help to increase employee wellbeing and build resilience. In sum, practices that are explicitly designed can have a positive impact on wellbeing, which in turn can affect individual, team and organizational performance and effectiveness.

Wellbeing is not just the role of HR and OD

Often, the responsibility for implementing wellbeing practices during a transformation sits with the HR department or with the OD team. However, placing the responsibility for wellbeing in one place neglects the fact that wellbeing is a multifaceted concept that involves multiple players. Although HR does have a responsibility to provide support for wellbeing during a transformation, the responsibility should also be spread across the organization and, importantly, include support from the executive leadership team and line managers. This requires a great deal of coordination across the organization in order to ensure that the right conversations and actions are taken by the right people in the right place at the right time, and it needs to involve not only the HR and OD team but also leaders, managers and other employees in their design, implementation and measurement.[17]

Formal employee wellbeing programmes such as mindfulness, stress management training, mental health awareness campaigns and 'email-free Fridays' can be immensely valuable when done well, especially when they destigmatize mental health challenges, support inclusive environments and promote physical activity. To monitor the effectiveness of such initiatives requires an assessment of factors such as: how many colleagues are actively engaged in the programmes; what kind of impact the programmes are having; whether or not people are using the tools and techniques suggested and sticking to them; what is making it possible to engage with the programmes and their proposed techniques; as well as what is making it hard to do so. It is not, however, enough just to launch wellbeing initiatives; they need to be assessed, monitored and improved continuously. Ultimately, investing in the wellbeing of people and monitoring the impact of wellbeing practices can have positive results, as research suggests organizations that invest in wellbeing see four times higher profits, more than 20 per cent gains in productivity and innovation, and are better prepared to handle disruptions with greater speed and resilience.[18]

In the following business insight, David Howell describes how to ensure that a business transformation, promotes and monitors wellbeing. Based on his experience with a police service in the Midlands, UK, David describes how this begins with the recruitment and selection of the transformation project team and the impact that this team can have on the wellbeing of others.

CASE STUDY

Business Insight: Wellbeing during change

I remember the day vividly! It was midday on a Friday afternoon and the new record management system was due to 'go live' the following week, but the project team had been called together for a hastily scheduled meeting. There had been a senior stakeholder meeting only hours before and the dozen or so people now huddled in the small functional meeting room were anticipating some major news.

The record management system was called Niche and the digital transformation was being implemented for a Midlands police service, removing some 14 separate operating systems and condensing them into just the one application. The Chief Inspector, who was the project manager for the £16 million project, entered the room in his uniform adorned with three 'pips' on his shoulder epaulettes looking somewhat stressed and sat down to deliver his news. The project was to be put on hold for several months and would not now be going ahead the following week.

What I remember was the tangible emotion in the room. Relief. People were actually close to tears. The Chief Inspector went on to elaborate on the decision-making process and then kindly invited comments and thoughts from each of the assembled team. Everyone who was crammed into that tiny room was in unanimous agreement that the difficult decision made by the Chief Inspector was a courageous one but the correct one. It would ultimately cost the police service more money, as contracted project members would require their contracts to be extended and the Deputy Chief Constable would have to explain to the whole force that the anticipated change would not now be going ahead as planned. The project went ahead some six months later. As the Business Change Manager for the project (and the only person left contracted onto the project team), I was given the task of preparing and delivering the post-implementation review. This was a fascinating opportunity for me to delve into some of the decisions made, including the one to postpone the 'go live' date.

One of the first people that I had the pleasure of speaking with was the Chief Inspector and he enlightened me as to why the postponement was authorized. He said that he had to fight hard to get the postponement and argue his case with some very senior officers who were the stakeholders and project leads. His argument was this: to have ploughed on with the initial 'go live' date would have seriously harmed so many good people both mentally and physically. He had observed how hard his team were working and understood the mental commitment being applied. Importantly, he had also seen how ill some of his staff were looking. To have pushed these people even harder, knowing that the project was simply not ready for implementation, would have caused so much harm to his already burnt-out team. What a brave decision, especially when you consider the lofty positions of the senior management whom he had to convince.

Having written the post-implementation review, and having since worked with innovative workplace and wellbeing assessments within teams and organizations, I appreciate that mental health has to become an integral part of every change project and not just a peripheral consequence of a project. We cannot keep leaving a trail of broken and collateral damage in the wake of change management projects. The success of any project will ultimately depend on the wellbeing and mental health of everyone involved. And, by 'everyone involved' I mean *everyone* involved! From the project team to the stakeholders to those experiencing the change within the organization.

So, how do we ensure that change management benefits from promoting and monitoring wellbeing?

It all starts with recruitment and selection of the project team – understanding their initial condition sensitivity and in the process aligning individual innate talent complexity potential with the complexity required to perform a specific role. That initial condition sensitivity takes into consideration each individual who makes up the team. What are their idiosyncrasies and biases? What is their current state of mental health and wellbeing, i.e., are they already in a state of burnout or living within a self-protectionist 'bubble' having been damaged and scarred from previous workplace experiences? How do they deal and cope with stress and are they more of a non-linear thinker than a linear one? So many questions, but by investing time to understand and appreciate these issues we 'get ahead of the danger' rather than experiencing them downstream once projects have commenced, which equates to additional time, money and poor mental health.

We can also start to get ahead of internal dangers by appreciating where potential individual conflicts may arise within a team. That self-awareness provides team members with a better understanding of their role and, importantly, how they contribute to the friction between people, now seeing problems from another person's context and no longer fearing being judged. At this critical initial stage constructive conversations can be facilitated, creating a dynamic context and trust within a safe non-judgemental environment. That shared awareness allows for issues to be surfaced and resolved, with people less likely to fight counterintuitive actions made by linear thinkers. All of the answers are undoubtedly in the room.

This initial condition sensitivity also takes into account the individual's own unique innate talent complexity potential. This unique individual insight allows us to understand and appreciate the very foundations that we are born with and the foundations on which we learn, and allows us to accelerate that learning. If we provide ourselves with this self-awareness then we are far better equipped and prepared to deal with and adapt to the complexity of the world around us. Individuals also tend to find it easier to sense what is easier or more difficult for them to adapt to and process, feeling less pressured to not speak up and finding it easier to ask for help. We can then make better choices and decisions as to which opportunities best align with our own unique innate talents, in the process respecting others around us and their own unique innate talents. Those innate talents require a holistic view of an individual's mind, body and soul from an inside to outside perspective, removing bias and subjectivity. If we do this, we then have a baseline from which to work from and monitor individual changes throughout the duration of any change management project. In effect, we have a fluid complexity risk matrix which reacts to changes in the team or the environment around them, including events at home. We also have to remember that changes in an individual's mental health may not be directly caused by the work environment but by events at home or within social circles. We cannot detach these two spheres of influence and feedback loops.

We also need to appreciate who is actually in a state of burnout even before the project commences. Within policing, and I am certain that it is no different in the corporate world, when staff are selected for project work it can be for any number of reasons. What I generally saw within this particular project was that departments who were approached to volunteer their 'best people' recoiled at the very idea as it would potentially create issues for that particular departmental team leader. 'Giving away' their most productive staff was simply not an option. This resulted in the project team being initially formed from those people who had returned from long-term sickness or stress leave, were approaching retirement or were a perceived departmental 'weakest link'. This then begs a serious question: how engaged would these people be, and how stable would a project team be, if it were formed of already burnt-out members of staff or people 'cruising' towards retirement? There is a caveat here. We must not forget that some of those people selected 'by default' will actually work fantastically well within a project management setting, as it was their previous workplace experiences within another team, department or under certain leadership that had caused that burnout. You are, however, potentially building in failure and serious risk to the project even before you start. Changes and hiccups naturally occur during any change management project, with new plans and new courses steered in order to negotiate issues on a regular basis during what can become a marathon. The project team need to be constantly aware of those complex changes and able to find innovative ways around them, so having good mental health and wellbeing is key to ironing out those bumps along the road.

By understanding who comprises the project team from day one and their initial condition sensitivity we commence change from a far stronger position, with the organization providing a duty of care to its staff in the process. The Chief Inspector was reliant on the visibly displayed behaviours to base his decision on, but that is a risk as it is subject to his own bias and subjectivity, along with the state of his own mental health. A different Chief Inspector could just as easily ignore the visible behavioural symptoms of their team, deciding to plough on regardless in order to save their own ego and professional standing. This may well have caused untold and lasting damage whilst compounding poor team decision-making within the change management process. What if that Chief Inspector had seen the role of project manager as being a unique opportunity to benefit their future career and next promotion, seeing the role as a high-profile challenge to impress leaders above them? A poor initial selection of the project manager or senior stakeholder all too often invariably creates those toxic environments where bullying and narcissism flourish, which in turn causes untold mental health and wellbeing issues to staff. I experienced this very outcome when police aviation was amalgamated within the National Police Air Service in 2013. The ramifications are being endured by those still working within that organization as well as officers 'on the ground' and the public themselves who experience a vastly reduced service and support.

To be able to get ahead of the danger and to reap the wholesale benefits of wellbeing throughout any change management project we need to have this initial baseline from which each person starts. We can then monitor periodically and have those important conversations in a timely manner. Importantly, we then become proactive to problems rather than reactive. Mental health and wellbeing then become an intrinsic part of any change management project rather than an extrinsic one, increasing the likelihood of successful outcomes and a healthy passage (mentally and physically) for all those involved.

Questions

1. What were the key lessons learnt about the importance of mental health and wellbeing during the transformation?
2. How were people effectively engaged with the proposed changes?
3. How might you ensure that wellbeing is an intrinsic part of a business transformation you are engaged in or one you are familiar with?

SUMMARY

Frequently, the people element of a business transformation is only considered once it has started, and often not until the process is about to finish. This is too late and will not create the necessary changes in working practices, skills, knowledge and behaviour which are needed to realize the benefits of a transformation. Such a sloppy approach may also adversely affect the health and wellbeing of individuals which, in turn, can have a detrimental impact on the overall effectiveness and success of a business transformation. In contrast, employees with higher levels of wellbeing are more likely to have higher levels of engagement and adaptability during a transformation and be able to implement organizational changes successfully. As discussed in this chapter, it is, therefore, crucial to have a people-centric approach to change that focuses on the wellbeing of individuals and teams. This means, firstly, recognizing the factors that impact on wellbeing and that can cause transformation saturation and fatigue such as uncertainty and a loss of resources. Then, secondly, building wellbeing into transformations at organizational, team and individual levels through practices such as:

- enhancing resilience and adaptability;
- chunking the transformation into smaller pieces;
- encouraging recovery time;
- listening to fears and concerns and identifying ways to address them; and
- tackling wellbeing from the bottom-up rather than the top-down setting up employee forums to identify and agree wellbeing initiatives

Furthermore, it comprises encouraging participation in the decision-making process (see Chapter 3) and providing adequate and effective information and communication (see Chapter 5) to help influence employee wellbeing during and following a transformation.

Promoting good wellbeing is a vital part of people-centric change, as it sends messages to staff that they are valued and appreciated. Designing wellbeing into a transformation cannot, however, be done by HR or OD alone. The incorporation of wellbeing into a transformation must be done as an integral part of the change process, championed by leaders and managers at every level and in every function if it is to make a meaningful difference. The design of wellbeing into business transformation is, therefore, a practice that must be developed, strengthened and flexed over time to be effective. As business transformations become more rapid, the ways in which an organization supports individual, team and organizational wellbeing must adapt in tandem, since wellbeing is no longer about balancing work with life but integrating work and life in a more flexible way. By giving wellbeing more prominence and viewing it as a vital part of people-centric change, so much more can be done in fostering and nurturing a healthy environment during business transformations.

PRACTICAL IMPLICATIONS

There are several practical implications which can be drawn from this chapter:

- *Reduce the impact of transformations on wellbeing.*
  To lessen the impact of a transformation on individual and team wellbeing there is need to be open and honest about what it will involve, in order to reduce the negative impact on the health of individuals. The following strategies can be applied to support this:
  - *Provide details.* Be specific about why there is a need for a transformation, how the changes will be made and when they are likely to occur. It is critical that as many details as possible are provided about the timeline and the steps of the transformation.
  - *Discuss the pros and cons.* Openly discuss the known challenges and concerns to make the transformation as positive as possible. Be honest and don't pretend that difficulties do not exist but engage stakeholders in identifying ways to address them.

- *Seek and act on feedback.* It is vital that employee feedback is sought and listened to, and actions are taken to address any fears and concerns as soon as possible.
- *Remind employees of other successful changes.* It is beneficial to link an impending transformation to previous positive ones. This can help to alleviate employees' anxiety by reminding them that the last transformation was successful. If this was not the case then it is important to remind people of the lessons learnt if a previous transformation failed.
- *Make the transformation in small steps.* Where possible, it is a good idea to break the transformation into small, incremental steps and provide some time for employees to complete and embed each step before moving on to the next one.
- *Be aware of what triggers stress.* Managers need to become aware of what triggers stress for themselves and others, and learn and share coping mechanisms. Whenever necessary, managers should also ask for support from HR and OD professionals to help them and their staff to cope with the pressures of transformation.
- *Maintain the energy levels.* Ensure that the energy of teams is maintained. To complement this, focus on showing appreciation when goals and priorities are completed. Celebrating wins, even short-term ones, such as 'wins of the week', can have a big impact during transformations.

- *Take individual responsibility and support others.*
  Be mindful about wellbeing needs – both your own and that of your team members – and check-in regularly, proactively and consistently with colleagues on their wellbeing needs and preferences. When it is evident that individuals are struggling with the pressure of a transformation, it is important to reach out to them. Although you can't put your arms around someone if they are online, you can make space for people to have personal conversations and to ask them not only what they think but also what they feel and how they can be supported during a transformation. If people are onsite, consider inviting them out to lunch or for a walk outside to discuss what they are finding challenging and what might help them. Adjustments need not be expensive. Typically they might include: changes to roles to incorporate the work needed for the business transformation; increased

support from managers in prioritizing and managing workload due to taking on additional work due to the transformation; or flexible hours or changes to start and finish times of working.

- *Role model.*
  Managers play an integral part when it comes to alleviating the negative impact of business transformations, for example by showing their commitment to avoiding excessive workloads and minimizing unpredictable hours during a transformation, and by role-modelling wellbeing behaviours such as taking breaks and time out to rest and recuperate.

Notes

1 Deloitte. 2020 Global Human Capital Trends report – *The Social Enterprise at Work: Paradox as a path forward*, Deloitte, nd. www2.deloitte.com/cn/en/pages/human-capital/articles/global-human-capital-trends-2020.html (archived at https://perma.cc/VJ24-R3E6)

2 K Alfes, C Truss and J Gill. The HR manager as change agent: Evidence from the public sector, *Journal of Change Management*, 2010, 10 (1), 109–27. www.tandfonline.com/doi/abs/10.1080/14697010903549465 (archived at https://perma.cc/RQU6-VYBF)

3 J Schwartz, K Eaton, D Mallion, Y Van Durme, M Hauptmann, R Scott and S Poynton. Diving deeper: Five workforce trends to watch in 2021, Deloitte, 9 December 2020. www2.deloitte.com/us/en/insights/focus/human-capital-trends/2021/workforce-trends-2020.html (archived at https://perma.cc/6YSV-KTJP)

4 J Greubel and G Kecklund. The impact of organizational changes on work stress, sleep, recovery and health, *Industrial Health*, 2011, 49 (3), 353–64. www.jstage.jst.go.jp/article/indhealth/49/3/49_MS1211/_article (archived at https://perma.cc/YHG6-KTL6)

5 V de Fátima Nery, K S Franco and E R Neiva. Attributes of the organizational change and its influence on attitudes toward organizational change and wellbeing at work: A longitudinal study, *The Journal of Applied Behavioral Science*, 2020, 56 (2), 216–36. journals.sagepub.com/doi/10.1177/0021886319865277 (archived at https://perma.cc/4DTK-V3EU)

6 M Fugate, G E Prussia and A J Kinicki. Managing employee withdrawal during organizational change: The role of threat appraisal, *Journal of Management*, 2012, 38 (3), 890–914. journals.sagepub.com/doi/10.1177/0149206309352881 (archived at https://perma.cc/D9K4-XN85)

7 Gartner. Gartner survey reveals leader and manager effectiveness tops HR leaders' list of priorities for 2023, Gartner, 12 October 2022. www.gartner.com/en/newsroom/press-releases/2022-10-12-gartner-survey-reveals-leader-and-manager-effectiveness-tops-hr-leaders-list-of-priorities-for-2023 (archived at https://perma.cc/Q6WQ-42BT)

8 J Harter. Percent who feel employer cares about their wellbeing plummets, Gallup, 18 March 2022. www.gallup.com/workplace/390776/percent-feel-employer-cares-wellbeing-plummets.aspx (archived at https://perma.cc/FEX9-WA2B)

9 N Furr and S H Furr (2022) *The Upside of Uncertainty: A guide to finding possibility in the unknown*, Harvard Business Review Press, Boston, MA

10 J B Bernerth, H J Walker and S G Harris. Change fatigue: Development and initial validation of a new measure, *Work & Stress*, 2011, 25 (4), 321–37. www.tandfonline.com/doi/abs/10.1080/02678373.2011.634280 (archived at https://perma.cc/6QK7-BVCF)

11 D E Guest. Perspectives on the study of work–life balance, *Social Science Information*, 2002, 41 (2), 255–79. journals.sagepub.com/doi/10.1177/0539018402041002005 (archived at https://perma.cc/E9B8-QN7L)

12 D Angrave and A Charlwood. What is the relationship between long working hours, over-employment, under-employment and the subjective wellbeing of workers? Longitudinal evidence from the UK, *Human Relations*, 2015, 68 (9), 1491–515. journals.sagepub.com/doi/abs/10.1177/0018726714559752?journalCode=huma (archived at https://perma.cc/A6KE-MDMG)

13 C O Morain and P Aykens. Employees are losing patience with change initiatives, *Harvard Business Review*, 9 May 2023. hbr.org/2023/05/employees-are-losing-patience-with-change-initiatives (archived at https://perma.cc/P7PU-993R)

14 Harvard Management Update. How to win the buy-in: Setting the stage for change, *Harvard Business Review*, 26 February 2008. hbr.org/2008/02/how-to-win-the-buyin-setting-t-1 (archived at https://perma.cc/CNB4-GRRV)

15 B Sethi and C Stubbings. Good work, Strategy + Business, 2019, 94, 41–49. www.strategy-business.com/feature/Good-Work (archived at https://perma.cc/62KW-37ZS)

16 C O Morain and P Aykens. Employees are losing patience with change initiatives, *Harvard Business Review*, 9 May 2023. hbr.org/2023/05/employees-are-losing-patience-with-change-initiatives (archived at https://perma.cc/G2JK-KYSJ)

17 J Hodges and M Crabtree (2021) *Reshaping HR: The role of HR in organizational change*, Routledge, London

18 A Robichaux. The key to a more resilient organization is more resilient teams, TecHR, October 2020. techrseries.com/guest-posts/the-key-to-a-more-resilient-organization-is-more-resilient-teams (archived at https://perma.cc/38ZT-FCUT)

09

Equality, diversity, inclusion and change

Introduction

In *Bully Market*, Jamie Fiore Higgins' eye-opening memoir of her time spent working at Goldman Sachs in New York, she highlights a dichotomy between the stated diverse and inclusive values of the company and the culture that dictates what really goes on.[1] Jamie describes how she was pinned against the wall by a male colleague who told her he wanted to 'rip [her] fucking face off'. When she reported this incident, her manager told her that he would not be getting rid of the man and warned: 'Imagine what your life will be like after you report him to human resources.' She didn't. Jamie's experience led her to the conclusion that there is a need for a shake-up of organizational cultures in order to make them fit for the future and not the past. The shake-up she proposes involves embedding equality, diversity and inclusion (EDI) objectives into everything that is done in the workplace. This pressing need to focus on EDI is also being driven by the social revolutions in the external environment, such as Black Lives Matter, which are putting a spotlight on the need for change. Whether highlighted in the business or wider community, there is a pressing need to embrace EDI within organizations because many employees still feel like outsiders, especially when it comes to inclusion in organizational change. This seems a contradiction, because to succeed business transformations need diverse, multidisciplinary teams that combine the collective capabilities of different experiences and skills, including those of younger as well as older workers, yet in many organizations EDI is rarely on the agenda of a business transformation.

Putting EDI at the heart of people-centric change is vital since people will only engage with a business transformation if they feel included, represented, valued and supported. Furthermore, a transformation that includes EDI will benefit from varying skillsets, perspectives, ideas and creativity.

The aim of this chapter is to focus on the importance of the equality, diversity and inclusion of the people inside a business transformation and consider practices for giving voice to the often voiceless. The chapter begins by discussing how biases can influence EDI during and after a transformation and goes on to consider how to mitigate bias and to ensure that all key stakeholders are included in a transformation in a fair and just way. Equality, diversity and inclusion are then each considered separately and suggestions made for how to enact each of them as part of people-centric change. The importance of integrating EDI into an organizational culture is outlined in the business insight written by Douglas Flory, a consultant in organizational change, about the challenges that a global IT company had in embedding EDI into its culture.

Unconscious biases

Issues of EDI are interconnected with the biases each person has, whether they are unconscious or not. Unconscious bias is when an individual makes judgements or decisions based on their prior experience, personal thought patterns, assumptions or interpretations, and are not aware that they are doing so. Consequently, this can have a significant impact on attitudes and behaviours, especially towards other people, and can influence key decisions about a transformation. In hybrid teams, unconscious bias can be reflected in proximity bias, that is, the tendency to prefer employees we see in-person over those who are more frequently remote. To address such biases there are a number of practical actions that can be taken, including the following:

- Regularly show that you value effective collaboration and innovation over location. This signals to people that you appreciate their involvement with the transformation even those working flexibly.
- Establish a regular check-in schedule with team members working remotely. This will help build in personalized one-to-one face time with people you would not otherwise see so frequently. Frequent check-ins will also provide visibility on the progress of individuals who are working remotely on a business transformation as well as what support they may need.

- Be honest with yourself. By increasing our awareness of unconscious bias, we can identify ways to address it in ourselves. As an individual, it can be important to recognize and understand what biases you may have, and to have discussions with others to explore those biases and how they can be alleviated.
- Be open to conversations and challenges around decisions and potential biases. When making decisions, take time to ensure that you justify decisions by considering the views of others and the evidence available. In addition, making decisions together as a team can help mitigate the biases of one individual.
- Question cultural stereotypes that do not seem to be correct. It is important to be open to seeing what is new and unfamiliar and increasing your knowledge of other people's perspectives and diversity of experience and thinking.
- Point out bias when you see it. We can often detect unconscious bias more easily in others than in ourselves, so being prepared to raise awareness of it when you see and hear it can help to raise awareness of negative bias.

It can be challenging to recognize our own biases and to behave in a way that is fair and just at all times. Nevertheless, to act in a way that ensures EDI is woven into a business transformation, there is a need to mitigate bias and ensure that people are included in a fair and just way.

Fairness and justice

Business transformations generate a heightened sensitivity about how people feel they are being treated based on the assessments that they make about what they perceive as fair or unfair. People will judge a business transformation to be fair, or not, based on a range of criteria such as: Do we trust that it is not biased by the self-interest of the decision-makers? Is it the right change for everyone based on reliable data? Does it represent the needs, values and outlook of all those it will affect? Is it ethical in the sense that it is compatible with individual, team and organizational morals and ethical values?

How individuals respond to the answers to these questions will be grounded in their assessment of the different types of justice, which comprise:

distributive; procedural; interactional; interpersonal; and informational.[2] *Distributive justice* involves judgements about the degree to which the outcomes of a transformation are considered to be fair; for example, the fairness of which roles are made redundant during a restructuring programme. *Procedural justice* is based on perceptions about the way in which decisions about the transformation are taken, the openness of the transformation process and the extent to which people's views are considered and whether or not they are treated with respect. This, in turn, is linked to *interactional justice*, which is the assessment of the fairness of the treatment people receive when procedures for the transformation are being planned and implemented. It also includes an individual's feelings of fairness and justice based on their interactions with managers and the way that managers behave towards individuals. Finally, *informational justice* is influenced by the communication and information that individuals receive about the transformation and that impact on levels of trust and fairness.

Ensuring justice and fairness is important within the different modes of working. In a virtual working environment fairness and a just approach can be built in a number of ways. First, by establishing trust as a core principle of the transformation process. Second, by being intentional about the design of the communication processes, because when working in virtual teams it is easy for individuals to hide or to not be visible, and therefore online communication sessions need to be frequently scheduled and effectively facilitated to ensure that everyone is included and has the opportunity to raise their voice. This also necessitates reproducing the serendipitous conversations that happen in-person by picking up the phone or connecting online and asking, 'How are you?' Third, behavioural nudges can be used to support people to do the right thing. For example, team leaders could regularly ask their team members about their ideas, concerns, hopes and fears in relation to the transformation process. Finally, reviews of fairness and justice need to be built into transformation processes, for instance during wrap-up sessions of meetings the following questions could be asked, 'In what ways are we acting with integrity?' 'How are we continuing to build and maintain trust during the transformation?' 'What can we stop, start and do differently to ensure fairness across all employees and other key stakeholders?' These questions (and others) can help to take a temperature check of how well fairness and justice is being enacted and any pain points which need to be addressed. Ultimately, employees are more likely to appraise a business transformation more favourably and as less threatening when they believe that it is being handled fairly and in a just way.

Equality

There is a Japanese proverb that says, 'A single arrow is easily broken, but not ten in a bundle.' In other words, a harmonious team is a real strength, and the equality, diversity and inclusion of team members can ensure better decisions are made, which are then more likely to be actioned. An environment of equality for a business transformation is one in which all individuals are treated fairly and respectfully, have equal access to opportunities to engage with decisions and to resources, and can contribute fully to the success of the transformation. Without broad and equal representation in a transformation process, there is likely to be insensitivity and a lack of awareness as to how the transformation will impact on different people. The lack of consideration and focus on equality is evident in how Unilever, a multinational consumer goods company, initially advertised its Dove body wash. The advert showed a black woman who removed a brown shirt and turned into a white woman in a light-coloured shirt. Although it was not the intention of Unilever to propose that after using the body wash the preferred state equated to being white that was, nevertheless, the perceived impact of the advert. Mistakes such as this are more likely to happen when the right mix of people are not equally involved in sharing ideas and making decisions. This brings to mind the example of the all-women spacewalk that never happened because the spacesuits were not suitable for females to wear, despite it having been assumed by the men on the design team that the male spacesuits would be fine for women to wear. There are innumerable similar examples of inherent design bias in Caroline Criado-Perez's book *Invisible Women*.[3] There is, therefore, a need to ensure equality of representation when it comes to the design and development of business transformations.

Equality initiatives

For equality to contribute effectively to business transformations there has to be a combination of a sense of belonging, transparency and fluency, and equal representation in place. Each of these is briefly discussed below.

A SENSE OF BELONGING

When there is true equality with a business transformation, employees perceive that the organization cares about them and their views and contributions. Creating a sense of belonging within a business transformation can result in greater effort and higher employee engagement and performance.

To build a sense of belonging requires eliminating outsiderness by bringing key stakeholders on board and valuing what each person can bring to a business transformation by caring for each other, listening to one another and advocating for everyone's voice to be heard. It is, therefore, important to encourage a culture of actively promoting debate about transformations and ensuring that the tone of debate counteracts the feeling of exclusion that is often experienced by underrepresented groups. Furthermore, stakeholders' input should be incorporated, whenever relevant, into the design of a business transformation in order to show individuals that they have an equal and meaningful role to play in the process and that their voices are being listened to and are of value.

TRANSPARENCY AND FLUENCY

Enabling challenging discussions about a transformation requires transparency around the issues which need to be tackled and the business imperative for them. Moreover, it requires fluency and commonality of language that enables people to equally discuss and challenge ideas. Developing a common language should, therefore, be a key part of a transformation because this will help to establish a climate of equity and trust as well as create a basis for clarity, and the ability to understand each other.

EQUAL REPRESENTATION

Teams working on a transformation should be assembled with members who will provide new perspectives on issues, foster innovation and be able to solve problems more effectively. When putting together such teams there is a need to consider the inclusion of individuals with different backgrounds and perspectives to ensure an equal representation of members. By building teams that are equally representative, the transformation will benefit from a diversity in thought and experiences.

Diversity

A business transformation must be designed to accommodate the full diversity of people, from a variety of backgrounds, that are represented in the organization. This is important because diversity is a great asset to business transformations in that it brings rich, vibrant and diverse voices to the process. Moreover, diversity creates wider perspectives that are essential for business transformations, especially because it can be dangerous if the decision-making is always done by the same people, often at senior levels. To avoid this happening requires creating an environment of compassion and empowerment that is accepting of diverse perspectives and unlocks people's creativity along with their diverse views and experience. Bringing diversity into business transformations, therefore, requires engaging a variety of relevant and diverse people who can contribute to the process.

Without diversity in business transformations, there is a significant risk that important things will be missed. For example, when a manufacturing company was conducting a process mapping exercise for a new operations system, the team leading the transformation completely forgot that those operating the system would need a lunch break, until the obvious mistake was pointed out by an operator who was not part of the design team. When designing transformations, it is, therefore, important to ensure appropriate diversity in the programme team, in terms of role, level, background and experience, as well as gender, ethnicity and disability. Without this diversity, mistakes can be made or vital elements missed that may then have to be addressed after the implementation has started, which can be costly. Diversity can bring a wealth of ideas, better decision-making and improved problem-solving capability, and can avoid issues such as groupthink that occurs when a consensus is reached without a diversity of critical thinking or evaluation of the consequences or alternatives. Creating an environment where a diversity of people feel comfortable, valued and free to express themselves can, therefore, lead to an increased richness of thought, creativity and enhanced critical thinking and evaluation.

Diversity is critical to all dimensions of a business transformation, especially in different organizational cultures. Being attentive to diversity means taking an organization-wide perspective, maximizing stakeholder participation and being mindful of differences such as age, gender and ethnic origin in order to avoid exclusion. It is important to recognize that exclusion and marginalization can happen even when managers are well-intentioned and value the inclusion of stakeholders. Taking diversity seriously avoids business transformations being based on incomplete analyses and limited ideas and solutions due to a lack of diverse representation. Hence, there is a need to be mindful of, and to stay open to, diversity in cross-cultural contexts, which requires the constant inquiry of individuals into their own motives and being willing to ask themselves: Am I open to learning and open to diverse views and approaches? If an individual's response is 'no' to this question, then they will need to make a conscious assessment of what that means for their role in the transformation and whether or not they are the right person to be involved with it.

Diversity is of vital importance for increasing the relevance and effectiveness of a transformation. This means recognizing that all employees cannot be developed and managed during a transformation in the same way since individuals, especially those from different cultures, genders, generations, disabilities, or at different life stages, will have different needs, goals and motivations. Furthermore, there must be an awareness of the dynamics of diversity and the ability, especially among managers, to effectively respond to different people in different situations during a business transformation.

Unlocking the benefits of diversity

To unlock the benefits of diversity, the members of diverse teams need to build safe environments, centred around framing, enquiry and bridging boundaries:[4]

- ***Framing.*** Framing focuses on helping people to reach a common understanding of the transformation and the rationale for it. In the case of diverse teams, it is particularly important to clearly define the purpose of meetings about the transformation and the value of individual expertise. People generally think of meetings as forums to share updates and make decisions. However, it is important to be mindful that some individuals may be reticent about speaking up, particularly to offer new ideas, especially in an online environment. To encourage people to talk, it is, therefore, vital to emphasize how the goal of the meeting is to share information and ideas, then invite people with different perspectives to provide input. All ideas should be carefully listened to, captured and evaluated before the group makes a decision. This means seeing and stressing differences as a source of value, for example by saying, 'We are likely to have different perspectives going into this meeting that will help us get a thorough understanding of the issues.' So, rather than becoming frustrated when someone voices a different opinion or perspective from our own, being explicit in framing differences as a source of value can help.
- ***Enquiry.*** The best way to help people contribute their ideas is to ask them. When managers genuinely enquire about every team member's ideas and listen thoughtfully to what is shared within a psychologically safe environment (see Chapter 4), this can encourage individuals to share their views, ideas, hopes, concerns and even their fears without feeling that they will be castigated and/or ridiculed.

- ***Bridging boundaries.*** In order to build relationships and trust during a transformation process, individuals need to get to know each other, which means finding out about each other. One way to do this is to ask about the following:
  - *Hopes and goals:* What do individuals/teams want to achieve from the transformation?
  - *Resources and skills:* What would be the best way for individuals/teams to contribute to the transformation?
  - *Worries and concerns:* What are the barriers to individuals/teams effectively implementing the change/s?

Through such a purposeful, direct and intentional approach steps can be taken to ensure that different voices and experiences are raised, listened to and considered.

In sum, people-centric change is based on a diversity of people and their ideas, knowledge and experience. To take full advantage of the multiple perspectives that a diverse team/group of individuals can bring, it is critical to learn how to embrace difference and utilize each person's strengths. Collaborative techniques, such as design thinking (discussed in Chapter 10), can provide a method for empowering people to work together and leverage the diversity of talent and perspectives brought by each individual.

Inclusion

As people-centric change relies on collaboration (see Chapter 10), there is a need to create inclusive environments for transformations in order to unlock the power of diversity. An inclusive work environment is one in which all individuals are treated fairly and respectfully, have equal access to opportunities and resources, and can contribute fully to the success of a transformation. Julie Coffman, the first Chief Diversity Officer at Bain & Company, has highlighted how much employees, investors, and consumers all value inclusion.[5] Yet research by Gartner shows that only 31 per cent of employees agree that their leaders promote an inclusive environment.[6] The challenge to achieving an inclusive environment is that it can be diverse without being inclusive. For instance, an organization in which women and minorities account for 40 per cent of the leadership team might, on the surface, be considered relatively diverse but the culture of that organization could also be characterized by a traditional, narrow-minded, boys' club mentality that excludes or is condescending to anyone considered an outsider. Such a lack of inclusion will impact on collaboration and directly hurt a business transformation.

Inclusion is a crucial part of people-centric change because it focuses on the role that stakeholders play in the process of a transformation. It also extends the practice of interactivity by enabling stakeholders to provide their own ideas rather than simply dismissing the ideas that others present. In this way inclusivity enables stakeholders to serve as frontline content providers of transformational change, creating its content (what needs to change) themselves and being proactive players in the process (how it will change). This is in contrast to traditional change models where leadership monopolizes the creation of change, usually from the top down, and keeps a tight rein on its content and process. In addition, this is juxtaposed to managers who resist the inclusivity of employees in a transformation because they believe that the process will be more efficient and quicker if fewer people are involved in it. This may well at times be the case, especially when change is emergent and urgent, such as during the early days of the Covid-19 pandemic, but a lack of inclusivity in planned transformations, and especially in decision-making processes, can be perceived by employees as signs of management's lack of appreciation and trust of the value and diverse views of employees. To prevent this from happening, managers (and others) need to embrace the wide range of experience, perspectives and goals that people can bring to a business transformation. Moreover, it means establishing a heterogeneous structure, mixing full-time, part-time, shift, contract, gig and remote workers as part of the business transformation. This demands no longer referring to 'us and them', which is often used as a reference to management and employees but only fuels division and a lack of inclusivity, and instead ensuring that there is a broad inclusion of all relevant people.

Creating an inclusive environment

Creating an inclusive environment within a business transformation is crucial. Consider for a moment the frustration we have all experienced of speaking on an online call and realizing that we are on mute. Just imagine being on mute permanently and you get a sense of what it is like for groups that are systematically excluded from decisions about organizational changes. Inclusion of relevant stakeholders in decision-making is likely to lead to enhanced co-creation because it provides the opportunity for individuals to share their ideas and opinions as well as concerns. According to research, inclusion in decision-making is associated with decreased opposition to change.[7] An important element of people-centric change is, therefore, to involve all relevant stakeholders/groups at the start of a transformation effort, especially people who are able to influence and inform the content and process of it. To enable this to happen means speaking to all key stakeholders, recognizing the underrepresented groups in the transformation process and acknowledging everyone's contribution. This is an important foundation for ensuring people-centric change.

For inclusivity to be effective there needs to be trust. When there is a lack of trust stakeholders may be sceptical about being involved in decision-making. For instance, this can occur when managers are perceived as manipulating employees to gain the outcomes they want or when managers seek open participation but circumvent this by selecting the employees who will participate to ensure managers get the outcome they want. Providing individuals with opportunities for inclusion is less likely to be perceived as manipulative if managers are considered to be authentic because this will generate positive perceptions of their true intentions for soliciting thoughts, information and concerns, and also help to build trust.

Inclusive techniques

To create an environment of inclusivity involves taking tactical steps that can help to drive inclusion and improve the overall engagement with a transformation. This can be done by: establishing the right level of ownership for the transformation, in other words ownership by stakeholders that have the greatest ability to influence the change and who will be impacted by it; spending time understanding the needs of stakeholders, starting with the key internal stakeholders; and putting initiatives in place to engage stakeholders in the transformation process deliberations, recognizing that the more that individuals are involved in the design of the process, the greater the chance that the transformation will have a positive and sustainable impact.

To help implement inclusivity in the decision-making process of a business transformation a suggested framework is as follows. First, consideration needs to be given as to how inclusivity in the transformation is to be implemented, whether it will be informal or formal, whether employees will have a direct say, or be indirect as in having voting rights. This means being mindful that some people will have a stronger desire for being included than others, although all key stakeholders should have the opportunity to be involved. Second, there has to be clarity on what issues employees can be involved in. For instance, will it be job design and working conditions or strategic issues? Employees also need to be clear on what level of involvement they will have. For instance, will they be able to express opinions and/or make decisions? In addition, they will need to know what decisions have already been made. Third, the process of decision-making needs to be clear so people know what to expect. For example, will decisions be made openly in teams, or in a confidential ballot? If their views are not taken on board then individuals will also need to be given a clear rationale as to why they have been rejected and feedback provided, such as, 'We have heard your ideas but due to budget constraints we cannot currently consider actioning them.' Through participating in decisions about business transformations, individuals and teams have the opportunity to question existing work practices and craft new approaches, and in so doing change the way that their work is done. Inclusion in decision-making and problem-solving will, therefore, increase individuals' perceived ability to influence business transformations as well as perceptions of fairness and justice.

Inclusion can be further enhanced when employees have the power to be innovative and implement ideas. For example, when a group of data scientists within the AI unit of Spanish multinational financial services company BBVA AI Factory raised concerns about finding time to explore opportunities outside assigned projects, the company launched an organization-wide programme allowing teams of three to four employees to devote several months to problem-solving projects beyond their job scope. As a result, teams have developed a number of new initiatives, including a data labelling tool that has cut time devoted to this task by 50 per cent.[8] Likewise, the crowdsourcing fintech company Dealmaker (based in Toronto, Canada) fosters internal inclusion and innovation through what the company co-founder and CEO Rebecca Kacaba calls 'adaptability quotient' – that is, the ability to determine what is relevant, deflect obsolete knowledge, overcome challenges and adjust to change. Companies also use approaches, such as boot camps and hackathons, to include stakeholders in idea generation.

In sum, to be effective inclusivity has to be an ongoing practice rather than a one-time event or a one-off process. It needs to be established as part of people-centric change where stakeholders are seen as central to a transformation and the focus is upon capturing the ideas of diverse stakeholders and securing their commitment. When done correctly, inclusivity goes far beyond the strategies for consultation and participation that most organizations embrace and instead re-imagines a business transformation so that it is collaborative and co-created (see Chapter 10). This lets people flourish within a transformation without barriers or biases and can make them feel respected and treated with dignity.

Inclusive leadership

Merely bringing together a mix of people does not guarantee success with a transformation. What is also needed is inclusive leadership, that is, leadership which ensures that all team members and other key stakeholders/groups feel that they are being treated respectfully and fairly, that they are valued, have a sense of belonging, and feel confident and inspired to contribute and engage with the transformation. According to research, teams with inclusive leaders are 17 per cent more likely to report that they are high performing, 20 per cent more likely to say that they make high-quality decisions and 29 per cent more likely to report behaving collaboratively.[9] To develop a more inclusive leadership approach requires a shift in behaviours to the following:

- showing visible commitment by articulating authentic commitment to diversity, challenging the status quo, holding others accountable and making diversity and inclusion a priority
- being humble and modest about capabilities, admitting mistakes and failures and creating space for others to contribute
- developing an awareness of personal biases and blind spots and working hard to overcome them
- listening to challenging and alternative views that are different from one's own
- being curious about others and being willing to listen to them without judgement but instead with empathy, in order to understand them
- learning about cultural differences and being attentive to different cultures and cultural nuances and adapting as required
- building effective collaboration by empowering others and creating space for, and paying attention to, diverse thinking (see Chapter 10 on collaboration)
- acknowledging team members as individuals by addressing them by name, and knowing the work that they do and how they are contributing to the business transformation

By demonstrating these behaviours, inclusive leaders ensure that representation and transparency are embedded throughout their teams, and that EDI and people-centric change are closely interwoven strands. Doing this in a purposeful way involves asking the following questions:

- How can we create the right atmosphere and spaces for EDI to flourish in business transformations so that team members are comfortable to challenge norms and preconceptions?
- How are we solving existing business problems with new solutions rather than identifying problems to fit with preconceived solutions?
- How are we really tackling the root cause and exploring dissenting opinions that may point us to more fundamental problems rather than quick-fix solutions?
- How can we ensure that EDI in teams is agile by continuously evolving to reflect stakeholders needs?

It takes energy and deliberate effort to create an environment of equality, diversity and inclusion, which is what Douglas Flory found when he was asked to help a global IT company integrate EDI into its culture. Douglas describes the challenges he faced in doing this and how he overcame them in the following business insight.

CASE STUDY

Business Insight: Change management + EDI = results that matter

How does a global IT company that specializes in VoIP, remote support, and videoconferencing integrate ethics, diversity and inclusivity into its culture? That was the question I was asked to address while working as the leader of a change management team in a USA based global technology company. To address this challenge, I partnered with a newly hired equality, diversity and inclusion (EDI) specialist, whom I will refer to as Terry. Once onboarded, Terry and I started a dialogue that grew over time to more of a close adviser. Our work together during the global pandemic brought change management and EDI together for positive results. This experience for me was eye-opening because I had never considered how these two functions could support one another.

When Terry joined the company, I reached out to welcome her and to learn more about the EDI programme. We instantly connected and aspired to reconnect in the near future. Terry advanced through the organization as she met with the people, business functions, leaders and regional offices. With the newly informed data and learnings, Terry was beginning to notice the need for her role. Such a polarizing topic was also heightened due to the social movements, personal impacts and worldwide events that catalysed civil unrest and the unnecessary deaths of citizens. We met regularly to support one another's efforts. During one of our dialogues, Terry began to share some of the concerns about an EDI programme she had launched in the company. For example:

> 'Generally, I think this is a good idea and support the cause, but do we really need an entire programme?'
>
> 'Our office and region are very homogeneous, so there really is nothing that we can do differently.'
>
> 'We've noticed that working with a certain office, there are a lot of stereotypes about us.'
>
> 'I feel like I am struggling each and every day to just make it through. As I see these events occurring in the news, I cannot help but feel sad and isolated. Yet, my manager and team are not talking about these racial acts and the resulting public reaction. I feel disconnected.'
>
> 'Our employee resource group is experiencing lower attendance at events and engagement via our communications. We're not even sure how many of our colleagues are in the company anymore.'

As our conversations continued, I began to learn more about the realities of our company's EDI challenges. Combining these types of challenges with the existing representation of employee resource groups was even more complex, yet we noticed that it was consistent across a majority of them. Our concern was: How to solve this many challenges? Which of them was a pattern and which were just random occurrences? What Terry was trying to solve did not have any formulas or approaches. After all, so much of this was new to all of us. As a change leader, I continued to think about our challenges and chats. It dawned on me that change management had some possible applications that could help, but initially I did not consider the crossover capability. To address the challenges, we started with a few fundamental pieces to see if they could make an impact:

- *Change education.* Education needed to occur for EDI to become a key competency in the company. Terry and the management team wanted to make this happen with a single event. However, as a change practitioner, I know behaviours could not just be changed with one event, and as a process occurs over time, people will be at different stages of change along the way. This is especially true when dealing with behavioural changes. After sharing this with Terry and the management team I proposed that we needed to consider how people transition through change, which might mean that Group A would be slower to adapt than Group B, C, D... in between current state to future state.

- *Data drives results.* Although Terry was hearing the 'voice of the employee', she also needed to capture the feedback from them in qualitative and quantitative measures. To help with this we created a digital survey. After conversations with stakeholders and employees, Terry distributed a series of questions for them to provide anonymized feedback. Using a 5-point Likert scale, most of the questions were built around a user-friendly approach to capturing their response via answers like:
    - strongly disagree
    - disagree
    - neither disagree nor agree
    - agree
    - strongly agree

  The questions also allowed participants to provide additional information to support their responses. The results meant that Terry had data that supported what she had heard in the conversations, which provided more in-depth empirical evidence of what people were thinking and feeling.

- *Sponsorship.* Since Terry's agenda was new, there was not an existing executive at the right level of the company to help champion the role and efforts. I therefore proposed that she had a sponsor to support her agenda, and to be accountable for the realization of the benefits of a change and to help align stakeholders to support and own a change. Once the sponsor was identified, this helped to elevate the conversation across the organization and made it OK to talk about previously taboo topics such as race, diversity and wellbeing.

- *Stakeholder identification and engagement strategy.* There were plenty of supporters and interested stakeholders in the EDI project, but there were also many who raised questions, doubts and even resistance/opposition. To create a process of addressing stakeholders' opposition to change, I proposed the need for stakeholder identification and mapping, and a stakeholder engagement strategy. This involved us:
    - identifying stakeholders across the organization
    - conducting a stakeholder analysis

- o determining the appropriate audiences to focus on for adoption
- o creating strategies for engaging target audiences with the right content

  We plotted stakeholders on a grid against their importance and commitment. Once the mapping exercise was complete, we targeted all of the stakeholders to varying degrees, but focused especially on the undecided ones in order to influence their decision and commitment.

- *Communication.* Communication strategy and channels were invaluable to help create conversations, but also to share multi-messaging approaches across the company. The communications plan helped to define our internal and external audiences, and the information and feedback requirements of those leading and affected by the change. It helped us address such questions as: When and where should Terry's blogs, posts, and updates occur? We found that there was great interest and reactions when we placed the messaging where the employees all had access to an existing channel and were actively engaged.

The key lessons I learned from this transformation initiative were:

- Change management is a cross-functional solution that can be applied across multiple roles and agendas.
- Change management can help EDI to be implemented across an organization and ensure that benefits are realized.

The application of the Association of Change Management Professionals framework was helpful. This includes: a definition of practices, processes, tasks and activities for change management without tools or templates; guidance for organizational change management, for any type of change; and generally accepted practices and processes used by practitioners across industries, organizations and roles. As a framework, the standard allowed us to build a working model orchestrated around managing change. It also allowed us to determine the appropriate change levers needed to address this new area of EDI. It was not about ticking boxes in a linear approach, but applying the framework to change in smaller, necessary components. Ultimately, this agility allowed us to navigate ambiguity and create a repeatable, scalable process.

My time working on this transformation project was one where I grew from learning, and discovered a passion for employee resource groups, which was followed up with my involvement with the implementation of the Association of Change Management Professionals' EDI statement.

Questions

1. How was EDI integrated within the culture of the company?
2. What challenges are faced when attempting to ensure a culture of equality, diversity and inclusion? How might these be addressed?
3. How might you implement EDI within a transformation you are engaged with, or one that you are familiar with?

SUMMARY

Equality, diversity and inclusion (EDI) are a key part of people-centric change and will make business transformations stronger and more agile. However, EDI is often ignored during a transformation due to unconscious bias which can occur when judgements and/or decisions are made on the basis of prior experiences, personal deep-seated thought patterns, assumptions and/or interpretations. This can have a significant impact on attitudes and behaviours, especially towards other people, and can influence key decisions about a transformation. While in hybrid teams unconscious bias can be reflected in proximity bias – the tendency to prefer employees we see in-person over those who are working remotely. There is, therefore, a need to be mindful of biases, unconscious or not, to ensure that EDI is centre stage during a transformation journey.

Unlocking the full value of diversity requires creating and fostering an environment of inclusivity and equality during a business transformation. That is an environment in which everyone feels they belong, are treated with dignity and encouraged to fully participate. To do this successfully demands EDI strategies that focus both inside and outside an organization's four walls and are based on an inclusive culture as well as strong external engagement in the marketplace and in the community. This means building EDI concepts and practices into business transformations, embedding EDI into transformation frameworks and making EDI part of managers' roles and responsibilities. Fundamentally, EDI can contribute substantially to transformation efforts and especially people-centric change by encouraging a diversity of opinion and views within an inclusive and equal environment.

PRACTICAL IMPLICATIONS

There are several practical implications which can be drawn from this chapter:

- *Value diverse perspectives.*
  This means prioritizing not only the diversity of those involved in the transformation in terms of gender and ethnicity, but also in terms of viewpoints, backgrounds and skill sets. The more diverse and inclusive those involved in a transformation are, the more adaptable and agile the transformation process will be. And remember to check your own unconscious bias.
- *Create formal and informal opportunities for idea generation.*
  Practices to create inclusivity in problem-solving and idea generation can be informal or formal. The former can occur face-to-face, such as coffee conversations where people gather round the coffee machine, or online (preferably with a cup of tea or coffee), and raise issues, concerns and ideas. As an idea comes up that may, in turn, spark other ideas, so in this informal way ideas can be generated and developed and perspectives encouraged that challenge the status quo.
- *Use inclusive language and images.*
  Using inclusive language and imagery ensures team members feel recognized as individuals and can help to build a more respectful connection. For example, some inclusive language practices that can be incorporated into a business transformation are saying 'all of you' instead of 'you guys' when addressing a group of employees and using 'people first' terms like 'people with disabilities' rather than 'the handicapped or disabled'. Instead of communicating the message 'we value your differences', focus instead on 'we value your strengths'. In addition to inclusive language, inclusive imagery can help to build stronger connections with the business transformation, for instance by highlighting the diverse range of team members who have achieved successful transformations in the past.
- *Incorporate inclusion nudges in meetings.*
  Nudges are soft, non-intrusive mental pushes that result in objective decisions and affect predictable behaviours to make them more inclusive. Some nudges that can be incorporated into meetings online and in-person in order to include and engage diverse teams comprise:
  - Broadening remote team members access and presence in meetings by making sure that they introduce themselves, allowing them time to speak, and pointing out any features for raising hands or chat boards for everyone to be aware of.

- Emphasizing individual employee contributions to the transformation and the value that they add. One way you can do this is by publicly recognizing an employee who practises inclusive behaviours and listens actively to others' points of view.

- *Deliberately seek out difference.*
  Give diverse groups of stakeholders the opportunity to speak up, invite them to discussions about what needs to change or to identify what needs to be done differently and how it can be done. Furthermore, seek out opportunities to engage cross-functional or multi-disciplinary teams to leverage diverse strengths. This is also important in hybrid and remote environments, where there are fewer opportunities for spontaneous in-person interactions. This means being more intentional in ensuring all appropriate and relevant stakeholders are involved with a business transformation.
- *Be more deliberate about creating inclusion in meetings.*
  Create rituals that encourage inclusion. For example, start meetings by checking in with team members. Ask how they are feeling. Bring people into the meeting by signalling in advance, for instance, 'Sam – next I am going to ask you'. Be intentional with positive feedback, for instance, 'Sam – that is an excellent suggestion which helps to address the issue we are currently discussing'.

Notes

1 J F Higgins (2022) *Bully Market: My story of money and misogyny at Goldman Sachs*, Simon & Schuster, New York

2 M Saunders, P Lewis and A Thornhill (2003) *Research Methods for Business Students*, Prentice Hall and *Financial Times*, Essex

3 C Criado-Perez (2019) *Invisible Women: Exposing data bias in a world designed for men*, Chatto & Windus, London

4 H Bresman and A C Edmondson. Exploring the relationship between team diversity, psychological safety and team performance: Evidence from pharmaceutical drug development (No. 22-055), Harvard Business School Working Paper, 2022. www.hbs.edu/faculty/Pages/item.aspx?num=61993 (archived at https://perma.cc/L5W3-8E29)

5 J Coffman. Making progress on DEI: Why inclusion and metrics matter most, Bain & Company, 14 January 2022. www.bain.com/insights/making-progress-on-dei-why-inclusion-and-metrics-matter-most (archived at https://perma.cc/4A3T-Q6QU)

6 Gartner. *Building Inclusive Leadership to Enable Future Success*, Gartner, 2020. emtemp.gcom.cloud/ngw/globalassets/en/human-resources/documents/trends/building-inclusive-leadership.pdf (archived at https://perma.cc/98ZK-R2MU)

7 R Lines. Influence of participation in strategic change: Resistance, organizational commitment and change goal achievement, *Journal of Change Management*, 2004, 4 (3), 193–215. www.tandfonline.com/doi/abs/10.1080/1469701042000221696 (archived at https://perma.cc/93CC-JQR3)

8 G Buono. Best workplaces for innovators 2022: 11 small company standouts, Fast Company, 2 August 2022. www.fastcompany.com/90769088/best-workplaces-for-innovators-2022-11-small-company-standouts (archived at https://perma.cc/Z2JF-RY2J)

9 J Bourke and A Espedido. Why inclusive leaders are good for organizations, and how to become one, *Harvard Business Review*, 2019, 29 (03). hbr.org/2019/03/why-inclusive-leaders-are-good-for-organizations-and-how-to-become-one (archived at https://perma.cc/4UPF-EFN7)

10

Fostering collaboration

Introduction

If you walk through an old forest, the diversity of trees that you see will be quite incredible. Douglas fir, pine, silver birch, oak and so on will be soaring into the sky, each individually competing with the others for sunlight and space. Or are they? Research suggests that beneath the surface of the soil the trees are actually collaborating and cooperating rather than competing with each other, with different species acting as a team to maximize the growth of the entire forest.[1] Scientists have discovered that trees and fungi form underground partnerships called mycorrhizae that connect the roots of diverse types of trees to one another to help share carbon, water and nutrients such as phosphorous and nitrogen. This helps to explain why when cleared forests are replanted with a single species such as oak trees, and where there is no competition for sunlight and space from other species, they do less well than when the same species is grown with other types of trees. The reason for this is that collaboration amongst diverse species fosters sustainable growth. Similarly, during business transformations a group of stakeholders only becomes truly engaged with the change when they are connected and collaborating with each other just like an old forest, and not simply working on their own like the replanted oak trees. This may also be why top-down mandates for business transformations often struggle, especially when there are stakeholders who want and expect to be active participants in any change that affects them. These individuals, who are the closest to the day-to-day operations and to customers, often know what needs fixing and how to change it and will also be able to come up with insights and opportunities that senior leadership might never have thought of. Building collaboration is a key element of people-centric change both onsite and offsite with people who are working virtually across geographical boundaries because this enables team members, and other stakeholders, to engage in generating ideas about change and taking them forward in an integrated and coordinated way.

The aim of this chapter is to explore how collaboration can be created among individuals and teams, including those working in a hybrid and/or remote way. The chapter begins by defining what collaboration is and why it is important within a business transformation. Consideration is then given as to how to establish a collaborative environment for business transformations when people no longer sit in the same space or are dispersed across many offices or working from home. The chapter introduces collaborative practices and principles as a means of engaging stakeholders and helping to foster the creation of innovative ideas that are beneficial for individuals, groups/teams and the organization as a whole. Techniques for collaboration are discussed, such as design thinking. The chapter emphasizes the importance of teaming for collaboration and the emergence of so-called superteams, which are combinations of people and technology using their complementary capabilities to pursue business transformations at a speed and scale not otherwise possible. The importance of collaboration as a key element of people-centric change is emphasized throughout and illustrated using the case of Lamu Island, Kenya, which spotlights that sustainable change is inclusive, collaborative and strengthens partnerships across communities, industries and national borders. The significance of collaboration is further depicted in the business insight written by David Maybin in which he describes his experience as a Senior Change Lead in implementing a new CRM system within a large Australian government department.

The importance of collaboration

In organizations, information and decision-making are often distributed among many people, making it exceedingly difficult to map a way forward. Even identifying and creating a shared understanding of problems can be arduous when a myriad of stakeholders have differing perspectives and motivations. To address this, there is a need to convene stakeholders to build common understanding and collective engagement and action. Tata, a global enterprise headquartered in India, has done this through the creation of a network or a 'wise crowd' that enables employees across the globe to have their voices heard through exchanging solutions to problems and sharing their innovative ideas. Moreover, Tata fosters collaboration by discouraging micromanagement, so although leaders are encouraged to define the end results and the boundaries for accountability and responsibility for a transformation, autonomy is created within these boundaries for people to work on solutions to implement them. The power of such collaboration is the ability to bring together stakeholders to identify interventions and to ensure that business transformations are successfully embedded by frontline staff.[2]

Collaboration is vital for ensuring effective transformations, especially as there is rarely just one change initiative happening in an organization. Instead there are often multiple changes occurring simultaneously across an organization. Research has shown that employees experience more efficacious implementation of change when they participate in collaborative implementation activities, as was found during a transformation to improve working processes within a healthcare organization where team activities provided hands-on opportunities for frontline staff and managers to explore how to improve work in their units.[3] For example, staff used a variety of techniques such as a mock-up activity and workflow maps to develop a new, more relevant shift report. They appreciated the opportunity to apply their expertise and to give feedback that was meaningfully incorporated into the design and implementation of improvements. The study found that collaborative activities encourage interactions between staff and managers, which combine into team dynamics that help to facilitate change. Collaboration can, therefore, increase engagement with change and commitment to implementing it successfully.

Collaborative practice

People-centric change involves providing, through collaborative practice, the opportunity for individuals and teams to be active rather than passive agents in a business transformation. Collaborative practice is a means of engaging stakeholders and of fostering the creation of innovative ideas in a way that is beneficial for individuals, groups/teams and the organization as a whole. This is important, because how people collaborate together is constantly changing due to businesses evolving, technology advancing and employees embracing different kinds of working arrangements and having different expectations of work and their employers.

Organizations are constantly searching for ways to improve how they encourage collaborative practice. This was the challenge faced by a global software company when it needed a better process for making decisions. In response to this issue, the company developed a decision framework, that provides guidelines for identifying who should be included when making decisions and how to include them. Rather than giving individuals more say based on rank and tenure, the framework proposes taking into account factors such as expertise, impact and customer-centricity, thus ensuring a level of transparency around how decisions are made and who is involved. As a result of this, no one is surprised by a decision, and everybody trusts it is the best option, even if it is not always liked. For the software company, decision-making using the framework works because it is a meritocracy, not a democracy, and the best ideas are taken forward no matter where they come from. This approach might slightly slow down decision-making, but the benefit is that the more time that is spent making better decisions, the greater the time savings during the implementation of the ideas.

Self-organized grassroots collaboration

Collaboration can be accelerated by groups coming together voluntarily themselves. This is what happened at IBM when a group of employees emerged, that had transitioned to working from home during the pandemic, and decided to establish guiding principles to help make work and life easier for themselves and their colleagues.[4] To start with, the group asked colleagues across the company for their views, then they collaborated with business and HR leaders to evolve their efforts into an organization-wide pledge. Within a few days, thousands of employees posted their individual pledges onto an internal social media channel and the then CEO Arvind Krishna shared his publicly on LinkedIn. This grassroots effort did more to accelerate the company's transition to productive remote work, and on a faster timeline, than any organization-led initiative could have done. Similarly, many race-based groups self-organized following George Floyd's murder in Minneapolis in 2020 to launch grassroots efforts, from hosting difficult conversations to lobbying for Juneteenth to be formally recognized with a day off to complement top-down diversity and inclusion activities. A self-organized collaborative process was also how a Kenyan organization, called Save Lamu, emerged when the local community were faced with the need to address external threats to their way of living (see the following section).

Case of Lamu Island

The story of Save Lamu[5] provides an example of two contrasting approaches to collaboration. It focuses on a transformation that was driven by the Kenyan government's decision to establish East and Central Africa's first coal-fired power plant, provided by the AMU power company on Lamu, a tranquil island off the north-east coast of Kenya that has an active fishing community and a thriving marine ecosystem that includes ancient mangroves. The decision by the government was a surprise to the local population, since Kenya has an abundant renewable energy resource and is Africa's leading producer of geothermal energy. To fuel its ambitions of growth, the government faced the dilemma of choosing between short-term exploitation of fossil fuels and the more sustainable approach of long-term investment in renewable energy. Furthermore, the country was facing a steep increase in public debt, with China its biggest foreign creditor accounting for a third of Kenya's external debt service costs. So cheap energy from coal would mean faster loan repayments for faster project completion, lower operating costs and higher profit margins. The reason why the government selected Lamu for a coal power plant, despite the country's apparent wealth in renewable resources, was the island's infrastructure development. The government's push for a coal power plant on the island was opposed by Save Lamu, a community organization that spearheaded a national campaign dubbed #Decoalonize Kenya.

When the coal plant was first proposed, the Save Lamu campaign team's knowledge about the impact and benefits of coal was limited. So, the first step the team took was to collaborate with experts such as the Natural Justice and The East African Institute for Constitutional Reform in order to enhance their expertise and to identify the key gaps in the government's environmental impact assessment. The campaign team also developed significant collaboration with the local community, who were the campaign's key stakeholders, by encouraging all those who supported the campaign to join and contribute in any way they chose. Furthermore, the team ensured that they had a relevant strategy that determined their actions and which they regularly reviewed with the involvement of the community. This approach was in sharp contrast to that of the government and the AMU Power Company, who proposed the change on behalf of the community without even consulting with the locals. In an attempt to take the project forward, the government sought to ignore and even stop the opposition to the changes and engaged only with individuals and organizations who supported the coal plant. AMU Power went as far as proposing that the Save Lamu campaign should not be recognized as a legitimate entity.

The campaign team appreciated that ignoring or striving to quiet the opposition would not dispel it but only make it louder, so they engaged with the community leaders who supported the coal plant. The team then leveraged their network of partners and supporters to send the community leaders to India and South Africa to see the effects there of supposedly clean coal plants. These field trips had a significant impact and not only changed the views of the local supporters of the coal plant but also resulted in the launch of a social media campaign in support of the Save Lamu campaign which included a video and testimonial evidence from those who had been on the field trips.

A legal battle resulted in a victory for the Save Lamu supporters, when the Environmental Tribunal of Kenya upheld a ruling revoking the AMU Power Company's licence to construct the coal plant. This remarkable story contains important lessons about working with stakeholders and cultivating collaboration and connections. On the one hand, the government's approach, potentially with good intentions and with a focus on Kenya's National Strategy, was single-minded and failed to engage those with a stake in Lamu's future and when they encountered resistance or new information, their response was to ignore it. On the other hand, the Save Lamu project team engaged and collaborated with a broad and inclusive group of people, including both the supporters and opponents of the coal plant, and continually adapted their campaign as concerns and new information emerged. This demonstrates that transformations need to be inclusive, collaborative and utilize partnerships across the organization and wider community when necessary.

Synchronous and asynchronous collaboration

Before the Covid-19 pandemic the majority of change was done in a synchronized way where people working on a business transformation tended to work the same hours and in the same place as their colleagues, often punctuated by in-person meetings. Communications were scheduled and real-time interactions took place by phone, video or in-person. Being synchronized and working at the same time and in the same place as others has real benefits. For instance, when people are connected to their colleagues this can boost productivity and means that team members or the whole team can speak together at certain times. However, it can also result in constant communications and interruptions that can disrupt focus on work.

The increase in more flexible modes of working has resulted in an increase in more remote and asynchronous working with employees working offsite and choosing their own hours, as opposed to having to work the same schedule as others in their team. For some this can boost their focus and concentration. However, it can also result in collaboration suffering because there can be little time for individuals to work with each other and in tandem naturally, without prior agreement. The risk is that fault lines can easily emerge between those who work together in-person and those who work remotely because of the extra effort required to collaborate with team members who are working remotely. This may mean that they are left out of conversations and decisions are made by those who are working together onsite. Those working remotely may also miss out on the casual and spontaneous rich interactions that happen in-person.[6]

To address such challenges companies have been finding innovative solutions to encourage collaboration across different modes of working. For example, Fujitsu, a Japanese multinational information and communications technology equipment and services corporation, has committed to creating an ecosystem of spaces that together make up what it calls the borderless office. These spaces take several forms: hubs that maximize cooperation; satellites which facilitate coordination; and shared offices which enable focus.[7] The hubs are located in major cities and designed with cross-functional cooperation and serendipitous encounters in mind. They are comfortable and welcoming open plan spaces, equipped with the advanced technologies necessary for brainstorming, team building and the co-creation of changes such as new products. When Fujitsu employees want to work creatively with customers or partners, they invite them to a hub.[8] The company's satellites are spaces designed to facilitate collaboration within and between teams that are working on shared projects. They contain meeting spaces where teams can come together, both in-person and virtually, supported by secure networks and advanced videoconferencing facilities. These satellites provide opportunities for collaboration, especially face-to-face, and also address some of the isolation and loneliness that employees may suffer when working from home. Shared offices which make up most of Fujitsu's ecosystem of spaces, are located all over Japan, often near or in urban or suburban train stations and can be used as short stopovers when people are travelling to visit customers, or as alternatives to working at home. They are designed to function as quiet spaces that employees can easily get to, thus reducing commuting time. The shared offices are equipped with desks and internet connections that allow employees to work independently and undisturbed or to attend online meetings. Such innovative and flexible workplaces enable collaboration on transformations when people no longer sit in the same space or in an office, or are dispersed across many offices, or working from home.

The benefit of more flexible approaches to working is that collaboration has gone omnichannel, which means it is now place agnostic. In other words people can be together face-to-face in-person – in a shared office, a hub or a coffee shop – or on a virtual platform such as Microsoft Teams or Zoom. The challenge in virtual teams is to create an environment for collaboration online, especially as disparate locations and time zones can make it difficult for team members to interact with one another at the same time. To address this, a shared style of leadership among members in a virtual team can be effective in encouraging collaboration. According to research, team members who are handed the baton of shared leadership show an increase in collaborative decision-making, trust and knowledge sharing.[9] Furthermore, shared leadership gives individual team members the autonomy and authority to deal with issues as and when they develop, instead of relying on one team leader to collate and interpret information from multiple sources and make decisions. This is important in business transformations since faster and situation-appropriate responses are critical, especially in highly volatile and uncertain environments.

To encourage collaboration in hybrid and remote workplaces also requires consideration of how change is done. For instance, a manager must not only consider the needs and preferences of individuals and teams but also coordinate the work they are doing on transformations with other stakeholders and functions. This kind of coordination and collaboration was easier when team members all worked in the same place at the same time, but it has become more complex with the advent of more flexible modes of working. Ways that this can be done in practice include boosting the use of technology to coordinate activities such as with state-of-the-art video and digital tools. For example, managers at Fujitsu use a range of digital tools to categorize and visualize the types of work their teams are performing as they experiment with new flexible working arrangements. This has enabled Fujitsu to improve their assessment of workloads, analyse remote working conditions and confirm work projections.

There is, however, a need for a word of caution here because, despite the increase in digital tools and online collaborative platforms, simply buying the technology is not sufficient. As studies of the adoption of technology indicate, whilst technological innovation is vital, to make a difference it has to be accompanied by innovation in organizational and managerial practices and processes.[10] This requires a flexible approach to working practices and processes. For example, being together in-person may be preferable when a transformation requires complex problem-solving or there is a need for tough conversations or resolving difficult issues. People may also prefer to be together in-person when they want to tap into the energy of being around other people, whereas they may want to stay at home for more routine work or tasks that don't require a lot of different perspectives. The combination of technological innovation and revised working practices are, therefore, required to ensure effective collaboration.

In order for spontaneous remote collaboration to happen, some degree of shared work time needs to occur between employees, even if they are in different time zones. However, that does not mean that employees in Asia should be forced to work at 3 am to be aligned with their American colleagues since there can be severe impacts on wellbeing when employees are forced to work unreasonable hours and for longer so instead, where feasible, employees should be encouraged to work reasonable overlapping hours. Such synchronicity with teammates can increase collaboration through means such as improved information sharing and idea generation. As a result, to maximize the balance of work quality and quantity, allowing for a combination of both synchronous and asynchronous work is vital. Beyond just aligning employee work hours, finding other ways to improve collaboration is also important. For instance, frequent video meetings using platforms such as Zoom can be beneficial. However, there is a need to be mindful of 'Zoom fatigue', which has led some companies to allow employees to turn off their cameras to help to reduce fatigue.

Collaboration remotely can be challenging, and some companies have decided to resort to more in-person working to encourage more collaboration. For instance, Apple has decided to adopt a hybrid work model because it believes that in-person collaboration is essential to its culture and its future. This is based on the view that the products and the launch execution of the company are built upon the work that employees do when they are all together in-person. However, this is not the view of many of the employees who point out that working from home delivers five key benefits: diversity and inclusion in retention and hiring; tearing down previously existing communication barriers; better work–life balance; better integration of existing remote/location-flexible workers; and reduced spread of pathogens. Many employees, therefore, feel that they have succeeded not despite working from home, but because of being able to work outside the office. Nevertheless, the CEO of Apple, Tim Cook, and other senior executives maintain that remote work is no substitute for face-to-face meetings.[11] So although some of the challenges of working remotely are being addressed, it would appear that there are still concerns from some leaders and managers about the impact of remote working on collaboration and connectivity.

Connectivity

The challenges of collaboration during a business transformation are not limited to problems with technological communication and the logistical coordination of hybrid and remote working but also to how people connect. Connections are important for triggering a sense of collaboration but the advent of remote working has weakened some connections. For example, connection points through email, team meetings or any other type of communication inside a team are called strong ties. In contrast, weak ties are when people meet unexpectedly at the coffee machine, in the lift, walking into the workplace or on the way to the car park or train station. It is these serendipitous connections that are becoming less frequent in hybrid and remote working environments, which means individuals have to work harder at generating them. One way to do this is to create nudges to help with weak tie connections online. Microsoft, for instance, has developed a tool called Microsoft Viva which tells you everything about an individual from their LinkedIn profile, which is their outside profile, to what they are working on including documents, presentations and projects as well as the expertise they have. Satya Nadella, the CEO of Microsoft, describes this tool as a new type of serendipitous discovery and says that 'It's not just I didn't run into them in the elevator this time and struck up a conversation. But I met them in an online meeting where they commented in a chat'.[12] Although there have been concerns that employees are missing out on the casual and spontaneous rich interactions that happen in-person, the approach used by Microsoft helps to compensate for the loss of those interactions by enabling impromptu meetings to happen remotely through creating direct connections among people across the organization. This shortens the time it takes to get things done and helps to build instant connections that allow employees to share important information, find answers quickly, and get help and advice from others.

Communities of interest

Since people who feel connected are more likely to be engaged in collaboration, there is a need to create opportunities in-person and online for people to connect formally and informally through networks. Many companies already have in place networks such as intranets – virtual communities where people can swap ideas and share experiences online, or they have built face-to-face communities where people can engage in purposeful ways. These communities of interest provide an outlet for colleagues to share and see all the information related to a transformation, including progress updates and informal commentary. They can also create an important esprit de corps. Specific tools can be used to build connectivity and collaboration with communities of interest such as shared dashboards, 'gamification' to bolster competition, and online forums where people can speak to one another, and discuss issues. For example, Tata Consultancy Services has developed its own social network called Knowe, a slang term related to the interpretation of DNA, that connects workers around the world in an online forum similar to Meta. Knowe is used by staff to collaborate, exchange information and ideas, upload blog posts and create communities with colleagues who share similar interests. A community network can, therefore, help to build a shared commitment and a greater willingness to connection and collaboration with others beyond functional boundaries.

Teaming

To enhance collaboration within a business transformation requires creating a teaming environment that fosters connectivity and sets clear expectations for communicating and implementing changes. Teaming was of vital importance when the Covid-19 pandemic forced organizational leaders to quickly pivot business and workforce priorities. To rapidly reorient their goals and operations, organizations turned to teams and teaming for transformational change. For example, Ford, an American multinational automobile manufacturer, formed special teams and set up new production lines in its manufacturing facilities to shift from making hybrid car batteries to making thousands of ventilators for hospitals. Teaming is, therefore, imperative as it enables organizations to reset and get work done amid turbulent and chaotic conditions.

Superteams

Since teams are built for adaptability rather than predictability and stability, they can learn and adapt faster than individual workers alone. Teams of motivated individuals will also challenge each other to come up with better, more creative ideas. In the post-pandemic world organizations have continued to increase their reliance on teams to navigate transformations and have learnt to multiply the value of teams even further through superteams, that is, combinations of people and technology leveraging their complementary capabilities to pursue outcomes at a speed and scale not otherwise possible.[13] Superteams are in their infancy because many organizations still tend to view technology as a tool and an enabler rather than as a team member and collaborator. This was evident in Deloitte's Global Human Capital Trends survey, where most respondents said that they saw artificial intelligence mainly as an automation tool that is a substitute for manual labour rather than a way to augment or collaborate with human capabilities.[14] This view is, however, slowly starting to change as debates are raging about how generative AI, such as ChatGPT, can be used in a collaborative way in sectors such as education. Deloitte's survey also found that the top three factors executives identified as important in transforming work were organizational culture, workforce capability and technology, which are all factors that must work together for an organization to envision and assemble effective superteams. The advantage of superteams is not just that they can get work done faster and cheaper but that they have the potential to re-architect work, using technology to change the nature of work so that it makes the most of people's distinctly human capabilities.

Superteams are most powerful when organizations use technology to empower teams in a way that improves work for team members and makes them better at work. When given the right environment to thrive, superteams of people and technology together can unlock organizational potential and achieve greater results than either people or machines can achieve on their own. Superteams, hold the promise of helping organizations bring human and technological capabilities together to re-architect collaboration.

Collaborative design of business transformations

The natural response in organizations is to want to control and plan the design of a business transformation from the top down. However, the complex and dynamic environments we are living in require a more experimental, collaborative approach rather than a controlling mode of design. A collaborative approach has its roots in social constructionism, which posits that organizational members partially create their reality through the retrospective stories that they share about their experiences and also through future oriented stories that they create as a pathway for action, and consequently the convergence of these narratives drives collective sense-making. Business transformations can be generated in this way through the sharing of stories and the building of consensus around images of the future.

Generative methods

The design of business transformations in a consensual way can be facilitated by methods such as a World Café (see Chapter 3), which is based on self-organizing principles that can lead to idea generation. With dialogic methods, interaction and conversation are the priority. Participants are given ownership and responsibility to bring up the issues and topics that matter most to them, individually and in groups, and the changes they want to take responsibility for. Managing a transformation in this way is more like coaching an improvisational jazz band than pulling levers and turning dials on a machine. It means not rigidly following the same set of rules through a well-defined process no matter what needs to be changed, but instead requires being inventive and creative with how it is achieved, and negotiating with different stakeholders to create the dialogues that need to happen for design options to emerge. In such a generative way the design will depend on fostering multiple levels of conversations formally and informally.[15] This can be done in informal ways, such as online conversations where people gather together and share ideas and suggestions. As an idea comes up it may, in turn, spark other ideas, so in this way ideas are generated and developed. Formally, ideas can be generated using methods such as scenario planning, which helps organizations prepare for uncertainty by envisaging and analysing plausible future outcomes. Scenario planning assesses critical uncertainties and macro forces influencing or impacting the market and enterprises, thus stimulating strategic thinking. It can be used to future test strategies, challenge assumptions and orthodoxy, and promote innovation by ideating opportunities, risks and actions. Design thinking (discussed below) is another formal method for stimulating ideas and generating collaboration.

Design thinking

At one point in the film *The Best Exotic Marigold Hotel*, Judi Dench, who plays a grieving widow, is connected with a customer-service agent at a call centre in India. Despite being told Dench is in mourning, the call-centre member of staff sticks to her script, with a sadly predictable result – hurt feelings and a customer who will not call again. By the end of the movie, Dench's character has moved to India and reinvented herself as a call-centre trainer. In her initial session, she conducts a role-play exercise in which she demands operators go off script and respond to customers as people first. As a result, instead of customers getting angry and hanging up, the call-centre staff make connections and customers for life. The lesson of this fictitious story for business transformations is that there is a need for flexible conversations and empathy.

Empathy is the foundation of design thinking, which is a collaborative tool which can be used for business transformations. As the Nobel Laureate Herbert Simon said, everyone designs who devises courses of action aimed at changing existing situations into preferred ones. Design thinking is characterized by user-centeredness, ideation and iterative prototyping, and focuses on designing *with* people, not *for* people. The process of design thinking is collaborative and based on the values of practicality, ingenuity and a concern for appropriateness; it focuses on interactions, using a participatory and a people-centric approach, emphasizing the perspectives of multiple stakeholders, and identifying solutions rather than analysing and assessing problems.[16] To achieve this, design thinking proposes an experiential approach which comprises exploring the end user's (stakeholder's) needs and perspectives, developing prototypes, testing, reflecting and re-testing to achieve the desired product. The tools that can be used for this include: need finding tools, such as ethnographic observations; in-depth contextual interviews; customer/stakeholder journeys to empathize with and understand needs; idea generation tools, such as brainstorming, to generate possible solutions to problems; and idea testing tools, such as rapid prototyping and experimentation, to test ideas on a small scale in order to determine their desirability, technical feasibility and business viability. Design thinking workshops can also use virtual reality goggles and rapid ideation techniques. The effective use of these various tools relies on an organizational environment that supports and reinforces the knowledge, visions and ideas that emerge from conversations. In this way, design thinking can be used to create intuitive and empathetic interactions between stakeholders in order to design a transformation. For example, Stockholm's international airport, Arlanda, used design thinking to create a system that would make its air traffic control system safer and more effective. A working group was set up which first identified the tasks and challenges of the air-traffic controllers, then the group collaboratively worked on prototypes and iterating, based on feedback, of the design of a new departure sequencing system that would enable air traffic controllers to do their jobs better. The new system reduced the time that planes spent between departing from the terminal and being in the air, which also helped to reduce fuel consumption.[17] Design thinking can, therefore, be used to encourage collaboration, resulting in a richer set of ideas and solutions, which can lead to increased adoption or acceptance levels by stakeholders involved in the design conversations.

In the following business insight, David Maybin, a change management and transformation leader, describes his experience as a Senior Change Lead generating a collaborative approach when introducing a new CRM system within a large Australian government department.

CASE STUDY

Business Insight: Going beyond process to engage the business

Organizational change is frequently approached through the lens of project management, which, despite being a robust approach, often lacks a focus on engaging key stakeholders. I was keen to ensure that engagement was a key element of a project I recently led in my role as a Senior Change Lead. The project was with a large Australian government department and involved the introduction of a new CRM system. The driver for the change was the need to improve the management of customer information and to improve the customer experience. This would also directly benefit the frontline staff in that they would have all the information they needed to be able to provide a better customer experience.

The government department had over fifty separate sources of information on customers, and these were stored on laptops, desktops and Access databases. No one really knew what information was available as it was maintained by individuals, some of whom had left the department. The project, which aimed to introduce a department-wide CRM system, adopted an agile delivery methodology and also used the basic awareness, desire, knowledge, ability and reinforcement (ADKAR) model. In order to develop a deeper understanding of the business and the challenges faced, I facilitated several discovery workshops with each business unit to: understand what problems the new system would need to address; identify the target audience; and find out if the solution would add value. This approach also helped to gain the initial engagement of the project team and the business and to define what success would look like. Furthermore, it helped the project team to develop a greater understanding of the user experience and the end-to-end journey of customers.

As part of my role, I was involved in educating and raising awareness of the need for change, which meant explaining what was required to achieve a successful outcome rather than just a technical solution. I also worked closely with the executive team and the project sponsor to ensure that they had a clear understanding of their roles in the project and what was expected of them. This involved coaching the executive team to not only take ownership of the change but also to provide an inspirational approach to the change. This was initiated through the facilitation of vision workshops with the leadership team, which aimed to ensure a shared understanding of the project and the expectations of the sponsor. These workshops were an opportunity to continue to build engagement as well as providing input into the design of the new system. This helped to emphasize the need for courage, ownership and a holistic perspective that focused on communication and not just the process of the change. The key communications included:

- Messages referencing the long-term health and wellbeing of the organization and the user experience. As we moved out of the pandemic this became even more important, and just taking the time to ask about the wellbeing of people involved in the project added a new dimension to all engagement activities.
- Throughout the project, every opportunity was taken to communicate and drive an inspirational message to generate confidence among a diverse group of stakeholders in order to build trust.

- The changes and the reasons for the change were continually explained by leaders, managers and by the team. We conducted interviews with staff to gain feedback on how effective the communications were and how we could improve on the 'what's in it for me' messaging. This also provided a greater understanding of how the change affected them.
- The discovery and co-design workshops and engagements also provided a direct communication channel to the business that enabled a greater understanding of the reasons for change, rather than just advising on the reasons why they should change.

In taking a more people-centric approach to managing change, I was able to prioritize not only the process but also the experience, health and wellbeing of people who were touched by the project. To help with this, we developed personas and journey maps, identified touch points and determined what motivated people in their day-to-day work through direct interviews and workshops. This provided the project team with knowledge on what people's critical concerns were about the new system. The showcases and demonstrations to business on the development of the system developed transparency and allowed for early feedback on the design. The involvement of users and customers in these showcases help to continue to build engagement and ownership. Comments such as 'We want to do better', 'We want to drive for positive feedback' and 'We are delivering a great outcome for customers' demonstrated ongoing engagement. It was also crucial to make sure that the user experience was aligned with the change strategy, which we workshopped with the frontline staff and also with customers in order to identify the potential impacts, including the impact on health and wellbeing. Listening, acknowledging and recognizing the valuable and insightful inputs from across the business helped to gain feedback about the implementation of the new system. Instead of just being handed a CRM solution, the business was involved from the beginning. For example, subject matter experts were involved in the co-design, showcased the solution, provided insights into the business and took ownership of the implementation. We were also able to use the insights and in-depth business knowledge that the frontline staff and customers brought to the project; for instance, the suggestion from a user at a workshop to link accounts helped to improve the engagement with the customer and created a 'one-stop shop' feature. The use of such suggestions and ideas inspired the user groups, as they could see how they could provide a much-improved service to customers.

The key lessons I learnt from this project include the following:

- *Communicate the 'why'*. Before the project even started, we focused on communicating the 'why' at every opportunity, making it clear why the change was happening and the direct benefits to different stakeholder groups across the department.

- *People have to be at the centre of any change.* We focused on the user experience and we listened to people, including customers. In the post-pandemic environment, concerns focused on more than just the process of change or the new system but also on wider concerns such as inclusivity, safety, and health and wellbeing.
- *Take time to understand the perspectives of others.* During the discovery and co-design workshops we continued to ask who else from the business should be involved so that we could gather as many different perspectives as possible. We didn't want to miss anyone in gathering valuable input and we also wanted to ensure engagement across all business areas. We kept talking with key staff all the way through the project to ensure we understood their needs, business processes and expectations of the new CRM system.
- *Listen.* Listening to all voices is important, especially with a large user base. Being able to address some of the issues and incorporate some ideas into the project helped to build trust and confidence in the system and in the project as a whole.
- *Communicate often.* We used a multi-channel approach to communications which included email, social media, showcases, stand-ups and town halls. The key stakeholder groups were identified and analysed so that we understood their motivation. We also kept people informed of progress and changes to the project. For example, when the training was reorganized around pilot sites, we let them know, and when the final user testing sessions were scheduled, we let them know. This built engagement and we saw that there was a growing excitement to get the system up and running.
- *Take ideas on board whenever possible to do so.* When individuals saw that their ideas had been incorporated into the project this helped to develop their ownership of the implementation.

To conclude, engagement at all levels can help to make a business transformation more effective and inspire greater individual performance, productivity, profitability and focus on customer experience. As was evident from this project, it is critical to keep building engagement and to focus on people throughout a transformation. The showcases, listening and incorporating people's ideas in the project, involving individuals in the discovery workshops, and the support and messaging from the sponsor and leaders all helped to build engagement at all levels and inspired the motivation for the system change. The impact of this was evident when one of the frontline staff came up to me during the implementation phase and said that this was different – it felt like he was an important part of this, and this was his system being implemented. It was not being done to him, but with him. He was engaged.

Questions

1. What was the impact of taking a more people-centric approach to change within the transformation?
2. What else might have been considered to ensure collaboration was fostered?
3. From the lessons learnt, which are the most important for you in creating people-centric change and how might you apply them in practice?

SUMMARY

There is an African proverb that says, 'If you want to go quickly, go alone. If you want to go far, go together.' This is often evident in an emergency; when people need to get pails of water to a fire or sandbags to a flood they will create bucket brigades – lines of people passing heavy items from one to another to put out the fire or stem the flood. This can be so much faster than everyone hauling a single bucket and is a classic example of how individuals can collaborate effectively even during a crisis.

Collaboration is a key element of people-centric change. As discussed in this chapter, to shift transformational change from being a top-down, mechanized, purely process-based activity to being much more people-centric, the focus must move from one of control to one of collaboration where stakeholders work to solve problems and address opportunities, using methods such as design thinking. Importantly, this also requires accepting the proposed solutions identified by stakeholders, if they are within the scope of the organization's strategy, values and purpose. Although, involving all relevant stakeholders in a collaborative way can be costly, demand additional resources and require detailed planning, these costs can be outweighed by the resulting benefits, because when people come together in a collaborative way, and share ideas and views with each other about a new product or service, the combination of ideas can be powerful. When different perspectives and knowledge combine, especially in teams such as superteams, then there is the possibility of developing something that is not only creative and innovative but also sustainable.

PRACTICAL IMPLICATIONS

The are several practical implications which can be drawn from this chapter:

- *Promote collaborative practice.* In order to promote collaborative practice the following approaches should be considered:
    - *Start with a collaborative approach* whereby stakeholders are constantly aware of the need for change and are able to voice their views and opinions in numerous formal and informal occasions.
    - *Create a no fear environment.* Create an environment that supports perpetual collaboration through collaborative behaviours by encouraging time for collaboration whether in formally allocated teams or through self-organized groups.
    - *Encourage stretching beyond the comfort zone.* An ability to stretch beyond a person's comfort zone is essential when it comes to encouraging collaboration, particularly across functions and silos. This involves asking individuals to work on projects that do not necessarily reflect the nature or level of their expertise but which will bring fresh perspectives to the creative process and also enhance the learning experience of employees.
    - *Celebrate individuality.* To be collaborative, individuals need to have autonomy over certain elements of the transformation and be able to voice their views, ideas and concerns during a transformation.

    Principles such as these can be incorporated into the way that collaboration is encouraged so that it becomes part of the culture of how transformations are enacted.
- *Use employee-led approaches.* Encourage teams to collaborate within and across the business and the ecosystem, and encourage them to experiment with technologies to deliver better value in what they do by applying people-led approaches around ideation and solutioning, such as appreciative inquiry and Design Thinking.
- *Develop superteams.* To create an environment where superteams flourish in business transformations the following practices will be of help:
    - *Set audacious goals.* Instead of focusing only on how to improve existing processes and outputs and focus on defining new aspirations and outcomes.

- *Avoid the instinct to use technologies only as an enabler for the work already being done.* Instead, take a broader view of technology's transformative potential to elevate the impact it can have on work and business transformations.
- *Encourage collaboration across teams* in order to break down silos across functions and the organization.
- *Make the creation of superteams a cross-organizational imperative,* leveraging the best thinking from HR, OD, IT, and other functions across the organization.

Notes

1 F Jabr. The social life of forests, *New York Times Magazine*, December 2020. www.nytimes.com/interactive/2020/12/02/magazine/tree-communication-mycorrhiza.html (archived at https://perma.cc/23ZW-2SD2)

2 J Hodges (2020) *Organization Development: How organizations change and develop effectively*, Bloomsbury, London

3 J Woiceshyn, J L Huq, K Blades and S R Pendharkar. Microdynamics of implementing planned change on organizations front line, *Journal of Change Management*, 2020, 20 (1), 59–80. www.tandfonline.com/doi/abs/10.1080/14697017.2019.1602553 (archived at https://perma.cc/2JTS-B689)

4 S J Clayton. An agile approach to change management, *Harvard Business Review*, 11 January 2021. hbr.org/2021/01/an-agile-approach-to-change-management (archived at https://perma.cc/AJR2-HFN9)

5 W Mungai, L White and Z Kinias. Lessons in sustainable change management: #deCOALonize Kenya, Insead Knowledge, 8 Februrary 2022. knowledge.insead.edu/responsibility/lessons-sustainable-change-management-decoalonize-kenya (archived at https://perma.cc/53H7-AQCN)

6 A Brodsky and M Tolliver. No, remote employees aren't becoming less engaged, *Harvard Business Review*, 6 December 2022. hbr.org/2022/12/no-remote-employees-arent-becoming-less-engaged (archived at https://perma.cc/55AK-SJEC)

7 L Gratton. Four principles to ensure hybrid work is productive work, *MIT Sloan Management Review*, 2021, 62 (2), 11A–16A. sloanreview.mit.edu/article/four-principles-to-ensure-hybrid-work-is-productive-work (archived at https://perma.cc/BKY6-U2EW)

8 L Gratton, How to do hybrid right, *Harvard Business Review*, May–June 2021. hbr.org/2021/05/how-to-do-hybrid-right (archived at https://perma.cc/38LL-V8UD)

9 J A Conger and C L Pearce (2023) Empowerment's pivotal role in enhancing effective self-and shared leadership, in *Principles of Organizational Behavior: The handbook of evidence-based management*, ed C L Pearce and E A Locke, Wiley, London, 293

10 C Baden-Fuller and S Haefliger. Business models and technological innovation, *Long Range Planning*, 2013, 46 (6), 419–26. www.sciencedirect.com/science/article/pii/S0024630113000691 (archived at https://perma.cc/9V97-Q72A)

11 AppleInsider. Apple to adopt hybrid work model despite worker pleas for more flexibility, AppleInsider, 30 June 2021. forums.appleinsider.com/discussion/222583/apple-to-adopt-hybrid-work-model-despite-worker-pleas-for-more-flexibility (archived at https://perma.cc/H6MD-JRL4)

12 S Nadella. Microsoft's Satya Nadella on flexible work, the metaverse, and the power of empathy, *Harvard Business Review*, 28 October 2021. hbr.org/2021/10/microsofts-satya-nadella-on-flexible-work-the-metaverse-and-the-power-of-empathy (archived at https://perma.cc/679Q-H3GA)

13 Deloitte. Using AI to turn your teams into superteams, *Harvard Business Review*, 5 March 2021. *hbr.org/sponsored/2021/03/using-ai-to-turn-your-teams-into-superteams* (archived at https://perma.cc/UC8R-NS4C)

14 Deloitte. 2020 Global Human Capital Trends report – *The Social Enterprise at Work: Paradox as a path forward*, Deloitte, nd. www2.deloitte.com/cn/en/pages/human-capital/articles/global-human-capital-trends-2020.html (archived at https://perma.cc/UFQ4-6PB2)

15 D Grant and R J Marshak. Toward a discourse-centered understanding of organizational change, *Journal of Applied Behavioral Science*, 2011, 47 (2), 204–35. journals.sagepub.com/doi/10.1177/0021886310397612 (archived at https://perma.cc/A97Z-K4FS)

16 T Brown. Design thinking, *Harvard Business Review*, 2008, 86 (6), 84. hbr.org/2008/06/design-thinking (archived at https://perma.cc/J327-EEHC)

17 J Rosenfield. Creating value through sustainable design, McKinsey, 25 July 2017. www.mckinsey.com/capabilities/sustainability/our-insights/creating-value-through-sustainable-design (archived at https://perma.cc/D8XM-HQ2B)

11

How to build a people-centric change strategy

Introduction

When a new business transformation starts it is often exciting but daunting. Along the way there will be pain points, like the infamous 'wall' in marathons, or moments of self-doubt, which are inevitable since a transformational change is complex and depends on people shifting the way they work and their behaviours often in dynamic and chaotic contexts. To assist with the management of change there are numerous frameworks which have been developed, all with various numbers of steps in them. Business transformations can, however, no longer be designed and managed as a discrete episode of staged linear steps because organizational change is no longer a single event experience. Instead, transformations require agility and adaptability, especially when there are multiple simultaneous transformation initiatives happening at the same time. Despite this, many change practitioners prefer to stick to what they have always used and cling to the certainty of what they know, relying on linear n-step process change frameworks that tend to be based on one-size-fits-all approaches or their gut instincts rather than on empirical evidence. Consequently, a successful business transformation is often due more to experience and practice and the achievement of short-term outcomes that may not be sustainable in the medium to long term. Such approaches are outdated and no longer fit for the environments in which we work. Instead, the design and delivery of business transformations must move forward to embrace the pace, nature and type of change that organizations carry out so that they are done in a way that is people-centric.

This chapter proposes a cyclical framework, supported with key principles, which moves away from the traditional linear approaches to change.

Through evidence-based research, the key elements of the framework and the supporting principles (many of which are covered in this book) have been identified as being necessary to achieve successful people-centric change. The chapter outlines each of the key elements of the framework and the supporting principles. To effectively implement the framework and the principles requires a supportive culture, and the chapter, therefore, begins by exploring the elements of a culture that are needed to support people-centric change.

Creating a culture for people-centric change

The scale and speed of change that organizations are facing requires agility and adaptability. Engaging people in organizational change has never been more important but to do that effectively the organizational culture needs to enable transformations to take root through a people-centric approach to change, since culture shapes the way that business transformations are done. When organizations create a culture that supports people-centric change and opportunities to develop the skills to do it effectively, they are able to take forward new initiatives and to respond to external trends and forces of change. Consideration needs to be given as to what needs to change in the culture to make it people-centric so that it shifts to a collaborative, engaging approach with a focus on seeing the opportunities of change and enhancing wellbeing and EDI. A starting point for this is to update the organization's mission statement, values and purpose to ensure that they reflect an explicit focus on people during business transformations. It is also crucial to ensure that the culture is rooted in the business context in which it operates, so that there is a clear link between the need for change and how it will impact on the strategy, purpose and stakeholders of the organization.

To nurture a culture which is open to business transformations and to develop a people-centric approach to change, it is important to encourage and sustain an organization-wide culture that promotes the generation and implementation of new ideas and also listens to employees. For example, LinkedIn, the business- and employment-focused social media platform, was forced to review its culture after adding this critical question to its quarterly employee survey: How are you? The honest responses that employees gave to that question, in particular, spotlighted that they were suffering serious issues with remote working, precipitated by the pandemic, such as burnout and deep feelings of isolation as they struggled to balance work and family life and greatly missed interactions with other employees. As a result, it took a hard look at what steps it could take not only to help employees move forward but also to reassert what the company's culture was about. Consequently, the company implemented several new employee-focused initiatives, including a programme called 'Lift Up' that gave almost all employees a week off, to fight burnout and help them deal with personal matters. It has also launched another programme called 'Reconnect', which encourages gatherings, with the company providing music and food.[1] Organizations such as LinkedIn with forward-thinking and change-receptive cultures thrive and grow, while companies with cultures that oppose change often take too long to adapt and adjust to new ideas and eventually wither away. To embrace a people-centric approach to change means changing elements of the culture by identifying the levers for doing so.

Levers of culture change

Changing an organization's culture is inextricable from the emotional and social dynamics of people in the organization, which means that it can be very difficult to change the entire culture. Instead, a more achievable approach is to change parts of it, which then, in turn, affect the whole culture. This is like dropping pebbles in a pond, where the ripples from each pebble create interconnecting ripples across the pond. In such a way, changing elements of the culture can happen through incremental changes, which have a cumulative impact on the whole culture of the organization rather than embarking on a massive culture change programme. Changing parts of the culture starts with a clear understanding of the organization's purpose and then driving behavioural change to match that purpose, which can only be truly effective when leaders and managers take responsibility for shaping and nurturing the culture, since the fundamental elements of an organization's culture are not changed by new thoughts or words but by behaviours and actions that reinforce desired cultural attributes. This takes time, and the message needs to be constantly reiterated in-person by leaders and managers role modelling the behaviours that they want their workforce to demonstrate by adopting a 'do as I do' way of behaving and working.

Training and development practices can also help to change behavioural elements of the culture by: creating an understanding of the drivers for a transformation and, the implications of not changing; a recognition that new behaviours and practices are required; and explaining how these new behaviours will have a positive impact on the culture. To ensure new behaviours stick, training and development interventions need to be followed up with ongoing support and coaching, especially for individuals who find it difficult to move out of their comfort zones and change their behaviours and ways of working. For some people, such a move can be very challenging and they may need additional help, while for others who just blatantly refuse to make changes to their behaviour despite support and development there may well be a need to exit them from the organization. Furthermore, it is important to recognize when the new behaviours are being enacted and provide subsequent positive feedback to individuals. Observing people doing things right and rewarding their positive behaviours are vital for ensuring that behavioural changes stick. Ultimately, integrating a people-centric approach to change into an organizational culture must be rooted in actions, norms, behaviours and practices over time.

The Business Transformation Framework

The idea that a transformation can be designed and managed as a discrete episode of activity with a set of top-down concurrent steps is no longer relevant for many organizations. Such approaches too often do not achieve the speed or new behaviours that organizations require. Well-known models (such as Kotter's eight-step process or Prosci's ADKAR model) are typically top-down, linear and process-heavy. The exact number of steps varies but the majority of such models describe similar activities, albeit with different names. In addition, these models propose that each step must be taken in order for change to progress, and that if one step is not completed or is not completed correctly then each subsequent step is in jeopardy as any errors, omissions or oversights will be carried through the remainder of the steps. It is a bit like ballroom dancing, where the end result is due to careful choreography rather than artistic licence. Admittedly, these models do provide helpful checklists for mapping out the process from the first recognition of the need for change through to the practicalities of implementation. However, there are limitations to such prescriptive approaches. For instance, they do not reflect the complexity and multiplicity of most transformation initiatives. Since a business transformation is a complex and dynamic process it cannot simply be solidified or treated as a series of linear events.

In contrast to a linear approach, a Business Transformation Framework is proposed for a people-centric approach to change (as shown in Figure 11.1). The framework is built on the key concepts outlined in this book and as an iterative cycle it is appropriate for ensuring agility and adaptability, since each element of the framework constantly informs the orientation of previous and subsequent phases. The framework is supported with eight key principles, which are covered in previous chapters in this book and are briefly defined in this chapter for continuity along with each of the elements of the framework.

FIGURE 11.1 Business transformation framework

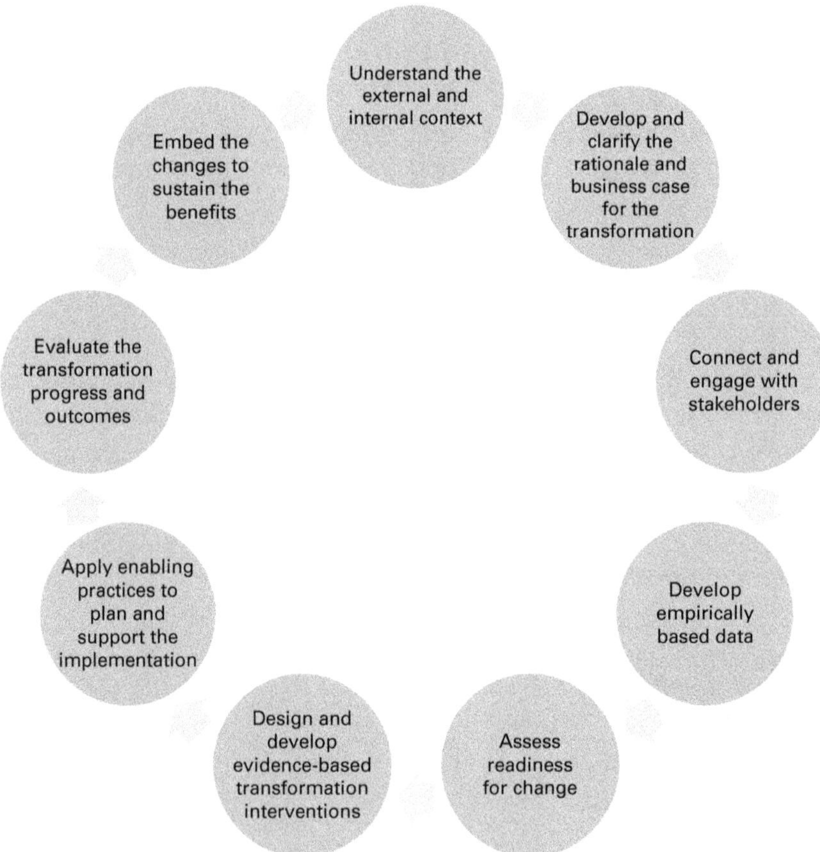

Elements of the Business Transformation Framework

UNDERSTAND THE EXTERNAL AND INTERNAL CONTEXT: IDENTIFY THE OPPORTUNITY/NEED FOR A TRANSFORMATION

A business transformation occurs at a certain point in time and against the context in which an organization is operating. The need for a transformation will be driven by internal and external forces for change (see Chapter 2) and should be grounded in an in-depth diagnosis/inquiry of the internal and external environment and potential challenges/opportunities, using tools and frameworks such as PESTLE (political, economic, societal, technological, legal or legislative, and environmental and ethical) analysis; and 14-S (see later in this chapter). Combining such frameworks with scenario planning (see Chapter 10) can provide a powerful combination to understand the need for change. The aim is, to recognize the initial opportunity/threat driving a transformation.

DEVELOP AND CLARIFY THE RATIONAL AND BUSINESS CASE FOR THE TRANSFORMATION

The focus of this element is on clarifying the reason for the change, why it is important that the transformation happens, and how the transformation links to the business strategy. The rationale for the transformation needs to be a clear, concise narrative and effectively communicated by addressing the following questions:

- Why is the transformation necessary? Why now?
- Why is it meaningful?
- Why is it the best thing for everyone?
- When does the transformation need to be achieved by?
- How does the transformation impact the strategy?
- How will the transformation serve the organization's vision and strategy?
- How will the transformation be aligned to business needs?

Along with clarity on the rationale for a transformation, there should also be a clear business case identified. Vital to the development of the business case is clarity on the purpose of the transformation, its outcomes and impact.

CONNECT AND ENGAGE WITH STAKEHOLDERS

Connecting and engaging with stakeholders (see Chapter 3) involves identifying and mapping who will be affected by the transformation and who can influence it, including their needs, motivations and commitment to the transformation, as well as how it will impact them. To identify who the key stakeholders are, the following questions should be asked:

- Who will be affected by the transformation?
- Who will be responsible for making it happen?
- Who will be accountable for it?
- Who will benefit from the transformation?
- Who can influence whether the transformation happens, or not?
- Who has the power to block the transformation?

After stakeholders have been identified, an action plan then needs to be developed for engaging and communicating with key stakeholders/groups throughout the transformation. There has to be clarity on who the key stakeholders/groups are internally and externally in order for actions to be taken to begin to connect and engage with them in order to start to build commitment and collaboration for the transformation.

DEVELOP EMPIRICALLY BASED DATA

To ensure that the right initiative is identified and structured in the most effective way, a transformation requires an assessment or diagnostic of the root causes of the problem/issue/opportunity to be addressed. This inquiry needs to include a mix of both quantitative and qualitative data and avoid any cognitive biases. Data should be gathered from multiple sources, including employees, customers, competitors, suppliers, partners, professional services and industry bodies. Frameworks such as the 14-S can be used to gather, categorize and code data. This model is based on the 7-S model, which focuses on the interaction of different parts of an organization and was initially developed by Pascale and Athos[2] before becoming popularly known as McKinsey's 7-S model. The model originally comprises seven interconnected organizational elements: strategy; structure; systems; staff; style; skills; and shared values, each of which is outlined below.

1 ***Strategy:*** The purpose of the organization and the way it seeks to enhance its competitive advantage.

2 *Structure:* The division of activities, integration and coordination mechanisms, and the nature of the formal and informal organization.
3 *Systems:* Formal and informal procedures and processes, such as financial measurement, reward, resource allocation, health and safety, and communication.
4 *Staff:* Employees' motivation, education and behaviour, as well as demographics.
5 *Style:* Typical behaviour patterns of specific groups, such as leaders, managers and frontline staff.
6 *Skills:* The core and distinct capabilities (knowledge, skills and attitudes) of employees.
7 *Shared values:* Core beliefs and values, and how these influence the organization's orientation towards customers, employees, shareholders, the external community and other key stakeholders.

Although these seven elements provide a comprehensive model, they are limited to a small number of internal factors and lack a focus on the external environment. In an attempt to address these limitations, the model has been expanded to include the following elements, to provide a deeper analysis:

1 *Stories:* These are told by employees to one another, to outsiders and to new recruits about the organization's history, events and personalities.
2 *Signals:* These are rituals and routines in how employees behave towards one another, that signal what is important and valued, such as recognition rituals (for instance awards for the best customer service).
3 *Structures of power:* These comprise the positional and relational power held by individuals. Positional power is dependent on an individual's role or position in the organization, such as Director of Finance, whereas relational power is based on the relationships and influence an individual has internally and externally.
4 *Symbols:* These include the visual representations of an organization, such as company logos, the layout and size of offices, dress codes, titles and the type of language and terminology used.
5 *Stakeholder satisfaction:* This is the satisfaction of those people who have an interest in, and are affected by, what the organization does, and how well it does it. This includes groups such as customers, employees, shareholders, partners and suppliers.

6 *Social responsibility:* This is the approach that the organization takes to internal and external ethical issues such as climate change and contributions to charity and local communities.

7 *Situation:* This is the external environment in which the organization operates. This includes factors such as: globalization; technological innovations; political, economic, social, regulatory and legal issues; customer expectations; shifts in demographics; and the competitive landscape.[3]

These additional seven elements result in the 14-S framework. They provide a focus on the external as well as wider internal components of the organization. To use the 14-S framework:

- Identify whether the focus of the inquiry is at an organizational, functional, departmental or team level and the relevant questions to use to explore each of the elements of the framework.
- Gather data on each of the 14 elements using primary and secondary methods of investigation, such as company reports, surveys, interviews, focus groups and observations.
- Identify the key themes from the data-gathering exercise.
- Summarize the findings, which can then be used to help understand the complex issues in each of the elements and where there is a need to focus attention.

Diagnostic frameworks such as the 14-S can be used as a structure for gathering data to identify the root causes of issues which need to be addressed through a transformation. There are other methods of investigation which can be used, including surveys, interviews and focus groups, while dialogic methods such as appreciative inquiry and a World Café can be used to generate conversations (see Chapter 3).

ASSESS READINESS FOR CHANGE

Readiness (or lack of) for a business transformation will influence whether or not stakeholders will engage in change practices. Readiness encompasses, firstly, the extent to which stakeholders have positive views about the need for change and believe that it will have positive implications for themselves and the wider organization. Secondly, readiness denotes stakeholders' beliefs about whether or not the organization has the capability and capacity to initiate a transformation and to successfully implement it. A lack of readiness can occur when there is: a poor understanding of the need for and the impact of change; limited focus on employee engagement in the planning

FIGURE 11.2 Assessing readiness for a transformation

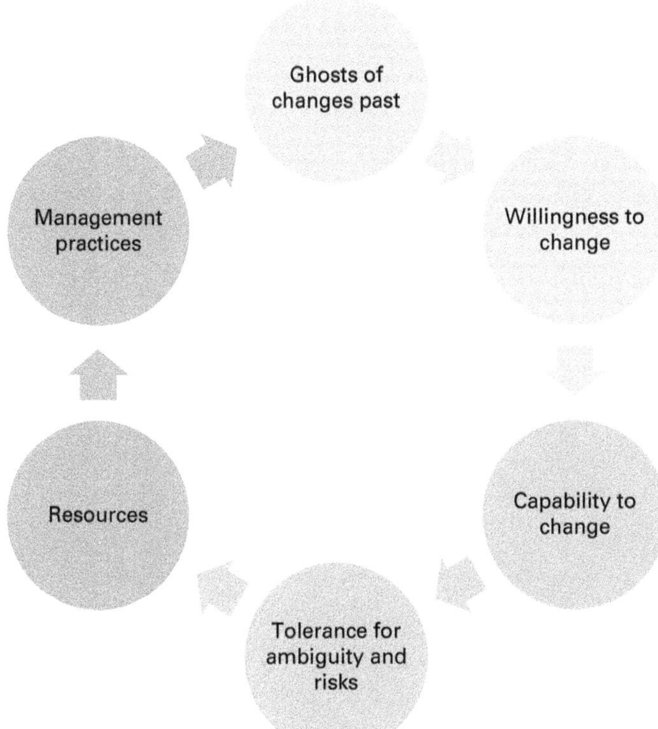

processes; and a lack of appropriate empirical data to provide evidence for the need for change. People also may not be ready for yet another change because of transformation saturation (see Chapter 8 on wellbeing).

Readiness for a transformation can be affected by a number of factors (see Figure 11.2), including:

- *Ghosts of changes past:* People remember the changes that have gone well but especially also those that have not gone well or even failed. This can have an impact on how ready they are for future changes, especially if they have had a bad experience of change in the past.
- *Willingness to change:* A willingness to change will affect how ready people are to change.
- *Capability to change:* Having the right skills, experience and knowledge can increase readiness for change. Likewise, if an individual feels that they lack the relevant skills then they may be less ready to embrace another transformation.

- ***Tolerance for ambiguity and risks:*** This relates to how much an individual is able to cope with the risks and ambiguity associated with another transformation.
- ***Resources:*** Having the necessary resources (financial and non-financial) to implement the transformation can impact on how ready people are for more change.
- ***Management practices:*** Having in place (or not) effective practices such as planning, engagement, collaboration, communication and so on will influence employee readiness.

Assessing the readiness for change allows an organization to tailor efforts to make success more likely. This can be done in a variety of ways, including:

- Observing employees for behaviour that will reveal their readiness. This should be relatively unobtrusive and focus on being attentive to rumours, increases in absenteeism and/or turnover, and any unusual behaviour associated with denial of, or opposition to change.
- Discussing with employees their reactions towards the change, either in one-to-one interviews or in team meetings.
- Conducting an organizational survey, consisting of responses to Likert-style items and open questions such as 'What...?', 'Why...?', or 'How...?'

Whichever method is used, it is important to collect feedback in an open, transparent and collaborative way so that employees feel that their voices have been heard and to ensure that valuable information is provided about the potential issues and concerns that are affecting readiness and which need to be addressed. However, measuring change readiness is not easy, especially because the surveys and methods that measure change readiness are complicated and often act as lagging indicators. Change readiness measurements are further complicated by the fact that the volume, variety and pace of change impacting organizations are increasing.

If an assessment identifies that there is a need to increase the readiness for change then this can be done in various ways, such as through:

- persuasive communications in which the urgency and need for the transformation is emphasized and repeated several times (see Chapter 5 on the communication of change)
- encouraging participation in meetings where key stakeholders can discuss issues such as the rationale for the transformation, what needs to change, and the impact this will have on their work

- ensuring participation in the co-creation of the design and implementation of transformations (see Chapter 10 on fostering collaboration)

Readiness for yet another transformation, needs to be assessed and, if necessary, ways identified to increase it. If this is not done then a transformation may kick off without the energy and enthusiasm needed to ensure its successful journey.

DESIGN AND DEVELOP EVIDENCE-BASED TRANSFORMATION INTERVENTIONS

Once it has been identified what needs to be transformed and why, the most appropriate intervention and how it will be designed has to be agreed. An intervention refers to the range of planned activities that can be designed and implemented during a transformation for the purpose of improvement. The stakeholders who will be impacted by the transformation and who can influence it should be included in the design process because this will not only enable them to share their ideas, it will also create more commitment and ownership for making the change happen (see Chapter 10 on collaboration).

To craft a solution that will effectively address the issues the intervention is seeking to resolve requires paying careful attention to the needs and dynamics of the organization and its stakeholders and ensuring that the intervention aligns with any other transformational initiatives that are happening across the organization. The design of the intervention should be a collaborative and an inclusive process which generates creativity (see Chapter 10) and addresses the following questions:

- What are we trying to achieve?
- What will it look like?
- What is in it for key stakeholders?
- What will drive the success of the transformation?
- What barriers might there be to successful implementation?
- What will need to be done differently as a result of the intervention?
- What resources are needed to change behaviours and to implement and embed the intervention?
- What will change and what will not change?
- What are the benefits of the intervention?
- What will people gain, lose, keep as a result of the intervention?
- What are the risks?

- What will be the impact of the intervention?
- What is required to change behaviours?
- What are the concerns about this intervention?
- How important is this intervention for the organization, division, team?
- How will the intervention add value?
- How will we support people through the transformation?

To ensure that the intervention is developed effectively identifying and adhering to design principles will be of help. This can be done, for example, by firstly agreeing that 'The design must be...', then confirming the rationale for the design, for instance 'The design must... in order to...', and finally identifying how the design will be measured, for example, 'The design will...' (add specific performance measures). The outcome of using this approach will be the design of a transformation intervention that has involved key stakeholders and is fit for purpose.

Ideally, the transformation intervention that is selected should have existing evidence for its efficacy and effectiveness and be closely monitored to assess its impact.[4] If there is no existing evidence base, or there is uncertainty, then experimentation can be encouraged and data gathered on its impact and outcomes.

APPLY ENABLING PRACTICES TO PLAN AND SUPPORT THE IMPLEMENTATION

Engaging stakeholders in the design of the transformation can help to support and accelerate implementation. Some of the activities that can be applied to do this include: tapping into the expertise of various people to get diverse thoughts and perspectives (see Chapter 9); inviting employees to co-create the change (see Chapter 10); and emphasizing open, two-way dialogue with employees to help them navigate the change (see Chapter 5).

With any transformation, it is vital to a have a plan for implementation but also to be open to that plan changing. To identify what might get in the way of the implementation (the barriers) and what might help it (the drivers), a force field analysis should be conducted (see Figure 11.3). Actions then need to be agreed on what needs to be done to build on the drivers and address the barriers.

The governance structure of the transformation will also need to be defined, ensuring clear roles, responsibilities and accountabilities so that the relevant stakeholders feel that they own the transformation intervention and are passionate about taking it forward.

FIGURE 11.3 Force field analysis

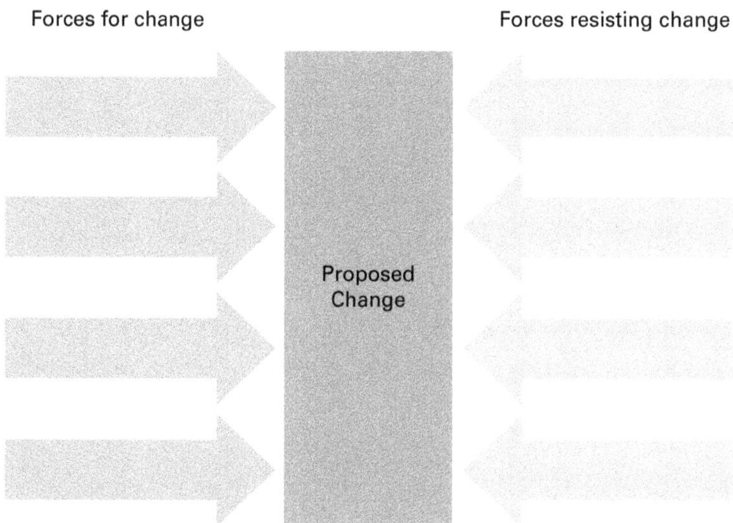

EVALUATE THE TRANSFORMATION PROGRESS AND OUTCOMES

Evaluation needs to be an ongoing activity throughout any transformation to determine what is being achieved and to demonstrate and tell a compelling and accurate story with the empirical data. At the start of the transformation, clear measures need to be agreed that provide timely and actionable goals and link behavioural indicators to business-focused key performance indicators. While the indicators will clarify the macro context for change, employees also need to understand the micro aspect, that is, what needs to change in their daily work and how they will need to function as a team. To avoid overloading people with metrics it is better to have a few key goals which will provide measurable results. It is also important to provide support for evaluation in practice by having:

- measurable, time-bound, sustainable goals and outcomes (key performance indicators) linked to the organizational strategy and tied to financial and business results, which should be communicated clearly
- regular reviews of actions
- time to capture lessons learnt – what went well and what could be done differently

Temperature checks which include reviewing:

- how far along the transformation is
- what needs to be adjusted
- what is helping and hindering the transformation
- how are people feeling about the changes

- feedback gathered from employees to identify challenges that continue to affect their work and productivity, and addressing the identified challenges and lessons learned
- success metrics tracked to assess the effectiveness of the implementation
- retrospective reviews conducted at the six-month and twelve-month mark and focusing on what has worked well and not so well, and what can be learnt from it
- consistent monitoring, learning and the celebration of results

EMBED THE CHANGES TO SUSTAIN THE BENEFITS

Once the changes that are part of the transformation have become business as usual and are operationalized, it is important to identify and implement the actions that will enable the benefits to be sustained. Practices for doing this include:

- Investing in staff by developing and providing support to help individuals and teams to adapt to and adopt new ways of working.
- Evaluating the outcomes of the transformation and ensuring that there is a follow-up improvement action plan.
- Assessing the ongoing impact of the changes and whether they continue to deliver value and, if not, what needs to be done differently. Reinforcements in place to prevent people reverting to old ways of behaving, processes and ways working.
- Continuing to reinforce the new behaviours and ways of working through role modelling them.
- Reinforcing and rewarding new ways of behaving and working.
- Celebrating successes.
- Recognizing mistakes and failure, identify what can be learnt from them and share the learning across the organization.

Each element of the framework outlined above constantly informs the orientation of previous and subsequent phases. Overall, the framework is

FIGURE 11.4 Principles for the Business Transformation Framework

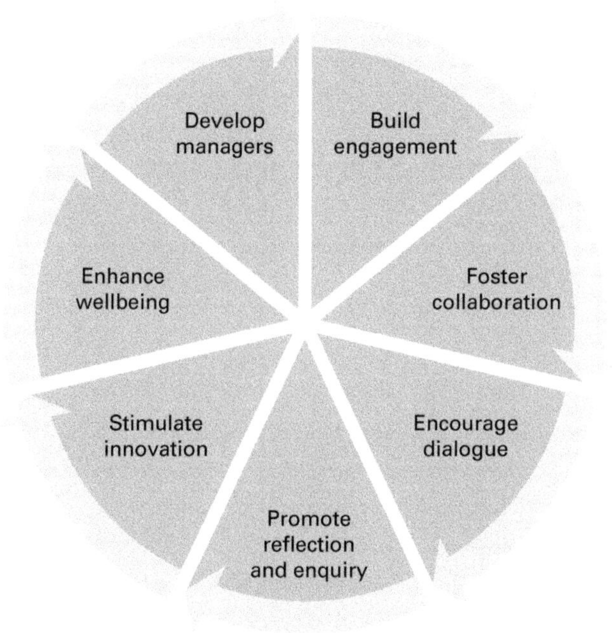

supported by eight key principles which flow throughout the framework and are briefly outlined below.

Key principles of the framework

The Business Transformation Framework is supported throughout by eight key principles (most of which are covered in this book), which comprise: build engagement; foster collaboration; encourage dialogue; promote reflection and enquiry; stimulate innovation; enhance wellbeing; develop managers; and build transformation capabilities (see Figure 11.4).

Build engagement

A people-centric approach to change is founded on stakeholder engagement (see Chapter 2). This means involving people in what needs to be done and how it can be done better rather than just telling them this is what has to change. Stakeholders, therefore, need to be involved in idea generation and in discussions about the specifics of the transformation and what it will mean for them, whenever feasible to do so (see Chapter 3 for further information on engaging stakeholders). This principle requires a focus on: who the key supporters and opponents of the transformation are; who will be affected; who needs to be involved; and who the key stakeholders/groups are who need to be involved and how they will contribute to it. This means engaging stakeholders in all the elements of the Business Transformation Framework, whenever feasible to do so. Engagement is , therefore, about having the right equality, diversity and inclusion of people involved (see Chapter 9 on EDI) and then ensuring that the right people have the capabilities and capacity to take ownership of making the transformation happen and ensuring that it is sustained.

Foster collaboration

Collaboration is a key principle of people-centric change, as discussed in Chapter 10, because it is important that, whenever feasible and relevant to do so, a business transformation is co-created and aligned across the organization. This means diagnosing, developing and implementing transformation interventions *with* rather than *for* stakeholders. A collaborative approach also recognizes that a business transformation is a team effort rather than being prescribed and imposed on people from the top-down, although there does have to be clarity on what can be co-created and what is non-negotiable.

Encourage dialogue

As discussed in Chapter 5, communication, especially dialogue, is vital for people-centric change because conversations lead to better understanding and action. Dialogue also enables key stakeholders to contribute to decisions about how to address challenges and opportunities, which helps to generate commitment to a transformation. Along with dialogue, other channels of communication are needed depending on the type of transformation, the message that needs to be conveyed and the audience to which it has to be communicated. The tone, content and approach to communication also has to be consistent across the organization as well as timely, open, continuous and transparent. Furthermore, communications need to be relevant at a team and individual level as well as an organizational level and messages must be clearly understood. Any type of communication is not, however, complete without building in opportunities for feedback since giving and receiving feedback is essential in order to monitor whether the transformation is working or not, and the impact that it is having on people.

Promote reflection and enquiry

Building learning into a business transformation enables individuals and teams at all levels to learn continuously and collaboratively, hence developing further their capabilities for engaging with transformations (see Chapter 6). To build and enhance a learning environment requires creating a culture favourable to continuous learning by enabling and encouraging people across the organization to take time for reflection and to learn from their experience of a transformation and to share it with others. Learning should, therefore, be seen as a continuous individual and collective process and time given to it so that people can reflect and share their learning. This can be done through traditional training and development methods as well as creating the time and space for reflective practice.

Stimulate innovation

Innovation is crucial for enabling organizations to be agile, competitive and adaptable to the accelerating pace of change. To stimulate innovation necessitates giving people across the organization the space and time to develop and share their creative ideas (see Chapter 6). Culturally, this also means organizations should be open to and acknowledge the potential for failure, where failure is considered an opportunity to learn. This can be done, for instance, through Action Research (see Chapter 3). Engaging multiple stakeholders in finding innovative solutions and helping to implement those solutions is a key element of people-centric change. However, it is important to be mindful that frontline employees often need an invitation to engage in innovation, and may need a high level of support, particularly within a hybrid environment which has not only changed the nature of innovation but also endangered it (see Chapter 6).

Enhance wellbeing

Badly implemented transformations can create significant employee stress, burnout, attrition, absenteeism, illness and poor change outcomes, resulting in negative employee sentiment and the loss of future employee engagement. Transformations that are unrelenting, without changes in pace or intensity, and have long time horizons can lead to excessive hours being worked and seriously impact employee wellbeing. It is, therefore, important to place wellbeing at the heart of any transformation (see Chapter 8) for without healthy, energetic and enthusiastic employees it can be difficult to implement and sustain a transformation.

Develop managers

The role of managers, as discussed in Chapter 7, is vital for people-centric change and, therefore, in implementing the Business Transformation Framework. The traditional command-and-control role of managers evokes a bygone industrial era in which managers functioned like cogs in a vast bureaucratic machine. This outdated perspective has to change. There is a need for a profound re-imagining of managers and their roles within business transformations so that they focus on people-centric change and move from a compliance and control stance to one of coaching and adapting. This requires a shift in mindsets and capabilities. Managers need to be seen as trustworthy, supportive, honest and transparent about the nature of the transformation. They also need to have the skills and capacity to apply a people-centric approach and the Business Transformation Framework.

Build transformation capabilities

The final key principle is the development of a skilled, knowledgeable, adaptable and agile workforce with the ability and capacity for business transformations. This requires building and enhancing capabilities (skills, knowledge, experience) to apply the people-centric change and the Business Transformation Framework at a number of levels in the organization such as strategic, operational, individual and team (Figure 11.5). Furthermore, it involves people having an awareness of how they can apply it in their work. At a strategic level, the application of the people-centric change approach and the framework requires commitment and leadership. This can be done through: role modelling the required behaviours; supporting and enabling people-centric change; creating the environment for engaging stakeholders with a transformation; and supporting the reframing of the role of managers. At an operational level the focus is on application, ability and adaptation. This means applying and adapting the framework as appropriate by: re-imagining the role of managers in transformations; facilitating the utilization of the framework; ensuring coaching is provided; setting up networks of practice; and encouraging collaboration across teams, functions and silos. Moreover, it means seeing transformation not only as a threat but also as an opportunity and, importantly, enabling the development of capabilities and capacity to ensure effective transformations. At team and individual levels the focus is on awareness and implementation. This is enacted by becoming

FIGURE 11.5 Enabling people to use and embed the Business Transformation Framework

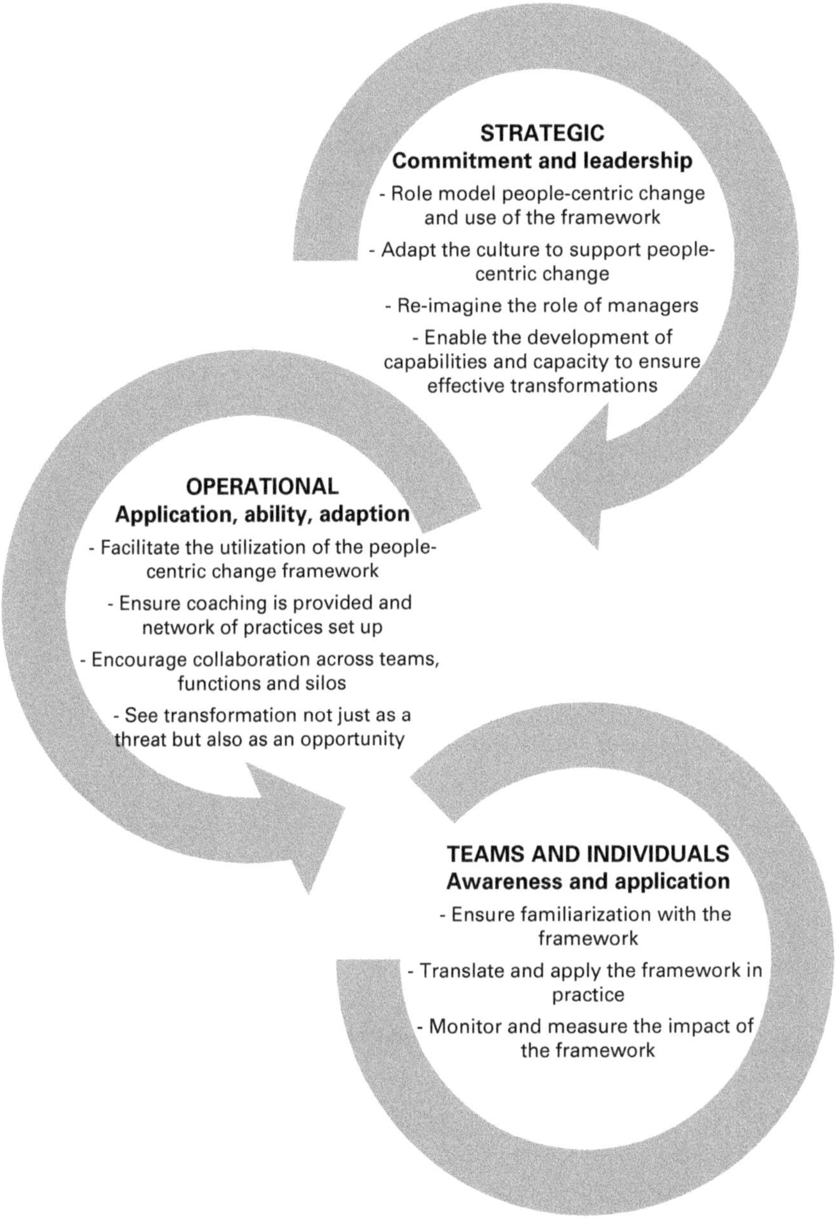

STRATEGIC
Commitment and leadership

- Role model people-centric change and use of the framework
- Adapt the culture to support people-centric change
- Re-imagine the role of managers
- Enable the development of capabilities and capacity to ensure effective transformations

OPERATIONAL
Application, ability, adaption

- Facilitate the utilization of the people-centric change framework
- Ensure coaching is provided and network of practices set up
- Encourage collaboration across teams, functions and silos
- See transformation not just as a threat but also as an opportunity

TEAMS AND INDIVIDUALS
Awareness and application

- Ensure familiarization with the framework
- Translate and apply the framework in practice
- Monitor and measure the impact of the framework

familiar with the framework and translating it into practice, as well as monitoring and measuring the impact of it.

SUMMARY

A business transformation is and should be people-centric, with individuals and teams engaging in the process of change from the start, whenever possible to do so. Unfortunately, the people element is frequently ignored during a transformation, despite the fact that people need to be included in it and be given opportunities to engage with it from its inception so that they understand the rationale for it, are committed to it and are willing to embed and sustain it. Too often, the people dimension is only considered after a transformation has started and, in many cases, not until the end of the process, which is often too little, too late and consequently can lead to the failure to create the desired changes in working practices, skills, knowledge and behaviour that are needed to deliver the business benefits.

This book proposes the need for a people-centric (and not just a process-centred) approach to business transformations due to the changing nature of the workplace and work and also shifts in employee expectations, with more people wanting to be active participants in transformational change in order to enhance and develop their sense of agency. Many employees no longer just want to let change happen to them, but instead they want to be able to affect, shape, curtail, expand and temper what and how it happens. In other words, they no longer want to be merely passive actors in organizational changes but instead want to be proactive in mobilizing their own part in the transformation process.

A people-centric approach to business transformations focuses on creating agency and engagement and is important to pursue not as an end in itself but as a means of improving change in organizations and hence working lives. People-centric change goes far beyond the strategies for consultation and participation that most organizations embrace and is not a one-time event or just a process. Instead, it puts people at the heart of business transformations, which is vital in order to enable agility and adaptability in organizations which are increasingly being forced to reboot due to the changing environments in which they operate. People-centric change is highly dependent on the advocacy of all relevant key stakeholders/groups because it is the link between strategic decision-making and effective implementation, between individual motivation and product innovation, and between delighted customers and growing revenues. Without stakeholder engagement the benefits of change will not be sustained, so keeping employees engaged, especially in a change-saturated environment, is vital to ensure that people are inside the transformation process rather than on the outside looking in. Putting people at the heart of an organization's decisions about changes related to their work and workplace entails creating a shared sense of purpose of change that mobilizes people to pull strongly in the same direction. Furthermore, it involves trusting people to engage with change in ways that allow them to fulfil their potential, by providing them with a degree of autonomy over what needs to change, why it needs to change, and how it will change and when.

A people-centric approach to change also means seeing change as not only a threat but also an opportunity and, importantly, enabling the development of capabilities and capacity to ensure effective transformations. Moreover, this provides the chance to rethink opposition to change and see it as a natural part of a transformation and as a potential source of energy and feedback (see Chapter 4). In other words, the power of opposition can be used to build support for a business transformation, and to improve the chances of identifying change initiatives that will be effective and alleviate some of the discomfort that people may be feeling about yet more change. Effective communications can help to shift the view of change from being only a threat to also being an opportunity.

Communications play a pivotal role in people-centric change before, during and after the transformation. Indeed, the management of communication processes that deliver key messages, at the appropriate time is a vital component for seeing transformations as an opportunity. The challenge is not to tell or communicate to people that the transformation is an opportunity but instead to enable them to see it for themselves through the application of tactics such as: adapting elements of the culture; making change meaningful; focusing on positive narratives; promoting employee-led creativity and innovation; and encouraging change as a learning experience. It is also vital to ensure that change will not adversely affect wellbeing.

Wellbeing is crucial to people-centric change since individuals and teams cannot function effectively, let alone adapt, compete and thrive when they are struggling and suffering. Promoting positive wellbeing is thus a crucial part of people-centric change as it sends messages to staff that they are valued and appreciated. Designing wellbeing into a transformation cannot, however, be done by HR alone.[5] The design of wellbeing into business transformation is a practice that needs to be developed, enhanced and ultimately championed by leaders and managers at every level and in every function. Along with wellbeing, equality, diversity and inclusion (EDI) need to be at the heart of people-centric change to ensure the inclusion of varied skillsets, perspectives, ideas and experiences. To create such an environment, EDI needs to be front and centre, especially since people will only engage with a business transformation if they feel included, represented, valued and supported.

A people-centric change approach has several benefits:

1. It is a way to ensure that business transformations achieve their purpose by driving positive and sustainable change with people.
2. A people-centric approach will elevate the employee voice and position people at the forefront of a transformation, thus giving voice to the voiceless and providing opportunities for diversity of thought and ideas, by including key employees in the decision-making process. Consequently, this will limit the amount of change being imposed on people and reduce the failure of change due to a lack of commitment and engagement.
3. Engaging stakeholders as integral participants within and throughout the transformation process can create conditions for more successful change outcomes, although this requires being mindful of the numerous factors which influence whether or not an individual and/or team will engage with change, including the history of change and the culture of the organization. Ultimately, engaging multiple stakeholders in finding innovative solutions and then implementing those solutions can contribute to more effective transformations.
4. Embracing a people-centric approach will help to fuel the shift that managers need to re-imagine their role in business transformations. People-centric change needs managers with a different way of thinking and a mindset that is faster, iterative and adaptable, requiring new, discontinuous and sometimes contradictory thoughts and behaviours. Managing transformations well needs compassion, adaptability, stakeholder agility, sense-making and coaching. The dichotomy is that, whilst the role of managers will need to become more important in people-centric change, the support and development of managers tends to take second place to that of leaders. So, until there is a reframing of the role of managers in business transformations, they may struggle to be in a position to support people-centric change.

To support people-centric change, this chapter proposes a cyclical Business Transformation Framework. Each of the phases of the framework is supported with the following principles: build engagement; foster collaboration; encourage dialogue; promote reflection and enquiry; stimulate innovation; enhance wellbeing; develop managers; and build transformation capabilities. To effectively implement the framework and the principles requires a supportive culture that drives people-centric change.

To create a successful transformation, people must feel that they are instrumental in influencing the direction of change, which means that employees and other key stakeholders need to be not just participants but also protagonists in business transformations. This means that, rather than using top-down linear change strategies, there is a need to adopt a people-centric approach that is less prescriptive, more collaborative and involves stakeholders throughout the transformation instead of simply telling them what will happen and what they must do. Shifting to a more people-centric approach to change is thus imperative in an era of disruption and transformation, for, as John F. Kennedy said, 'Change is the law of life and those who look only to the past or the present are certain to miss the future.'

PRACTICAL IMPLICATIONS

There are several factors which need to be considered when applying the Business Transformation Framework and the supporting principles in practice:

- *Build a culture that embraces people-centric change.*
  The fundamental elements of an organization's culture can be changed by changing the behaviours and actions that reinforce desired cultural attributes. This takes time and the message needs to be constantly reiterated in-person by leaders and managers role-modelling the behaviours that they want their workforce to demonstrate by adopting a 'do as I do' way of behaving and working.
- *Implement training and development practices.*
  Training and development practices can help to change behavioural elements of the culture. To ensure new behaviours stick, training and development interventions need to be followed-up with ongoing support and coaching. It is also important to recognize when the new behaviours are

being enacted and provide subsequent positive feedback to individuals. Observing people doing things right and rewarding their positive behaviours is vital.

- *Adapt the Business Transformation Framework to local contexts, and provide opportunities for applying it and learning from the application.*

  Ensure that people at all levels have the opportunity to become familiar with using and adapting the Business Transformation Framework, as appropriate, with the support from managers as well as development interventions such as training and coaching.

Notes

1 B Horovitz. How companies have evolved their cultures in response to the pandemic, *Time*, 14 October 2022. time.com/6222082/company-culture-pandemic (archived at https://perma.cc/9YPG-LAKN)
2 R T Pascale and A G Athos. The art of Japanese management, *Business Horizons*, 1981, 24 (6), 83–85
3 J Hodges (2017) *Consultancy, Organizational Development and Change: A practical guide to delivering value*, Kogan Page, London
4 J Hodges (2020) *Organization Development: How organizations change and develop effectively*, Bloomsbury, London
5 J Hodges and M Crabtree (2021) *Reshaping HR: The role of HR in organizational change*, Routledge, London

GLOSSARY

action research Occurs through a process of examining and reflecting on how people interact with each other and the world, as well as the discourses in which they interpret and understand their world. This leads to practical changes.

adaptability paradox Occurs when managers most need to learn and change, but stick with what they know, often in a way that stifles learning and innovation.

appreciative inquiry An organization can heighten positive potential by crafting an unconditional positive question in this approach.

authentic informal leaders Can be found at any level of the hierarchy and are influential not because of their position, but because of their capability, energy and commitment.

co-creation Constructing or negotiating change with, rather than for, stakeholders, thereby reflecting the plurality of stakeholders' interests.

cognitive dissonance Occurs when people discover that their beliefs are inconsistent with their actions.

collaborative practice A means of engaging stakeholders that helps to foster the creation of innovative ideas which are beneficial for individuals, groups/teams and the organization as a whole.

culture An organization's culture can be defined as the artefacts, espoused values and shared tacit assumptions.

design thinking Proposes an experiential approach where problems are looked upon as system problems with opportunities for systemic solutions involving different procedures and concepts to create a holistic solution.

diversity Taking an organization-wide perspective and maximizing stakeholder participation but being mindful of differences in terms of age, gender, ethnic origin and so on, in order to avoid exclusion.

equality Individuals are treated fairly and respectfully, have equal access to opportunities to engage with decisions and to resources, and can contribute fully to the success of the transformation.

force field analysis Provides a framework for understanding what factors will support a given change effort and what opposition will prevent the change from being adopted. Driving forces are conditions that have an impact on a situation and try to urge it in a specific direction. The driving forces are restrained or reduced by the restraining forces.

health circles Workers can explore solutions to reduce or eliminate health hazards and other stress factors in systematic, organized workshops.

human moments When a manager is present for, and provides their full attention to, stakeholders, be these affected people or colleagues who show signs of distress during a business transformation.

inclusive leadership Leadership that guarantees that all members of the team as well as other stakeholders feel appreciated, treated with respect and equity, have a feeling of belonging and are encouraged to contribute to and participate in the transformation.

inclusivity All relevant and appropriate individuals are included in the transformation process from its inception, enabling them to provide their own ideas rather than simply dismissing the ideas that others present.

loss aversion bias Rather than being thrilled about acquiring something new that might be even better, one is more worried about losing what one has.

mindsets The frame of reference through which an individual views a transformation, provides guidance for action and determines how to react and behave.

proximity bias The tendency to prefer employees you see in-person over those who are more frequently remote.

psychological safety A sense of permission for candour.

readiness for change The beliefs, attitudes and intentions of employees regarding the extent to which changes are needed, their capacity to undertake change successfully and their belief that change will have positive outcomes for the job they do and their working environment

reframing The practice of deliberately and systematically examining a complex situation from multiple perspectives.

scenario planning A method for defining and explaining numerous potential scenarios.

sense-making Constructing meaning through the conversations and dialogues that take place between people in organizations.

stakeholder agility Being able to engage and build rapport and support with stakeholders as well as being able to deal with multiple stakeholders in a variety of ways.

stakeholder capitalism Stakeholder capitalism proposes that organizations should serve the interests of all their stakeholders, and not just shareholders. Stakeholders can be customers, employees, suppliers and communities. The focus is on long-term value creation, not merely enhancing shareholder value.

stakeholder theory Stakeholder theory emphasized the relationships between an organization and its customers, suppliers, employees, investors, communities and others internal and external to the business who have a stake in the organization. The theory argues that an organization should create value for all stakeholders.

transformational change An organizational paradigm shift involving multidimensional, multi-level changes.

unconscious bias Lack of awareness that judgements or decisions we make are based on our past experiences, personal beliefs, assumptions or interpretations.

wellbeing A state of being in which an individual is aware of their own potential, capable of coping with the normal stresses of life, capable of working productively, effectively and actively contributing to the organization where they work.

World café Creates an environment in which people can express their ideas and insights openly and creatively, identifying collective knowledge, sharing ideas and understanding how to resolve specific issues or make necessary changes.

FURTHER READING

Blackman, D A, Buick, F, O'Donnell, M E and Ilahee, N (2022) Changing the conversation to create organizational change, *Journal of Change Management*, 22 (3), 252–72

Dewar, C, Kellar, S and Malhotra, V (2022) *CEO Excellence: The six mindsets that distinguish the best leaders from the rest*, Nicholas Brealey, London

Feiler, B (2020) *Life is in the Transitions: Mastering change at any age*, Penguin Press, New York

Furr, N and Furr, S H (2022) *The Upside of Uncertainty: A guide to finding possibility in the unknown*, Harvard Business Review Press, Boston, MA

Gratton, L (2022) *Redesigning Work: How to transform your organization and make hybrid work for everyone*, Penguin, London

Gregersen, H (2018) *Questions are the Answer*, HarperCollins, New York

Hodges, J (2020) *Organization Development: How organizations change and develop effectively*, Bloomsbury, London

Hodges, J (2021) *Managing and Leading People Through Organizational Change: The theory and practice of sustaining change through practice*, 2nd edn, Kogan Page, London

Hougaard, R and Carter, J (2022) *Compassionate Leadership: How to do hard things in a human way*, Harvard Business Review Press, Boston, MA

Nooyi, I (2021) *My Life in Full: Work, family and our future*, Hachette, London

Polman, P and Winston, A (2021) *Net Positive: How courageous companies thrive by giving more than they take*, Harvard Business Review Press, Boston

Schwartz, J and Riss, S (2021) *Work Disrupted: Opportunity, resilience, and growth in the accelerated future of work*, Wiley, New Jersey

Söderlund, J and Pemsel, S (2022) Changing times for digitalization: The multiple roles of temporal shifts in enabling organizational change, *Human Relations*, 75 (5), 871–902

Vani, S and Harte, C A (2021) *Jacinda Ardern: Leading with empathy*, Simon and Schuster, London

INDEX

Page locators in *italic* denote information contained within a Table or Figure.

Printed in the USA
CPSIA information can be obtained
at www.ICGtesting.com
JSHW071255041024
71098JS00009B/200